IMPERIAL WAR MUSEUM REVIEW

ARTICLES ON ASPECTS OF
TWENTIETH CENTURY HISTORY
PRINCIPALLY BY THE STAFF OF
THE IMPERIAL WAR MUSEUM

PUBLISHED BY:
THE TRUSTEES OF
THE IMPERIAL WAR MUSEUM
1988
GENERAL EDITOR:
SUZANNE BARDGETT
HISTORICAL EDITOR:
PETER SIMKINS
DESIGNED BY
GRUNDY & NORTHEDGE DESIGNERS
DISTRIBUTED BY LEO COOPER IN ASSOCIATION
WITH WILLIAM HEINEMANN LTD.
PRINTED BY:
BAS PRINTERS LTD
© TRUSTEES OF THE IMPERIAL
WAR MUSEUM AND THE AUTHORS
BRITISH LIBRARY CATALOGUING IN PUBLICATION DATA
IMPERIAL WAR MUSEUM REVIEW.—NO. 3–
1. WARFARE. HISTORY. SERIALS
I. IMPERIAL WAR MUSEUM. *TRUSTEES*
355'.02'09
ISBN 0-901627-46-1
ISSN 0951 3094

Cover illustration: stills from *The Battle of the Somme*, 1916 Q 70164, Q 70167, IWM FLM 1645

Contents

Unless otherwise stated, all photographs and historical sources cited are from the Imperial War Museum's archives.

'A Wonderful Idea of the Fighting': The Question of Fakes in *The Battle of the Somme*

Roger Smither

Roger Smither joined the Museum as a film cataloguer in 1970, and since 1977 has held the post of Keeper of the Department of Information Retrieval, the department which supervises the computerised cataloguing of the Museum's collections.

The caption announces *The attack. At a signal, along the entire 16 mile front, the British troops leaped over the trench parapets and advanced towards the German trenches, under heavy fire of the enemy.*[1] The screen shows a dozen men in a trench: one moves behind the others then leads them over the parapet, but two fall back. The scene shifts – from a low camera angle, some 15 men are seen advancing slowly through barbed wire; again, two fall. This was the visual climax of the film *The Battle of the Somme*, the moment at which the British Army goes 'over the top' in the long-awaited 'Big Push'. Though not the conclusion of the film, it was still the moment on which all attention was concentrated as it played to packed audiences in the late summer and autumn of 1916, mere weeks after the events portrayed. Reactions encompassed shock ('Oh God, they're dead!' cried a woman in the audience), and outrage ('I beg leave respectfully to enter a protest against an entertainment which wounds the heart and violates the very sanctity of bereavement,' wrote the Dean of Durham) but the most common was a kind of stunned approval. The author Rider Haggard wrote in his diary '. . . it does give a wonderful idea of the fighting. . . . The most impressive [picture] to my mind is that of a regiment scrambling out of a trench to charge and of the one man who slides back shot dead. There is something appalling about the instantaneous change from fierce activity to supine death. . . . War has always been dreadful, but never, I suppose, more dreadful than today.'[2] Yet the sequence that provoked these reactions is almost certainly not genuine.

The case against it is extremely strong. The shallow, un-wired trench and the lush grass below the wire through which the men advance do not look convincing as part of a battle zone, and the troops are not carrying any of the heavy equipment with which the attackers on 1 July were notoriously weighed down. The camera positions, especially for the second shot, are dangerously exposed: in a real attack, a cameraman so placed would be at risk as much as the attackers, standing still in the face of enemy fire. The supposed casualties 'fall' very easily, and one in the second shot crosses his legs and looks back at the camera. If this is supposed to be the opening of the attack at 7.30 am time presents a major problem, as the cameraman Malins had at 7.20 am been filming a mine explosion from a position above and behind the front line and could scarcely have reloaded and moved his camera and set up in two new positions in just ten minutes, although this is effectively what he claimed to have done in his autobiographical account *How I Filmed the War*. There is, finally, direct contradictory evidence: another cameraman, Brooke-Carrington, interviewed by Kevin

Brownlow for his book *The War, the West and the Wilderness*, described meeting a soldier who had 'died' for Malins in a trench in a mortar school well behind the lines.[3]

There is a case for the defence. The testimony quoted by Brownlow is no more automatically credible than Malins's own account, being hearsay evidence with professional jealousy a possible additional factor, and proving, if anything, only that Malins filmed a staged attack, not that that attack is the sequence used in the film. As to timing, the sequence continues after the two opening shots with some long shots entirely compatible with Malins's earlier camera position. Since he claims to have filmed several waves of attackers during the course of 1 July, the dishonesty might amount only to an editorial merging of several attacks blurred by a slightly misleading caption. The comfortable casualty might be genuinely seeking comfort or even shamming death in a real battle, the cameraman could be a genuine hero or a naive novice who did not understand the reality of danger, and the 'typical' trench and the 'proper' equipment are the products of historians' hindsight not contemporary reality.[4] Such arguments are not without value, but in this case they appear somewhat laboured. The sequence is now generally accepted to be a fake, and its development into a classic part of the imagery of the First World War is one of the ironies of popular culture.

The film that contains this famous scene – although it may be acclaimed with hindsight as the first feature-length British battle documentary and thus the direct ancestor of such notable Second World War films as *Desert Victory* and *The True Glory* – came into being in some senses almost by accident. The machinery for the taking of official (or indeed any) film in British front line areas had only recently started up. After the initial outright ban imposed by Lord Kitchener in September 1914, it took over a year to evolve a working arrangement between the War Office and the trade, under the auspices of a body called the British Top-

The first part of the 'over the top' sequence from *The Battle of the Somme* – the scene that so impressed Rider Haggard.
Q70164 and Q70166

The second part of the sequence : note how the casualty (second from the right in the first picture) appears to fall carefully and later to compose himself comfortably on his back.
Q70169 and FLM1654

ical Committee for War Films. The first two cameramen allowed in the British sectors of the Western Front arrived in November 1915 and the various series of short information films resulting from their work were thus still relative novelties in the summer of 1916.

Since these early films were considered rather dull, there may have been suggestions to the cameramen to work for more exciting action film. There is, however, no evidence to indicate any intention to change the format of short informational films before the nature of the material returned from the Somme itself suggested that something more ambitious might be attempted. There was no concerted, planned or scripted effort coherently to cover a major offensive for posterity – merely the continuing efforts of just two cameramen, with bulky equipment and dependent on the officers in charge of the positions where they filmed for information and assistance, to make the most of the events unfolding around them. Nonetheless, the skill and, to a large extent, the luck of those cameramen (that luck including a two-day postponement of the attack, which gave more time for filming preparations) combined with the inescapable drama of the events portrayed made it possible to produce a major film. The effect of that film would be all the greater because of the absence of any similar previous film with which it could be compared.[5]

As has already been seen, the initial impact of the film was considerable and there was little inclination to question its authenticity – the *Illustrated London News* wrote 'Never before has a battle been filmed at such close quarters' while the trade paper *Bioscope* claimed some of the credit for having goaded the authorities into producing this more exciting film: 'if the Trade press had shared Fleet Street's artificial ecstasies over those early films, the authorities might not have made the effort which resulted in the present splendid series'. Nonetheless, the audience for which *The Battle of the Somme* was prepared was not wholly naive, and there is what one writer has termed 'negative evidence' to suggest the existence of some suspicions. This evidence takes the form of the emphasis given in the publicity for its successor films on authenticity: for example the publicity leaflet for the opening of *The Battle of the Ancre and the Advance of the Tanks* (the film of the end of the Somme campaign in the autumn of 1916) starts with the words 'General Headquarters is responsible for the censorship of these films and allows nothing in the nature of a "fake" to be shown. The pictures are authentic and taken on the battlefield.'[6] Such comments, with their implied criticism of earlier films, must have been made for some purpose.

Whatever the attitudes of 1916, the staff of the Imperial War Museum in the immediate post-war years were already fully aware of their responsibility in the matter of film, and arranged screenings in the early 1920s to obtain the views of experts on the films they held. *The Battle of the Somme* was screened on 4 May 1922 to a panel of experts who appear to have been unanimous in their suspicion of the 'attack' sequence. One of them, Colonel R G Finlayson, suggested 'any parts which are considered to be "fakes" – such as the scene showing the troops actually going over the top – should be so labelled in the explanatory notes' although this excellent suggestion does not seem to have been acted on at the time.[7] Their comments interestingly also link the suspect passages to a trench mortar school, confirmation of the story related by Brooke-Carrington to Brownlow.

Against this background of early cynicism or realism, it is hard to explain the apparent need for more recent generations to rediscover the fact that this powerful image was less than fully authentic. Possibly it is the major BBC television series *The Great War*, produced for the fiftieth anniversary of the outbreak of that war, that is responsible. It is at least arguable that awareness of fakery in First World War battle film was obscured by *The Great War* at the same time as the series was rediscovering for the public the very existence of that film.

At the suggestion of the Imperial War Museum, *The Great War* carried a disclaimer stating 'A very small part of the film material used in this series is reconstructed, usually by Official Photographers two or three days after the events depicted. Material of this kind is used only where it faithfully reflects the reality, and where no genuine film exists'.[8] The Museum made this suggestion because *The Great War* was at times regrettably cavalier in its use of film – in fact, considerably more so than the disclaimer intimated. Sequences were used out of their correct temporal or geographical context, feature film material was imported wholesale and without acknowledgement to make up the deficiencies of the actuality footage available, and individual shots were manipulated to 'help' the audience – for example, film was reversed to ensure that on the whole the Allies advance left-to-right across the screen and the Central Powers right-to-left as on maps of the Western Front even if this resulted in whole regiments of left-handed soldiers. Because of the disclaimer, because of the impressive production values – the series was an important part of the launch of the new (and some would say highbrow) BBC second channel, and featured a solemn credits sequence, episode titles based on 'significant' though not necessarily helpful quotations, imposing music, challenging scripts, 'big name' stars voicing the narration and the words of the statesmen and commanders, and the usage of skilfully edited interviews with redoubtable and eloquent survivors – and especially because British television had not seen anything on quite this scale before, the series carried with it a strong aura of authority. This aura carried over to the original film which the series makers had utilised.

'Once bitten, twice shy.' The viewer aware of

having been taken in by one sequence is anxious not to be fooled again. To be thought cynical or over-suspicious is less embarrassing than to be thought unduly credulous. Those who (re)discover the inauthenticity of the 'attack' sequence in *The Battle of the Somme* are likely to comb the remainder of the film for further evidence of sharp practice by the film makers, and to think they have found it. Before considering these further candidates for denunciation, however, a moment should be spent considering the criteria against which 'truth' or 'accuracy' are to be measured. There are, effectively, three distinct yardsticks. First, there is that established by the film itself – the extent to which the images match what is promised by the captions which introduce each scene to the audience. Next, there is the level established by the makers of the film and their contemporaries in the documentation that has come down to posterity together with the film itself. Finally, there is the test of objective truth, so far as historians can establish such a thing, in matching the visual evidence of the film against alternative visual, oral and written testimony.

The standards of precision set by the film itself are not high. The captions conform to the interpretation of the balancing needs of propaganda and censorship current at the time. They offer little in the way of specific geography: only six towns or villages are named. The suggestion of time is no more informative – after early references to five days of preparations, most captions suggest only the eve or the day of the attack or the day after. No individual is named in the captions – de Lisle (the only general officer seen) is identified simply as 'a Divisional General'. To preserve secrecy about the significant fighting units, the captions never identify Battalions and only once mention a specific Division. In contrast, they are used to the greatest extent possible to name Regiments and so to maximise the national empathy which the county identifications of the British regimental system naturally promoted. Eighteen Regiments are named, with additional less specific references to 'Highlanders' or 'a Lancashire Battalion' etc.

The documentation attaching to the film provides a rather higher standard of identification. The Museum's Department of Film possesses a listing compiled sometime between the production of the film and the aforementioned screening to experts which allocates each sequence to a precise date and location (and occasionally unit), as well as attributing each to one of the two cameramen – Geoffrey Malins and J. B. McDowell – responsible for the film.[9] This document, conventionally if not quite appropriately known as the dope sheet, makes significant claims about the film and it is to be regretted that more is not known about its origins. Some of its identifications are demonstrably wrong, and many more are only partially right (for example, plausible for one

The roll-call of the Seaforth Highlanders: an enlargement of a photograph taken by Ernest Brooks which may include a previously unrecognised picture of Geoffrey Malins (the figure taking notes to the left of the Sergeant conducting the roll call) and his camera (above the helmet of the soldier on the extreme left) on the evening of 1 July 1916. Although this identification is not certain, the film sequence of the roll call was filmed from a camera position directly compatible with the position of the supposed Malins figure. Q746 (enlargement)

A likely story? The 'Hull Commercials', according to their Battalion History, dragged away from their mail on 3 July 1916 after participating in a battle and sent on a long route march laid on solely to please the cameramen – but still looking very happy about it. From the sequence following caption 14. FLM1657 part of a sequence but not for all of it): although far too helpful to be dismissed out of hand, it is a document which should be used cautiously.

Also preserved in the Museum are the still photographs taken by the official photographer Ernest Brooks, which were frequently taken at almost the same moment and from very much the same viewpoint as the film. The captions attaching to such photographs offer for those scenes a kind of second opinion to that provided in the film captions or dope sheet. Some significance may be attached to the fact that there are no still photographs equivalent to episodes of suspect film, including the 'over the top' scenes, but this argument must be used with care: there are also no still photographs matching several film scenes of unquestioned authenticity, just as there is no film matching some of the classic photographs. Perhaps more interesting in the context of the 'attack' sequence is the existence of a series of photographs showing explosions filmed at a trench mortar school in a landscape very reminiscent of that sequence.[10]

Of comparable vintage is the personal account *How I Filmed the War* by one of the cameramen, Geoffrey Malins. This book, originally written in 1917, was not published until 1920: even so it retains some gestures towards wartime censorship, including the deletion of certain personal and place names (though these are often reinstated in the photograph captions). More seriously, it provides ample illustrations of its author's tendency towards boastful exaggerations of his own heroics, amounting at times to demonstrable falsehood, which leave the reader obliged to question its overall credibility. With reference to 1 July 1916, for example, Malins describes in terms which generally ring true his filming of two events which are undeniably authentic (the Lancashire Fusiliers in the sunken road and the explosion of the mine under the Hawthorn Redoubt) but then provides an account of filming the attack itself which bears little relation to any known film, including the 'over the top' sequence.[11] Unfortunately, neither Brooks nor McDowell left an autobiography of his own.

Aids to the person who seeks to establish objective truth are numerous, from the *Official History* and battalion or regimental histories of the units involved to a number of modern studies of the battle frequently based (after the pattern of the original work of this kind, Martin Middlebrook's *The First Day on the Somme*) on oral history interviews with survivors. These works occasionally mention the filming or photography of the war, and provide detailed accounts of events which the film and photographs covered, but they do not always prove as helpful to the researcher as might be expected. More recently still, the columns of publications such as the journals of the Western Front Association *Stand To!* and *Gun Fire* have begun directly to consider the authenticity

of the visual record of the war.[12]

As with the 'over the top' sequence, the other scenes in *The Battle of the Somme* on which suspicion falls are those where something is thought not to 'look right' or where the camera position is considered incompatible with authenticity, and those where there is some outside evidence suggesting dishonesty in the film. A catalogue of these scenes would include the following:

The vicious bark of the Canadian 60 Pounders adds to the din of gun fire. (Caption 13)

The sequence shows a 60-pounder Mark 1 field gun firing from a heavily sand-bagged gun emplacement, filmed from both inside and outside. Challenges based on the 'exposed camera position' argument have been made against this scene because of the outside shots. Such arguments, however, overlook the fact that the 60-pounder's range was over 6 miles and that a cameraman filming one in action was thus scarcely risking being sniped. A more subtle challenge is that the emplacement is much more elaborate than those seen elsewhere in the film: this may suggest that the film derives from a training ground, or simply that the gunners concerned had time to take pains on a static front.

Meanwhile, more troops are started for the trenches. London Scottish and East Yorkshires. (Caption 14)

The sequence shows kilted troops marching, led by bagpipes, then a column of infantry on the march looking very happy, waving to the camera etc. The problem is that neither of the units filmed, though correctly identified, 'belongs' near any of the others seen in the film and on this occasion the dope sheet (which suggests filming by McDowell near Beaumont Hamel on 26 June – a combination incompatible with the known movements of both cameraman and the units concerned) does not help. However, Malins, in *How I Filmed the War*, describes meeting the London Scottish on his way to Gommecourt on 26 June and although his account describes a General's speech rather than a marching column the match is close enough with the Battalion's movements to suggest a satisfactory explanation.[13] More problematic are the East Yorks.

The book *A History of the 10th (Service) Battalion of the East Yorkshire Regiment (Hull Commercials)* contains a detailed anecdote concerning an episode on the morning of 3 July. The Battalion was resting and enjoying its mail after involvement in the opening of the Somme battle (though not itself in the attack) when it was called out in full battle order and at next to no notice – consigning the contents of parcels to an incinerator – to be sent on a very long route march. It transpired that this was solely for the purpose of passing the official cameraman with a cheery smile. The story con-

The camera angle outside the emplacement for the 60-pounder gun in the sequence following caption 13. Compare the elaborate emplacement with that of the 'Vimy Queen' in the accompanying still photograph below. FLM1651 and Q2

The scene in the mortar pit in the sequence following caption 16. Note the foot of an onlooker at the top of the frame (centre). FLM1653

The still photograph bearing the caption 'shell bursting at the Trench Mortar School St Pol, July 1916' that exactly matches the sequence in the film following caption 17 'Bombarding the Germans with 9.2 inch howitzers' attributed by the dope sheet to Malins filming near Beaumont Hamel around 27 June. Note also the similarity in the landscape to the second part of the 'over the top' sequence. Q784

cludes with humorous reflections of the 'What a pity it was before the time of sound pictures!' type; an accompanying still photograph confirms that this scene is the result of the filming described.

It is hard to know how to react to this: the film researcher would normally treat a battalion history as an authoritative source and seemingly no clearer evidence of trickery could be required. Despite its origins, however, this account does not ring altogether true. On the circumstantial side, no other evidence places Malins or McDowell as far north as 31st Division on 3 July while the London Scottish material just described does confirm Malins's account of his passage through the northern sector before the attack opened.

(The original captions to still photographs of this scene date it as 28 June.) It must moreover be questioned whether a commanding officer would do anything so unnecessary, so unfeeling, and so disruptive of morale as to give to resting troops orders such as those described solely to oblige a cameraman, and whether the men would look so cheerful if he had. The scene is, however, entirely consistent in tone with others of columns marching towards the front before the attack. On balance, it seems that it may be the battalion history that needs to be taken with a pinch of salt: it was not published until 1937, and possibly a good story had been developed over twenty years of telling.[14]

Firing 'plum puddings' from trench mortars.
(Caption 16)

In a trench mortar pit, the mortar is fired twice. Malins describes taking this material in 29th Division trenches on 29 June: his account is quite detailed, and describes the mortar misfiring three times (there are no misfires apparent in the film, though there are several cuts).[15] This scene is open to several of the same types of criticism as the 'over the top' sequence, and it is noteworthy that the context recalls the trench mortar school associated with that sequence. An extra piece of evidence in this case is the foot of someone apparently standing on the rim of the mortar pit at the end of the scene – an unlikely position in genuine combat. The evidence seems to suggest another fake.

Bombarding the Germans with 9.2 inch howitzers. The shells tearing up the enemy's deep dug-outs.
(Caption 17)

The scene concludes with shellbursts filmed through barbed wire – a shot previously considered authentic and indeed on occasion used by the Museum as a contrast to more dubious shellburst film. The dope sheet attributes it to Malins near Beaumont Hamel about 27 June. The shot, however, exactly matches a still photograph with the caption 'shell bursting at the Trench Mortar School St Pol, July 1916', and thus seems likely to be a stock shot.[16] The similarity of the landscape to that seen in the second shot of the 'over the top' sequence has already been commented on.

Cold nights or heatwave summer? The men in cold weather kit who appear in the sequence following caption 18. FLM1652

The Royal Warwickshires – in shorts – in the sequence following caption 21. FLM1658

The famous still photograph of the Lancashire Fusiliers fixing bayonets, commonly captioned 1 July 1916 but recently shown to have been taken a day or two earlier, and a frame from the film following caption 28 demonstrating that the action continued after the photograph was taken. Q744 and Q79491

The Royal Warwickshires were having a meal in camp on the evening of the great advance. (Caption 18)

The scene conforms to the caption, though the dope sheet gives the date of 29 June rather than the 30 June the former implies. Suspicion here attaches to a shot cut into the sequence, in which some soldiers in cold weather kit are seen sharing out cigarettes. In the context of 'the heat wave summer' of 1916 this does indeed seem anomalous, and probably suggests a stock shot introduced for padding. It is, however, worth pointing out that the scene is quite long already and hardly needs padding; that the 'heat wave' had in fact included such heavy rain on and before 28 June that the attack was postponed for two days from the planned date, and the nights were still cold (Malins on 30 June: 'I lay shiver-ing in my blanket and could not get warm'[17]), and that – on the other side – some of the men in the background to this shot look quite comfortable in ordinary kit. The shot seems to deserve curiosity more than denunciation.

A further moving up of troops. A new Battalion of the Royal Warwickshires resting on their way to the trenches. (Caption 21)

Interest in this sequence (besides the point that the men, despite the caption, are marching not resting) lies in the fact that the troops are all wearing shorts. This has been used to justify suspicion that the scene is merely a stock shot of route-marching troops, on the grounds that in 1916 shorts would not have been worn into battle. This, however,

The mine crater from the sequence following caption 29 – where it cannot be the result of the 'Hawthorn Redoubt' mine, though this is what is implied – which is used again after caption 51. FLM1659

The camera angle – and the gun angle – from the sequence following caption 30. Q79496

The soldier on the extreme left still has the protective cover on his rifle (though the others do not): how close to combat should we believe he is? From the sequence following caption 32. FLM1650

The 'rescue' scene from the sequence following caption 34. Q79501

is not battle but moving up towards battle and, in any case, the truth is that shorts *were* worn in combat – a Private in the Worcestershire Regiment won a VC on 3 July while wearing shorts.[18] Thus there is no reason to doubt the authenticity of this scene.

A Lancashire Battalion awaiting instructions fixing bayonets, and passing through communication trench to the first line. Bombers taking up supplies.
(Caption 28)

The sequence shows, first, a group of men and officers against the background of a sand-bagged position, then a long scene at the junction of a communication trench and a reserve trench in which a Corporal, a Warrant Officer and their men fix bayonets and move up the communication trench followed by several pairs of soldiers carrying boxes slung from poles over their shoulders, and more troops arriving from right and left at the double. The dope sheet lists this material as 'White City' (opposite Beaumont Hamel) on the morning of 1 July.

For the historian, this sequence recalls the problems of caption 14. Although one of the officers in the first scene has a Fusilier hackle on his helmet, these are not Lancashire Fusiliers. They are more probably the 16th (Public Schools) Battalion, Middlesex Regiment – the Battalion history uses a similar still photograph with a caption confirming White City on 1 July.[19] Even this identification is problematic, however, as the Battalion should have been in its assembly positions, not at White City, on the morning of the attack: possibly the troops are some men detached the previous day as reserves, or perhaps the date is wrong – a possibility the earlier Hull Commercials anecdote, or indeed the second part of this sequence, may illustrate.

The scene for the second part has shifted from 'White City' to the nearby junction of 'King Street' and 'Esau's Way'. Here the troops are definitely the 1st Battalion, Lancashire Fusiliers. This scene (or the exactly matching photograph) is another classic image of the Somme: the *Lancashire Fusiliers Annual* reproduces it with a caption identifying the NCOs and confirming the date as 1 July, and it is widely used elsewhere. Recent testimony, however, suggests dope sheet, photograph caption and unit history are all wrong. A Corporal of the Battalion, George Ashurst, in an interview by the Museum's Department of Sound Records and in his autobiography, describes being asked to cooperate in staging the bayonet-fixing scene to oblige a photographer a day or two before the attack ' "Lancashire Fusiliers going over the top" – we weren't at all, we went back in the dugout after that'.[20] This account does not explain the other ingredients in the film sequence (which do not of course feature in the still photograph), and these might be considered more

than would be laid on just to oblige a cameraman. The basic account is, however, plausible – it also makes the point that on the morning of the actual attack the trenches were far more crowded than in this scene – and it seems probable that for once the non-specific film caption is less misleading than normally more authoritative sources.

It may be noted that both the *Lancashire Fusiliers Annual* and the Public Schools Battalion history cite Malins or his work among their references.[21] The task of disentangling the credible from the misleading is made all the more difficult by the knowledge that people's memories of events come to be coloured by the preserved images with which they also become familiar: the film and the photographs themselves thus become sources for the sources which researchers then use to decipher them. It is no wonder the result can be so confusing.

Just before the attack. Blowing up enemy trenches by a huge mine. Royal Engineers rushing off to wire the crater for occupation by the advance troops.
(Caption 29)

The sequence shows men carrying tackle and wire equipment at 'White City', the explosion of a very large mine, several shell bursts filmed through wire, and panning shots over a large crater which is being explored by a small group of unarmed personnel. Despite some criticisms that the mine explosion (another classic image) was almost too good to be true – doubts were expressed by one member of the Museum's 1922 review panel – the explosion is now generally accepted as authentic coverage of the detonation at 7.20 am on 1 July of 40,000 lbs of ammonal laid under the German positions at 'Hawthorn Redoubt'. It is in fact partly belief in Malins's account of filming the explosion that makes it impossible to believe he could have filmed the 'over the top' scenes ten minutes later. Doubts about this sequence attach to the mine crater seen at the end – it most certainly is not the crater resulting from the explosion, as that was not captured until months after the film had first been shown to the public. In fact this footage is re-used later in the film in a sequence (number 51) captioned *A mine crater 40 feet deep*. The dope sheet attributes the second appearance to Malins filming near La Boisselle on 5 July, a plausible descripton which suggests identification of the crater as that at 'Lochnagar' and which removes the justification for the darker suspicions that have sometimes been entertained about its first appearance.

Setting up machine guns. Firing from top of trench parapet. (Caption 30)

The sequence shows troops setting up a Vickers gun on a trench parapet: one of them, wearing shorts, sits on the parapet to do so. The gun fires short bursts (some film apparently from outside the trench) then a sustained burst from which the camera pans over no man's land to the enemy lines beyond. The 'exposed camera position' argument has been brought into play against this scene, with 'shorts not worn in combat' in support. As has been shown, the shorts argument is not valid while the pan from machine gun to enemy lines does carry conviction. It is the cameraman's seemingly recklessness that requires explanation. The clue is provided by Martin Middlebrook, who uses this scene as an illustration in *The First Day on the Somme* and points out that the angle of the gun suggests it is laying down long-range harrassing fire over the heads of attacking troops.[22] If this is so, the range would be such (and the enemy sufficiently distracted) that the cameraman – or others leaning over the parapet – would not be unduly at risk.

Warwickshires advancing up a captured trench to relieve the Queens in the front line. (Caption 32)

One or two of the troops seen moving up a communication trench in this scene still have mud-covers on their rifles: this may be considered unlikely for troops approaching combat and so suggestive of fakery or a scene from training, or it may be basic care of weapons for troops approaching combat but not yet in it.

British Tommies rescuing a comrade under shell fire. (This man died 30 minutes after reaching the trenches). (Caption 34)

Despite (or possibly because of) a detailed circumstantial account by Malins, this scene, with a wounded man being carried on another's back along a trench towards the camera is another one that has been thought 'too good to be true'. The Museum, however, received a letter in 1978 from the daughter of the rescuer, positively identifying him as RSM George Wood of the West Yorkshire Regiment.[23] The 21st Pioneer Battalion of the West Yorks were part of 4th Division, in the line next to 29th Division, to which the wounded man visibly belongs (he wears the Divisional shoulder flash): both Divisions feature prominently in Malins's filming.

Bringing in the wounded (British and German) on stretchers through the trenches during the height of battle. (Caption 35)

A cataloguer working at the Museum once constructed the hypothesis that one shot in this sequence shows a British soldier lying at his ease on a stretcher wearing a captured Pickelhaube to impersonate a wounded German. While it is true that he looks quite comfortable, with his hands behind his head and a contented expression on his face, examination of a clearer print of the film shows that the 'Pickelhaube' is in fact a standard British helmet liner. The

anecdote illustrates the dangers of over-zealous fake-spotting.

One of five unsuccessful German counter attacks at La Boisselle. (Caption 38)

The complaint about this sequence is that the visual material fails to live up to the excitement promised by the caption: the foreground shows only troops resting and a stretcher party. There is, however, a major artillery barrage going on in the distance, and it is presumably to this the caption refers. Another problem is that the dope sheet dates this scene as 9 July, which is late for the cameraman's assumed stay in the area: Malins himself offers the more probable date of 3 or 4 July.[24]

Officer giving drink, and Tommies offering cigarettes to German prisoners. (Caption 42)

The scene conforms to the caption: it merits mention in this context because the offerings are obviously made in direct response to promptings from the camera position, so that it provides a perfect example of the extent to which the very presence of a camera can influence events.

Clearing the battle field of snipers and hidden machine guns. Routing Germans from dug-outs. (Caption 46)

The scene shows British soldiers moving between trenches: there is no sign of any casualties, of German prisoners, or even of discarded equipment. Although the dope sheet ascribes this to Malins at Montauban on 1 or 2 July, the scene is totally unconvincing, and gives every sign of having been staged for the camera well away from any recently fought battle.

A labour battalion of the Duke of Cornwall's Light Infantry repairing road on day following battle. (Caption 52)

The troops seen in this footage – filmed at Fricourt on 5 July according to the dope sheet, though the caption implies 3 July – are never close enough to identify clearly. No confirmation of a DCLI presence has come to light in any source so far consulted by film cataloguers: the caption may thus be an instance of the use of unit names for propaganda purposes only, without any historical justification. If this is the case, it is the only such case in the film, and the possibility should not be overlooked that the research, not the caption, may be in error.

Royal Fusiliers cleaning up after the successful advance. (Caption 57)

Several panning shots across an encamped unit, the 13th Battalion Royal Fusiliers, filmed between 7 and 9

The helmet liner mistaken for a Pickelhaube in the sequence following caption 35. FLM1660

The distant counter-attack, from the sequence following caption 38. FLM1655

According to the caption these men are clearing the battlefield of snipers and hidden machine guns after a recent battle. Note, however, the absence of debris or of caution – by the soldiers or the cameraman. From the sequence following caption 46. FLM1656

The scene described by Guy Chapman, from the sequence following caption 57. FLM1648

July. Some people looking at the sequence think it combines film from two different scenes, though this is by no means a universal opinion; the dates are also a little late compared to the rest of the film taken. To counteract these suspicions, however, there is ample confirmation of the authenticity of these scenes in the shape both of a matching set of still photographs and, more entertainingly, in the trench memoir *A Passionate Prodigality* by Guy Chapman who served with the Battalion. He is describing the Battalion encamped and exhausted after their participation in an attack on 7 July: '. . . there was a sudden stir. A few men rose, others woke and joined them, collecting in a mob around a khaki figure with a camera. Pickelhaubes, German helmets, Teutonic forage caps, leaf-shaped bayonets, automatics, were produced from haversacks. The faces which ten minutes earlier had seemed those of dying men were now alight with excited amusement. "Come on, come an' have your picture took," echoed from man to man: and amid much cheering the official press was obliged with a sitting.'[25]

Seeking further laurels. A 'sample' of the British Army (the Worcesters) off to continue the advance.
(Caption 61)

A battalion in column of fours on the march, very clean, waving helmets, equipment etc (including a large mallet). These are virtually the last British troops seen in the film: the caption makes the purpose of the shot obvious, and the dope sheet optimistically dates it as 9 July. The tone of the shot is, however, absolutely consistent with the 'moving up' shots from before 30 June, and an exactly equivalent still photograph in the Museum is captioned 28 June.[26] These are indeed troops hoping to 'continue the advance', but they were filmed before 1 July, not after.

Besides the piecemeal analysis of individual shots, there are some general comments to be made about the issue of faking in *The Battle of the Somme*. Most obvious is the question why, if there are fakes in the film, is the resulting film not more exciting? While the film holds the interest – especially of the informed viewer who has an idea what to look for – it scarcely overflows with dramatic incident. Some such incidents are clearly fakes or highly suspicious (the attack and the trench mortar) but there are not many of them, while some other moments of drama (the sunken road, the mine, the wounded) are considered authentic. The remaining 'suspect' scenes are actually at best of only average visual interest, and one is obliged to ask why the cameramen should bother to fake or stage material – especially material involving troops on the march or encamped – when such scenes were happening all around them in any case.

The film returned from France was assembled in London in circumstances which remain a little obscure: the credit for the film appears to belong to William Jury (of Jury's Imperial Pictures before the war, and a member of the British Topical Committee) although roles have been claimed on behalf both of Charles Urban (another Committee member) and Malins himself. As noted earlier, the grandeur of the subject matter seems to have suggested the compilation of a major film. There is no evidence of a more definite propaganda motive, such as an attempt to conceal the absence of success and the heavy casualty list behind a triumphant veneer. The only goal openly stated for the film is that in the letter from Lloyd George (then Secretary of State for War) read to the audience at the first screening: 'that every one of us at home and abroad shall see what our men at the Front are doing and suffering for us and how their achievements have been made possible by the sacrifices made at home.'[27]

Whatever its intentions, the film overall does not convey the impression of great editorial sophistication. Several times, the editors appear almost wilfully to destroy the logical development of events – for example in the build-up to the (admittedly fake) attack on the morning of 1 July, or in the roll call of the Seaforth Highlanders on the evening of that day when a scene which Malins recognised as potentially 'one of the most wonderful, the most impressive that can be conceived'[28] is ruined by being split over two sequences either side of the Royal Fusiliers encampment. The re-use of the 'Lochnagar' crater film, the retention of the blatantly orchestrated 'cigarettes to prisoners' scene, the charmingly inept use of the ambiguous caption *Manchester Pioneers waiting to go down to the German trenches when captured*, and the attempt to pass off film from 28 June as being troops 'seeking fresh laurels' are all difficult to reconcile with a production we are supposed also to believe capable of organising extensive faking and of perpetrating cunning confidence tricks on the public.

In general, it seems fair to conclude that, while *The Battle of the Somme* does contain some faked film, the proportion of such film to the whole work is actually quite small – much smaller, for example, than the proportion in the average episode of *The Great War* or many other subsequent documentaries. The makers of the earlier film are on the whole guilty – if guilty is the word – not so much of fakery as of the lesser misdemeanour of 'improvement'. Improvement can take place both at the filming stage – with the cameraman encouraging participants to do more interesting things – and in the editing process, with scenes juxtaposed or dressed up with captions or music to provide an appearance more exciting than the reality. With the difference only that modern filmmakers have more technology at their disposal (including sound effects and speech to help blur the visual impact), these practices continue in 'actuality' filming to this day, and the question of how far they compromise the underlying truthfulness of the film record is an issue wider than this paper can encompass. In the specific context of *The Battle of the Somme*, it can only be said that excessive zeal in crying 'fake' does an undeserved discourtesy to the original makers of the film and, in obscuring a very real achievement in pioneering the battlefield documentary, a serious disservice to the modern viewer.

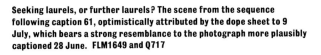

Seeking laurels, or further laurels? The scene from the sequence following caption 61, optimistically attributed by the dope sheet to 9 July, which bears a strong resemblance to the photograph more plausibly captioned 28 June. FLM1649 and Q717

Notes

1. Caption 33 of *The Battle of the Somme*. The film is preserved in the archival collection of the Imperial War Museum's Department of Film, archive number IWM 191; video cassette copies are available for purchase, together with a *Viewing Guide* booklet. This article derives from work done in the preparation of the booklet and has borrowed extensively from the expertise of two colleagues associated with that work, Chris McCarthy of the Department of Exhibits and Firearms and Philip Dutton of the Department of Information Retrieval. Their help is gratefully acknowledged.

2. *Bioscope*, 24 August 1916, p 671; *Times*, 1 September 1916, 7d, letter from H Henley Henson; D S Higgins, Editor, *The Private Diaries of Sir H Rider Haggard 1914–1925*, Cassell, London, 1980, p 84.

3. Lieut. Geoffrey H Malins, *How I Filmed the War*, Herbert Jenkins, London, 1920, pp 162–164; Kevin Brownlow, *The War, the West and the Wilderness*, Secker and Warburg, London, 1979, pp 64–65.

4. Many of these arguments are advanced in Nicholas Reeves's, *Official British Film Propaganda during the First World War*, Croom Helm, London 1986, pp 160–161. On the dangers of hindsight relating, for example, to unrealistically lush grass, consider the reference to 'the wild flowers and rank summer grass' of no man's land in Martin Middlebrook, *The First Day on the Somme*, Allen Lane, London, 1971, p 124.

5. For an account of the origins, intentions and effect of the film see Reeves, op cit, pp 56–62 and 94–113, and S D Badsey, '*Battle of the Somme*: British war-propaganda', *Historical Journal of Film, Radio and Television*, Vol 3 No 2, 1983, pp 99–115.

6. *Illustrated London News*, 26 August 1916, pp 240–241; *Bioscope*, 17 August 1916, p 577; A J Peacock, 'The Somme Film – some notes', *Gun Fire*, Vol 1 No 1, 1984, pp 9–16; Scala Theatre leaflet for the programme commencing 15 January [1917] – copy in the Department of Film.

7. 'Particulars of "Battle of Somme" film screened on 4 May 1922 before Imperial War Museum Trustees and comments thereon by technical officers of the Navy and Army' – document preserved in the Department of Film.

8. Copies of *The Great War* are held in the Department of Film, archive numbers IWM 1065/1–26. The disclaimer appears on the first episode and some others.

9. 'Battle of Somme 1st July–18th November 1916' [sic] – document preserved in the Department of Film.

10. Five photographs each captioned 'Shell bursting at the Trench Mortar School, St Pol, July 1916', Department of Photographs Q784–788; see also others in the Department's 'Q' series.

11. Malins, op cit, pp 153–165.

12. Brigadier-General Sir James E Edmonds (compiled) *Military Operations France and Belgium 1916*, Macmillan, London, 1932; second volume, covering events from 2 July, compiled by Captain Wilfrid Miles, 1938; Middlebrook, op cit; *Stand To!*, journal of the Western Front Association; *Gun Fire*, journal produced by members of the Northern Branch of the Western Front Association.

13. Malins, op cit, p 122; Lt-Col J H Lindsay, *The London Scottish in the Great War*, Regimental Headquarters, London, 1925, p 102.

14. *A History of the 10th (Service) Battalion of the East Yorkshire Regiment (Hull Commercials) 1914–1919*, Brown and Sons, London 1937, pp 92–93, photograph opposite p 96; 'The 10th East Yorkshire Regiment marching to the trenches; near Doullens, 28 June 1916', Department of Photographs Q743.

15. Malins, op cit, pp 148–150.

16. Q784 etc – see note 10.

17. Malins, op cit, p 153; striking visual evidence of bad weather in late June is provided in the film following Caption 25 *Operating the 15-inch howitzer ('Grandmother') manned by the Royal Marine Artillery*.

18. 'Private T G TURRALL, VC. NOTE. The Battalion bombers wore shorts, and Private Turrall used his own puttee as a bandage for the wounded officer' – caption to illustration, Captain H Fitz M Stacke, *The Worcestershire Regiment in the Great War*, Cheshire and Sons, Kidderminster, 1929, facing p 170. Men wearing shorts in or near the front line are also visible in the film, for example in the sequences following captions 30 and 35.

19. H W Wallis Grain, *The 16th (Public Schools) Service Battalion (The Duke of Cambridge's Own) Middlesex Regiment and the Great War, 1914–1918*, Lewingdon (printer), London, 1935, caption to photograph facing p 38 'parading in the White City before the attack on Beaumont Hamel, 1st July, 1916'; Middlebrook, op cit, facing p 125, in his caption to the same photo suggests 'the eve of the battle'.

20. 'Battle of Albert. The 1st Lancashire Fusiliers fixing bayonets prior to the assault on Beaumont Hamel. July 1916.', Department of Photographs Q744; Major B Smyth (compiled and edited), *The Lancashire Fusiliers Annual 1916, Number XXVI*, Sackville Press, Dublin 1917, pp 35–37 and 43; Department of Sound Records interview with George Ashurst, accession number 9875/22; see also George Ashurst, *My Bit*, Crowood Press, Marlborough, 1987, and R B Grundy 'Q744', *Stand To!*, Number 17, 1986, pp 10–11.

21. Wallis Grain, op cit, title page and pp 43–44; Smyth, op cit, p 35 and p 43.

22. Middlebrook, op cit, p 205.

23. Malins, op cit, pp 167–168; letter from Mrs G Sweeting to Imperial War Museum, 15 August 1978, held in the Department of Film.

24. Malins, op cit, photograph facing p 176.

25. 'Battle of Albert. 13th Royal Fusiliers resting after the attack on La Boisselle, on 7th July 1916. Near Albert, on the Albert-Bapaume Road', Department of Photographs Q775–777 and Q797–798; Guy Chapman, *A Passionate Prodigality*, Nicholson and Watson, London, 1933, p 114.

26. 'The 4th Battalion of the Worcestershire Regiment (29th Division) marching to the trenches; Acheux, 28th June 1916', Department of Photographs Q716–717.

27. Reeves, op cit; Badsey, op cit; *Bioscope*, 17 August 1916, p 576.

28. Malins, op cit, p 171.

Further Reading

On the background to British official film:
Rachael Low, *The History of the British Film 1914–1918*, Allen and Unwin, London, 1950.
Kevin Brownlow, *The War, the West and the Wilderness*, Secker and Warburg, London, 1979.
Nicholas Reeves, *Official British Film Propaganda during the First World War*, Croom Helm, London, 1986.
On the making and reception of *The Battle of the Somme*:
Lieut. Geoffrey H Malins, *How I Filmed the War*, Herbert Jenkins, London, 1920.
S D Badsey, '*Battle of the Somme*: British war-propaganda', *Historical Journal of Film, Radio and Television*, Vol 3 No 2, 1983, pp 99–115.
On the events depicted in the film:
For a general guide to the more significant of the numerous books on the Somme battles, see the Department of Printed Books' booklist No. 36, *Military Operations, 1914–1918; The Battle of the Somme 1916*, 1986.
The Official History, ie Brigadier-General Sir James E Edmonds (compiled), *Military Operations France and Belgium 1916*, Macmillan, London, 1932; second volume, covering events from 2 July, compiled by Captain Wilfrid Miles, 1938.
Martin Middlebrook, *The First Day on the Somme*, Allen Lane, London, 1971.

The Evacuation of Cape Helles, Gallipoli

Peter Hart

IMPERIAL WAR MUSEUM

REVIEW

This article attempts to provide a picture of the evacuation of the Helles position on the Gallipoli Peninsula, using excerpts from the collections held by the Departments of Documents, Printed Books and Sound Records in the Imperial War Museum. It is not intended to be a comprehensive survey of all the sources or of all the differing types of experience available but rather to interlock the differing strands of individuals' experiences on Cape Helles during that long and anxious first week of January 1916.

'We are living in exciting times,' wrote Major General Archibald Paris on the morning of 8 January 1916.[1] As he wrote the troops of the Royal Naval Division under his command along with the VIII Corps under Lieutenant General Francis Davies were about to undertake the extremely dangerous evacuation of Cape Helles at the foot of the Gallipoli Peninsula.

This marked the end of the disastrous Gallipoli Campaign which had begun on such high hopes with the landings at Helles and Anzac Cove the previous April. The landings under the command of General Sir Ian Hamilton, were a catalogue of blunders, missed opportunities and slaughter, made worse by a serious underestimation of the Turks' ability in defence, and further assaults by both sides had done little more than swell the casualty lists. On 6 August a last effort had been made with diversionary actions at Helles and Anzac and a new landing was made at Suvla Bay four miles north of Anzac Cove. Initial opportunities soon

Cape Helles

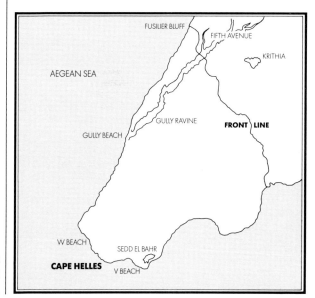

Peter Hart is a research assistant in the Department of Sound Records.

evaporated in the hot August sun, however, and the stalemate was confirmed. With the failure of the August attack it became clear to many that an evacuation was inevitable. Hamilton, who opposed such a move, was recalled on 16 October and replaced by General Sir Charles Monro who, having assessed the situation and secured Kitchener's agreement, recommended evacuation which the Cabinet sanctioned on 7 December. The evacuation of Anzac and Suvla began, using every method of subterfuge possible, and culminated on the night of 19 December in near total success, with the Turks seemingly totally unaware of their opportunity in the final stages.

Four divisions, amounting to some 35,000 men, remained on the Helles bridgehead. Their mood on hearing that their position was to be retained is perhaps best summed up by Able Seaman Thomas Macmillan of the Drake Battalion:

> It was common talk that our Divisional Commander had reported to his superiors that the men of his division were anxious to remain on the Peninsula until the operations had been brought to a satisfactory conclusion. If our Divisional Commander was reported correctly, either he did not know the mind of his men, or it was a case of wishful thinking on his part. Our position appeared hopeless to any man with a spark of intelligence . . .[2]

Similar fears were being expressed in London, and, on 27 December, the final decision was taken by the Cabinet to evacuate Helles.

As with the previous evacuations secrecy was of paramount importance – all the more so now since it was felt that the Turks were unlikely to be fooled twice. As part of the deception process Lieutenant General Sir F J Davies issued an order which would allow the troops in the field to prepare for evacuation but, in case of any leaks, maintain the illusion that Helles was to be retained. Able Seaman Joseph Murray of the Hood Battalion, RND, who had been attached to the VIII Corps Mining Company, remembers chancing upon a copy of the order on a noticeboard in an abandoned dugout whilst pinning up waterproof sheets in the support lines, 'I found a note in one of the dugouts . . . to say that the "VIII Army Corps will be relieved by the IX. Inform all concerned". That was the only information we ever had of any evacuation proceeding or otherwise'.[3] Macmillan's memoir refers to the order too although perhaps with the benefit of hindsight: 'To the discerning eye it was evident that a general evacuation was intended. It was soon common knowledge that the Ninth Army Corps did not exist'.[4] In fact

IX Corps had been the force evacuated from Suvla and one of its constituent parts, the 13th Division, replaced the 42nd Division at Helles. As such the order was a reasonable ploy.

Lieutenant McGrigor of the Royal Gloucestershire Hussars, who had been attached as General Birdwood's ADC at Army Headquarters based at Imbros, took a fairly critical view. In his diary entry for 30 December, he wrote:

> Although it is not supposed to be known, one can't help putting two and two together, and the latest decision is that Helles is now to be abandoned. It does not do to criticise and is not politic, but it does strike one as weird that the decision could not be come to before, and the three places given up together . . . By jove though, this new operation will be ticklish in the extreme; one can surely not hope to get away a second time without fighting, and it does appear that if this evacuation does, and it might easily do, cost us many men, stores, and some guns, it will entirely destroy all the wonderful success of the withdrawal from the other two places.[5]

Some of the factors which were causing concern can be seen in a letter written by Lieutenant Colonel Norman Burge commanding the Nelson Battalion of the RND on 4 January:

> Since the Anzac and Suvla shows are no more – and the Turks have full liberty to concentrate on us here, things have not been too pleasant, in fact they have been, and are, most damnably uncomfortable. We get shelled far more than we've ever had before and with heavier guns and we wallow in the mud and wish we were flatter.[6]

Lieutenant Lavell Leeson, an RAMC officer at the 17th Stationary Hospital, had real fears that some of the hospital staff might be left behind. These were fuelled by the issue to them of notes in French and Turkish which translated 'I am not a fighting soldier; my only work is in connection with the wounded and sick in hospital and in the field under the protection of the Geneva Convention.'[7] Following further orders of 1 January, which left only a skeleton staff of eight (later reduced to six) officers and twenty four other ranks at the hospital, he remarks, 'We were expected to hold off the Turks, take care of roughly 35,000 men, and stay alive,'[8] and later, 'We were stunned by the finality of all the arrangements; it seemed to fit into such a tidy pattern, with absolutely no room for a mistake.'[9]

Matters were not helped by the circulation of

reports or rumours of Turkish foreknowledge of the evacuation. Thus McGrigor at AHQ recorded on 30 December, 'This morning a message thrown into our trenches contained the following rather feeble German joke:-"When are you going? Will meet you again soon on the Canal. Our bully beef is better than yours". We presume the latter part referred to some tins that had been found at Anzac or Suvla.'[10] Whilst Burge wrote on 5 January, 'I heard a yarn today (from a General too) that the Turks catapulted a note into the 52nd Div trenches last night which reads "Goodbye you swine – we know you are going". Pleasant ain't it if it's true?'[11]

Even before the final decision to evacuate had been made 'periods of silence' had been introduced. Thomas Macmillan explains the ruse as it developed in January:

> Throughout the campaign it had been a first principle with us on taking over trenches to secure fire mastery: for every shot fired by the enemy, we returned two where possible. Now, during the hours from dusk to dawn he was allowed to fire to his heart's content without challenge. This made him inordinately curious, and patrol after patrol was sent towards our line.[12] Orders were given that the Turks were to be allowed to come right on to our wire and that, even then, fire was to be opened only on the instruction of a responsible officer.

To help make the silence periods as effective as possible the troops were ordered to wear sandbags on their feet which Joseph Murray found 'bloody awkward.'

In December and early January the remaining French units and the 42nd Division were evacuated from Helles. For the troops who remained the once busy Peninsula became a strange place. Joseph Murray noticed the difference whilst on a working party to collect ammonol from a dump:

> It was really frightening, we leave Fusilier Bluff . . . and come down at the Geogheghan's Bluff you see, that's alright, but there was nobody behind us, there was no troops to be seen anywhere, and we used to walk down to this dump through empty trenches, nobody there, and I thought to myself, 'Well I don't know where the hell everybody's gone . . .'.[13]

From his vantage point at the hospital Lieutenant Leeson observed:

> There were sounds and signs of withdrawal all about us, in spite of the seemingly strong security that we were following. It was a sobering thought, watching the men slipping away down the cliff's edge to the beach, and becoming aware that their disappearance meant we were less protected every minute.[14]

The measures taken at 17th Stationary Hospital to disguise its partially evacuated state are typical of those used throughout the period:

> The Red Cross flags continued to flutter bravely and outwardly our Tented White City looked as busy as ever; there were stretcher bearers supposedly bringing in patients from the Front, there were parades and work parties, and we even took the precaution of keeping lights ablaze at night, to lull the Turks into believing that our lives went on as usual.[15]

A panorama of Lancashire Landing and the four piers constructed on it, numbered from right to left 1–4. In the centre the two sunken ships forming the breakwater at the seaward end of number one pier have been disconnected from the shore. During October and November 1915 the winter weather had frequently caused this kind of damage to the piers built on all the beaches. On the right of the picture the inland edge of the ring of terraced dugouts hewn out of the cliff where Hill 114 dropped into the sea can be seen culminating in the office of the Military Landing Officer. In front of this the road which passes into the centre of the picture led up the gully at the rear of the beach towards the base camp and eventually to the front line nearly three miles away. The remains of the terraces and the piers embedded in the shore can still be seen today. Q25738

On the beaches there was a hive of activity as troops, guns, pack animals, stores and munitions were evacuated and what had to remain was got ready for destruction. One of those detailed to supervise the work was Lieutenant Campbell of the Ayrshire Yeomanry who had been evacuated from their positions on the night of 30 December:

> . . . I have had the rather unpleasant but none the less honourable duty thrust upon us, of being left behind and attached to the embarkation staff, fortunately under a brick of a General, beside whom it would be an honour to be killed should the worst come to the worst. It is a most wonderfully calm and cool staff this, considering the difficulty and extent of the operation and the most unwelcome attention of Asiatic Annie, Puking Percy, Quick Dick and sundry other long barrelled visitors.[16]

The 'brick of a General' was Brigadier General J W O'Dowda who arrived to take control of W Beach on 1 January. In notes prepared for a lecture after the war he recalled how he had 'found a great deal of confusion and lack of organisation reigning on the beach. This I proceeded to remedy as soon as I could, parcelling off areas of the shore to my various assistants and advising them how to create some order out of the confusion.'[17]

The embarkation staff faced a perplexing task and Campbell recorded his frustration:

> We are engaged, as you may judge, in infernally difficult work, and on two nights the weather has played the deuce with everything. I never had more difficulty in keeping my head in my life. Dealing at night with refractory piers, refractory boats, refractory Indians, and more refractory mules, and meanwhile shells at the rate sometimes of three to the minute, from two different directions and from as many as seven guns, is just about the limit.[18]

There were other problems of discipline for General O'Dowda to cope with:

> . . . I noticed a good deal of looting going on. I had therefore to arrange for police and patrols to look after the dumps to stop this practice. Not that I minded the stores being taken, as I realised that thousands of tons would have to be destroyed, but it was very bad for the discipline of the area . . . But on one occasion a very exalted General Officer and his Staff paid us a visit to see the progress we had made, and on their departure the General asked for some bales to be opened when he knew what the contents were, and in front of a considerable crowd of onlookers he and his staff proceeded to loot them properly.[19]

For the efficient usage of the lighters and for easy access to larger vessels it was crucial that an effective system of piers, breakwaters and blockships be constructed and maintained for the duration of the evacuation period – whatever the weather conditions. Lieutenant G M C Taylor of the 3rd Field Company, RND had the task of building and maintaining No 1 Pier and the breakwater on W Beach. The breakwater could not be finished in time and a gap of two hundred feet remained to the two breakwater ships from which the troops could embark on to the larger ships without the need of lighters. The Royal Navy was called in but their efforts were not appreciated by Taylor, who wrote to his father describing how:

> The Navy produced an old Greek ship and said they would sink her and close the gap in the breakwater. They did it at night and to our horror in the morning we found it . . . really did more harm than good as it diverted waves on to the line . . . we wanted to bridge . . . . I was given the job of building the floating bridge. It was in 6 sections 30 ft long and a sloping gangway up the side of the inner hulk supported from the hulk and a gangway through the inner to the outer hulk alongside which came ships that could hold 2000 troops each.[20]

On 7 January it was ready, '. . . the first night was dead calm and at dusk we floated out our sections and the whole thing was most successful . . .'[21]

Despite such efforts it soon became apparent that not everything of use to the Turks could be got away and that what could not be removed would have to be destroyed. General O'Dowda remembered the scene:

> There was a large cavern in one of the cliffs jutting out near to the beach which was crammed to its mouth with all the surplus guncotton, shell SAA, grenades, limbers full of shell etc, etc all ready to be blown up. There were about 25 dumps of stores, drenched with petrol and oil, ready to be set alight by means of fuses, and all these fuses were timed to last for half an hour.[22]

W Beach, or Lancashire Landing, photographed on the day before the Helles evacuation 7 January 1916, showing the remaining stores and equipment piled up on the edge of the shore. The permanence of the piers and the extensive clutter on the beach clearly show how much the beach had been developed as the main British base since the 1st Battalion Lancashire Fusiliers landed on it on 25 April 1915. From that moment on, the whole of the beach had been vulnerable to shell fire from both the Asiatic shore, visible through the mist on the horizon, and from the north beyond Achi Baba and the burst of a shell falling short into the sea underlines the latent threat presented by these guns throughout the whole evacuation. In addition to the stores the long train of mules pulling wagons across the foreground highlights a further problem faced by the organisers of the evacuation. Eventually it was agreed that many of the mules and horses could not be taken off and so they were destroyed during the course of the last afternoon. Q13692

Further inland a variety of military preparations was in hand. In Lieutenant Colonel N O Burge's view the problem was not the Turkish infantry but their artillery:

> Of course we hope that even if they do discover that we are retreating from our front lines pretty soon after we have commenced to go, that they won't come after us too quickly. In fact we are discouraging little schemes of that kind by leaving large numbers of contact mines behind us and various other little booby traps, which should throw a considerable amount of cold water (otherwise melanite) on any thrusting and inquisitive spirits.[23]

But such tricks could not silence artillery, and 'every gun here and on the Asiatic side will at once be brought to bear on our communication trenches and the beaches. So it's a gamble.'[24]

Dixon Nuttall was a Royal Engineers officer working in the Fusilier Bluff sector. Among the tasks allotted to him was the preparation of barbed wire entanglements, to be positioned as soon as the last troops had passed through. He was also ordered to destroy all water tanks and pumps except where the din might be heard by the Turks; and the next day to prepare three mines behind the British lines at Fusilier Bluff and to lay various trip and tread mines; and to bury stores of barbed wire and iron stakes in old dugouts or disused trenches.[25]

As the Royal Engineers' work continued it became more and more difficult to move around the Peninsula. Joseph Murray remembers his frustration,

> '. . . we'd been up and down these trenches hundreds of times, and – bless my heart and soul – we come off today carrying our rations and, "Oh, trench blocked, what the hell's done that?" And you have to go, walk back and find another way and find *that* one blocked. We got lost, because *all* the trenches that we knew were blocked. Some at a convenient place had this concertina wire over on the side ready to be pulled in . . .'[26]

One method of deception practised during the evacuations of Anzac and Suvla and now repeated at Helles was the skillfully improvised use of self-firing rifles to give an illusion of fully-manned front lines. A pair of kerosene cans were positioned one above another, a hole punched in the base of the upper can, allowing water to drip slowly into the lower can, which, when full, exerted its weight on a length of string looped around the trigger of a gun, causing it to fire after a long interval.

The final element of the military preparations was to build up the beaches' defences in case the Turks should break through during the evacuation. O'Dowda describes the defences at W Beach, 'The far side of the crest of the semi-circular beach was fully entrenched and strengthened by a double apron barbed wire fence. Six hundred men, naturally called the Die-Hards, held these trenches to the last ie. until I gave them the order to retire as rapidly as possible to the beach . . .'[27]

The evacuation was proceeding reasonably smoothly when, on 7 January, the Turks launched a heavy bombardment on the Fusilier Bluff sector of the front. In his book *Gallipoli – as I saw it*, Joseph Murray recorded how:

> At about eleven in the morning the Turks began an intensive bombardment of both sides of Gully Ravine. It was soon obvious that this was the prelude to an attack. The question was – 'How long did we have to wait?' As the hours passed, thousands of shells crashed into the empty sup-

port trenches and those that fell in the front line took their toll. It was by far the most severe and prolonged shelling I have ever experienced.[28]

At Area Headquarters the atmosphere was tense: 'The General much worried in the evening,' wrote McGrigor, 'as the Turks have bombarded our left flank heavily for four hours, and have shown signs of preparing to attack. There may be nothing in it. Hope to goodness not, but the bombardment has been a very intense one.'[29] Further along the line Dixon Nuttall described events as he saw them in a letter of 20 January:

> ... the Turks shelled very heavily all day and about 4 pm after a frightful culminating bombardment attempted to attack ... Probably the Turks knew we were preparing to evacuate and imagined there would be very few infantry in our line but as a matter of fact we had more men there than usual. The bombardment ceased at 3.45 pm and then the Turks were apparently to attack, but only about 4 or 5 came over out of their trenches and were all killed. We must have hit a lot of them, but most only showed their bayonets over the parapet and fired in the air and did no more. All was quiet about 6 and I had to send our sappers to repair our trenches.[30]

Major General F S Maude, the 13th Division commander wrote in his diary of this attack, 'At 4 pm they sprung two mines near Fusilier Bluff, and at 4.15 they attacked Fifth Avenue and Fusilier Bluff resolutely. The attack was handsomely repulsed by the North Staffords, who however lost Walker, their Colonel, one of our best commanding officers. The Turks tried to attack all along our front, but the officers could not get their men forward elsewhere'.[31] Murray and a few sappers were with the Staffordshires at the centre of the attack:

> The Turks charged over, shouting wildly. They had about a hundred yards to cover before reaching my particular part of the line though they had less ground to cover a little further to the left. After their four and a half hours' warning, we were ready for them ... They came in their hundreds, some carrying timber for use in bridging our trenches. Perhaps they thought that after these hours of shelling there would be no one to stop them, but they had not reckoned with the Staffordshires of the 13th Division and eight sappers who could handle rifles as well as the rest.[32]

On 8 January, the final day, the evacuation of the troops was to take place in three waves. Burge in command of the RND rendezvous point described how he went about getting the first wave away:

> My first job was to get rid of the troops in bivouac, of which there were 2000. The difficulty was that they must arrive on the beach in bodies of 100 exactly and as no unit was exactly that number, it meant adding a few of this battalion on to that and chucking in a few RE or something of that sort as a make-weight. Still, not so difficult so far. BUT I'd only got one narrow road to form those troops up on – no one could move or show himself till 5.45 pm and the whole body must start off at 6.15. So it meant falling in in the dark and detaching bodies to join other bodies, and in short doing most unmilitary things which, if I'd done in a promotion exam would have ploughed me straight away. Well, they fell in at 5.45 – representatives of 11 units, ranging in numbers from 559 of my own battalion to 10 Medical Unit. At 6.10 they commenced to move off and at 6.20 the bivouacs were clear.[33]

Not surprisingly Burge was pleased with this achievement. After clearing the first wave troops he had been ordered to command the RND rendevous point.

It was now time for the second wave to come through. Murray, who was a member of the RND, though attached to the sappers on the extreme left of the line, seems to have been evacuated through the RND rendezvous point. He left the front line area shortly after dusk.

> All the gear that we had that jingled – water bottles, entrenching tools, even your bayonet scabbard – was taken away because it made a noise. We still had our sandbags on our feet ... and we were told well empty the breech and you got to make your way to Krithia Road ... we had a day's iron ration with us, a little bag with some small dog biscuits in ... to keep us going for a day ...[34]

As they departed Murray, who had been at Helles from almost the very start, was profoundly depressed:

> I thought to myself, 'Well I don't like sneaking away like this after all this bloody trouble ...' I was really distressed, in my own mind, I was really sad. First of all about leaving the men

behind, and then of course I thought . . ., 'We're stealing away. We stole away from Blandford . . ., we stole away from Egypt, we've stole away from Gallipoli . . . stealing away all the time.'[35]

On arrival at V beach there was an agonising wait in an exposed position:

There was a bugler on top of Sedd el Bahr fort and he could see the flash of the gun – whether it was Asiatic Annie we don't know – but the moment he saw the flash he used to blow a low G and that meant to say, 'on its way'. Now, as soon as that went everybody dashed to the cliff – that was the instructions – we had twenty eight seconds I think – that was the time it took the shell to come over . . . that's not a lot of time to get back and then all of a sudden BANG . . . .[36]

Eventually at about midnight Murray boarded a lighter using the River Clyde hulk as a jetty but an alarming departure followed of which he recorded his vivid if slightly disjointed recollections:

We were so packed we couldn't move our hands up at all we couldn't . . . I remember the chap in front of me was as sick as a dog . . . Half of them were asleep and leaning . . . we were packed up like sardines in this blinking lighter . . . . Its dark of course, apart from being dark it was dark inside, no lights, no portholes . . . I remember a couple of fellows behind me pushing and shoving, and I thought to myself, 'Do as you bloody well like' . . . and all of a sudden the damned thing started to rock, and it did rock, there must have been a shell. I couldn't hear it, there must have been a shell dropped pretty close, and you know we laughed at V Beach shelling, we laughed, and here we are – no reason for laughing . . . . There must have been hundreds in this blinking lighter, ... And every now and again it was rocking . . . . Those that were asleep were half awake and those that were sick were still being sick and, oh dear me, it was stifling hot, stifling hot . . . . We left there like a lot of cattle being dumped into a lighter and just pushed to sea and nobody gave a tinker's cuss whether we lived or died . . . .[37]

For Burge back at the RND rendezvous tension mounted with the departure of the second wave '. . . and then came the anxious time. The Firing line was left most dread-fully thin and if the Turks attacked or found out we were going – we – the last ditchers would of course have been done.'[38]

Macmillan had been given a place amongst the 'last ditchers': 'I was to take position on the extreme left of the Divisional front at a traverse called "Stink Point" and "bring up the rear" . . . . At 8.0 pm I took position on the firing step, having my boots swathed in the blanket strips, while on my left forearm was fixed a piece of white bandage which was to serve as a mark of identification'. The Turks at least seemed oblivious of their opportunity. 'That all seemed normal to the Turk was proved by his periodical rifle flashes from various fire positions; this to show that his sentries were not sleeping. Little did he know that, at the moment, his rifle crackle and the rap-tap-tap of his machine guns were to us the sweetest music under Heaven. Had he remained silent how ominous it all would have seemed to the anxious watchers of the skeleton garrisons.'[39]

At last at 11.45 it was time to depart with only the dead left behind:

Rushing on I caught a glimpse of some of the boys who had lost their last chance of escaping and who waited in death the arrival of the enemy. Dr Macewan and his faithful assistants had found old stretchers for them and with tender care had covered them over with blankets, leaving only their tackety boots to view. Running as fast as my legs would carry me I eventually got up with my party as they were leaving the communication trench for the open. There we halted and removed the blanket strips from our feet. When freed from our fetters, the gallop was resumed . . . we found that the road had been broken up purposely by our engineers, and at frequent intervals we were precipitated, at times headlong into holes of considerable depth. The wisdom of this precaution was not challenged, and we endured uncomplaining. On clearing the road, from which it was impossible to stray by reason of directing belts of wire, we were halted at the first blockhouse. The officer in charge and Pincher Martin satisfactorily accounted for our party to cool and calculating engineer non-commissioned officers, and on we passed to the next blockhouse.[40]

Macmillan also got away safely from V Beach.

Leeson too had been waiting for the order to leave at 17th Stationary Hospital. When it came:

We made a rather pathetic sight as we staggered

The view inland from No 3 Pier towards W Beach on 6 January 1916, showing the breadth of the beach from the cliffs below Hill 114 on the left to those below Hill 138 on the right. The wide perspective of the panorama invests the beach with a deceptive air of space and size. In fact the length of the shoreline on which the Lancashire Fusiliers landed was only 350 yards and by the time of the evacuation despite extensive development of the surrounding area this remained little changed. On the left of the picture the edge of the terraced dugouts can be seen on the cliff face above the road leading up to the base camp and the derrick built on the landward edge of the pier features clearly in the other views of the beach. Q25131

to the cliff edge, laden down, weary, forlorn; our pockets filled with last minute items we could not leave in the tents. Our orders had called for the lights to be left burning in the hospital area; how strange it was, walking away from our Tented White City, with lights blazing cheerfully, and not one person left behind.[41]

As we have seen the troops were being successfully got back to the beaches from the forward areas. But how were they coping on the crowded beaches? O'Dowda describes the embarkation procedure on W Beach:

> The troops were met at the entrance of the defence works of the beach, which were on the top of the cliffs. From that point they were guided to forming-up places where they were sorted out and detailed for their respective troop carriers. Then they were marched to the beach by guides and either sent to the hulks by the floating pier or embarked in lighters alongside the jetties.[42]

O'Dowda was working in close cooperation with his naval opposite number on W Beach:

> I had to produce the men, animals and stores at the right time, and at the right jetty, or at the floating pier leading to the hulk. The naval transport officers took over everything at what is termed 'High Water Mark' and were responsible that the men, animals and stores were taken to their respective ships.[43]

But though the arrangements were all made there was one problem not under staff control: the weather. The embarkation proper had started at 6.30 pm and Taylor, who had concealed the floating bridge by the pier, '. . . floated out the raft and connected up and had it ready by 7 o'clock when there was quite a swell on. It was an odd looking thing formed of steel tanks, steel barrels and wooden barrels'.[44] It was on this structure that any really successful evacuation of W Beach depended. Gradually, as O'Dowda reports, the weather worsened, 'At 7 pm the breeze, which had been a gentle one, freshened. At 8 o'clock it had stiffened considerably, and by 9 pm the wind had reached a velocity of 35 miles an hour and was increasing, and W was a very open beach . . .' .[45] Taylor and his men struggled to keep the bridge intact, '. . . by about 9 o'clock the sea was getting up in rather an alarming fashion and there were signs of breakdown on the raft in more than one place. To help matters a great big unmanageable hospital barge bumped into us . . .' .[46] As O'Dowda describes it, '. . . then as the wind continued to gather force, the lighters became more and more unmanageable till finally one of them charged the floating pier and damaged it badly. However the Navy were able to repair it and again we went ahead. Then to make quite sure two lighters crashed into the pier simultaneously and carried it away altogether.'[47]

Coxswain Powell who was in command of a lighter attached to HMS *Talbot* was working from No 2 Pier W Beach:

> By 11 pm the wind had freshened blowing from the South, and a slight sea got up, and was causing much inconvenience on the beach. A floating bridge got carried away on W Beach necessitating us to make a trip to the destroyer with troops. The Turks seem very quiet. I only noticed about six shells fired up to the present, but I found that

one of these shells dropped on the last section that was coming aboard my lighter, one was killed three injured.[48]

This seems to contradict claims that no casualties were suffered during the night of the evacuation.

Powell and his lighter worked through the night carrying troops out to the naval ships:

> 11.15 pm we were busy being loaded up as full as possible; still we made progress and by 11.45 I moved out after some difficulty for the wind and sea was blowing right on. I was ordered to the HMS *Mars* but it was a rather long trip uncomfortable for us and certainly so for the soldiers who had marched down five miles through trenches. We had great difficulty in getting alongside, and also remaining on. It was hard work for the troops to climb the ladders with 100 lb pack and rifles, for the sea was very nasty.[49]

Corporal Herbert Lamb described such a climb in his diary:

> About three am we were taken out to HMS *Talbot* a very difficult and dangerous job getting on board. Wind and sea rising: the sailors swung wooden ladders over onto which we had to cling for dear life as the lighter was swept at intervals away from the ship's side. We had full kit on and a roll of blankets in our hands which made it more dangerous; one man fell into sea between ship and lighter but was rescued. 500 of us got on board up these ladders . . .[50]

After unloading, Powell's lighter returned to No 2 Pier. Having picked up 400 troops ordered to W Beach apparently after a lighter had been wrecked at Gully Beach and taken them to a destroyer he went in for a last time. He was to face a very dangerous situation:

> . . . soon the wind and sea was playing tricks with me and I went ashore my bows on No 2 Pier and stern on or by No 3 Pier. The Turks had dropped a few shells around and we wondered if it was going to increase, also the fires had just started and I knew that the fuses for the magazine had probably been fired . . .[51]

Over at Gully Beach the 13th Divisional Commander General Maude was encountering a variety of prob-

lems. One of the two lighters intended to pick up 13th Divisional Headquarters and a number of other troops had been wrecked forcing them to go to W Beach to embark. According to Maude:

> We had all the kit of headquarters with us, for which we had provided two steamboats, but as the horses had been shot and the vehicles destroyed, it was somewhat of a problem to get it along. Luckily however the ADMS remembered that there were three or four vehicle-stretchers lying handy, and these we got and loaded up. We could not go by the beach route as it was too heavy going, so we started up hill on to the plateau, and very hard work it was. We all puffed and blew like grampuses, especially as we were all warmly clad. I then sent Hildyard by the beach route to try and notify W Beach that we were going, and the ADMS and I and party pursued our weary way across the top.[52]

On the beach O'Dowda was about to leave:

> I packed up my dispatch case, and leaving my office, brought up the rear of the last party. Just at that moment a GSO very disturbed, rushed up and told me that General Maude . . . had not yet arrived . . . I asked what had happened and was informed that, after they had left Gully Beach General Maude discovered that his bedding roll had been left behind. He said that he was hanged if he was going to leave his bedding for the Turks, got two volunteers with a stretcher and went back for it . . .[53]

It is perhaps not altogether surprising that Maude's untimely concern for his bedding is not mentioned in Callwell's biography! O'Dowda continued, '. . . The time was now 3.50 am and there was no sign of the missing General. I therefore sent an Officer and a couple of men, who knew every inch of the beach and gave them ten minutes to retrieve him. Fortunately they found him almost at once . . .'.[54] Maude himself was still struggling across the top:

> All went well until we came to the inner defences (except for an occasional fall in the dark), but, once there, we found that the garrison had been withdrawn and had embarked, and that the wire had been hermetically closed. One of the party however produced some wire cutters, rather like a pair of nail scissors, and after much hacking we

No 17 Stationary Hospital – Lieutenant Leeson's 'Tented White City' – on an exposed site halfway between V beach and Gully beach. Achi Baba can be seen in the background. Q25132

managed to carve an opening. The Turks now began to pitch some shell about us which accelerated our movements a bit, and then we were again brought up by the Inner Defence trenches. As we could not get the stretchers over the ditch we had to abandon them and the very heavy stuff, and the men carried as much as they could over. Finally we reached W Beach . . .[55]

Leeson remembered their arrival, 'In the darkness, we heard the approach of General Maude, his fellow officer, and a wheeled stretcher carrying his suitcase. Having been in a state of near panic over the idea of leaving a general behind, the embarkation officer had composed a little verse:

"Come into the lighter, Maude,
For the fuse has long been lit,
Come into the lighter, Maude,
And never mind your kit" '[56]

Whoever was the author of the doggerel O'Dowda was relieved:

Being in command of the Beach and the embarkation arrangements, I was in a position to give my own Divisional Commander a piece of my mind . . . the manner in which I restrained myself on that occasion should be placed to the credit side of my account when my sins are being recorded.

And so at last:

It was now nearing 4 am and time for the cliff explosion ominously close. So after hustling the last two or three men and General Maude on board the last lighter, I too, stepped, with what feelings of relief perhaps you can imagine, off the Gallipoli shore.[57]

Powell's lighter had been struggling to get away from the beach:

The sight ashore now was becoming very fascinating but it also told us of our danger, also a few large shells had come too close to be comfortable so we now had to get clear of shore, as the only lighter in W Beach now was the hospital one about 300 yards down . . .[58]

Leeson had made for the hospital lighter:

We scrambled to reach the hospital lighter tossing in the cruel waves, helping each other with supplies and kit bags. Were we in time? 'Leeson!' shouted Thomas, 'Get down'. I saw Thomas crumpled on the deck, and the air was filled with mud, sand, clods of earth, pieces of shrapnel and the most incredible noise I had ever heard . . .[59]

Powell's lighter was also caught in the explosion:

Being the weather side of the pier, with a nasty sea running and strong wind I found it a task to get out . . . . The time now was about 4.40 am and we were about half a mile from shore, when suddenly an awful tremendous explosion occurred, everyone was dumb for a while, did not know whether it was a torpedo or mine or shell, soon there was splashes in the water and the falling on deck of stone, earth and pieces of iron, marvellous not one of us on deck got hit, it's a mystery how we escaped. We soon found the reason of it, on looking ashore the whole point was covered in smoke of all shades . . . on the beach was flames of every colour, and now and again a column of smoke and flame would rise up illuminating the place like day. The sight ashore is difficult to describe, it was terrible, it was beautiful, one wanted to look at it, and one wanted to be away out of it, the whole place seemed full of revenge spreading its fury, and increasing as time went by, and the sea breaking up on the shore added to the awful sight.[60]

O'Dowda had a vivid memory of the explosion:

We had not gone 200 yards from the jetty when the expected terrific explosion nearly blew us out of the water. Thousands of tons of debris, rock, shell cases, bits of limber wheels, and other oddments hurtled over our heads. I could never understand how we escaped injury. The men had been battened down in the hold of the lighter and were safe, but the few of us who were on deck escaped I imagine because we were within the cone of the explosion ie the mass of stuff fell all round us like the outside of an open umbrella. At the same time the beach was lighted up as if for a Carnival, and would have delighted Mr Brock of fireworks fame. It truly was a magnificent sight.[61]

The evacuation was over. It had been successful in its aim of evacuating Cape Helles with the minimum possible casualties. But perhaps we could leave the final word with one of the more embittered evacuees. Thomas Macmillan wrote:

General Paris was justly proud of his division, and whether it was his intention to visit all battalions in turn in order to express his appreciation, I know not. Suffice it to say that the 'Hoods' were paraded for the General's inspection; and after saying some nice things, he announced his intention of giving the officers leave in England and the men, if they cared, leave to Malta. His speech was listened to in silence, but when the acting commander called for three cheers for the General the gallant 'Hoods' gave him the 'raspberry'. The General went pink and, in a fit of choler, cancelled all leave for the battalion and confined all ranks to camp for seven days.[62]

Notes

1. Department of Documents, letters of Major General Sir Archibald Paris, letter to Mrs Pilkington, 8 January 1916.
2. Department of Documents, papers of Able Seaman T Macmillan, 'The War to End War: 1914–1918', pp 109–110.
3. Department of Sound Records', Joseph Murray interview, 1985, 6201/42 Reel 27.
4. Macmillan, op cit, p 110.
5. Department of Documents, diary of Captain A M McGrigor, 30 December 1915.
6. Department of Documents, papers of Lieutenant Colonel N O Burge, letter to family, 4–10 January 1916.
7. Department of Documents, diary of Lieutenant Colonel L H Leeson, edited by D Thompson, p 115.
8. Ibid, p 121.
9. Ibid, p 125.
10. McGrigor, op cit, 30 December 1915.
11. Burge, op cit, 4–10 January 1916.
12. Macmillan, op cit, p 115.
13. Murray, op cit, Reel 26.
14. Leeson, p 126.
15. Ibid, p 126–127.
16. Lieutenant P M Campbell, *Letters from Gallipoli*, T A Constable, p 89.
17. Department of Printed Books, typescript lecture notes on the evacuation, almost certainly by Brigadier General J W O'Dowda, contained in the book *Letters from Gallipoli* by Lieutenant P M Campbell, qv.
18. Campbell, op cit, p 91.
19. O'Dowda, op cit, p 7.
20. Department of Documents, papers of Captain G M C Taylor.
21. Ibid, p 9.
22. O'Dowda, op cit, p 14.
23. Burge, op cit, 4–10 January 1916.
24. Ibid.
25. Department of Documents, papers of Major W F Dixon Nuttall, orders from CRE 13th Division to Dixon Nuttall, 3 and 4 January 1916.
26. Murray, op cit, Reel 27.
27. O'Dowda, op cit, p 13.
28. Joseph Murray, *Gallipoli as I saw it*, William Kimber, London, 1965, p 188.
29. McGrigor, op cit, 7 January 1916.
30. Department of Documents, Dixon Nuttall, op cit, letter from Dixon Nuttall to family, 20 January 1916.
31. Sir C E Callwell, *The Life of Sir Stanley Maude*, Constable, London, 1920, p 181.
32. Murray, *Gallipoli as I saw it*, op cit, p 188.
33. Burge, op cit, 4–10 January 1916.
34. Murray, op cit, Reel 27.
35. Ibid.
36. Ibid.
37. Ibid.
38. Burge, op cit, 4–10 January 1916.
39. Macmillan, op cit, 4–10 January 1916.
40. Ibid.
41. Leeson, op cit, pp 146–147.
42. O'Dowda, op cit, p 10.
43. Ibid, pp 9–10.
44. Taylor, op cit, 12 January 1916.
45. O'Dowda, op cit, p 11.
46. Taylor, op cit, 12 January 1916.
47. O'Dowda, op cit, p 12.
48. Department of Documents, papers of Coxwain P Powell, 8 January 1916.
49. Ibid.
50. Department of Documents, diary of Second Lieutnant H A J Lamb, 9 January 1916.
51. Powell, op cit, 8 January 1916.
52. Callwell, *Life of Maude*, op cit, p 184.
53. O'Dowda, op cit, pp 14–15.
54. Ibid.
55. Callwell, op cit.
56. Leeson, op cit, pp 150–151.
57. O'Dowda, op cit, pp 15–16.
58. Powell, op cit, 8 January 1916.
59. Leeson, op cit, pp 151–152.
60. Powell, op cit, 8 January 1916.
61. O'Dowda, op cit, p 16.
62. Macmillan, op cit, p 128.

Further Reading

C F Aspinall-Oglander, *Gallipoli (History of the Great War: Military Operations, 2 Volumes)*, Heinemann, London, 1929–1932.
Robert Rhodes James, *Gallipoli*, Batsford, London, 1965.
Alan Moorehead, *Gallipoli*, Hamish Hamilton, London, 1956.
Eric Wheeler Bush, *Gallipoli*, Allen & Unwin, London, 1975.

Kamp Kufstein: A Record of International Refugee Work in Austria during 1945

Ann Lane

Between 1944 and 1946 numerous refugee camps were set up in the western occupied areas of Central Europe under the auspices of the United Nations Relief and Rehabilitation Administration (UNRRA). The diaries, correspondence and photographic collection of the director of such a camp, Thomas Hall, deposited at the Imperial War Museum by his family in 1986, provide a rare and interesting insight into the organisation and daily life of an UNRRA refugee camp, and the problems that beset its administration in the aftermath of the European War.

The refugee problem at the end of the Second World War was unprecedented in its scale and complexity. An estimated 11 million people had been displaced by the Nazi occupation; many more were uprooted during the liberation as the Allied armies advanced on two fronts across Europe. To meet this problem the United Nations Relief and Rehabilitation Administration (referred to hereafter as UNRRA) had been created.[1]

Wartime planning for coping with the problem of refugees had been in progress since the earliest days of the Second World War, both in Britain and the United States.[2] Indeed, even as early as 1938, the US Government had set up a committee to research the question, and the American President, Franklin D Roosevelt, had predicted that between 10 and 20 million people might have to leave Europe at the end of a conflict there. Roosevelt's belief that large numbers of people would be displaced by the fighting was soon to be borne out as the British forces encountered vast numbers of refugees during their operations in Egypt and Libya between

Thomas Hall, director of Kamp Kufstein. HU 51541

Ann Lane is a research assistant in the Department of Photographs and has completed a doctoral thesis on the subject of British foreign policy towards Yugoslavia between 1945 and 1949.

1940 and 1942. In order to deal with this problem, Britain set up a Middle East Relief and Refugee Administration with headquarters in Cairo. By mid-1944, it had cared for some 46,000 refugees, most of whom had fled from the Axis occupation of the Balkans.

In Britain, wartime planning for the refugee problem was undertaken initially by the Committee on Surpluses, which was established by Prime Minister Winston Churchill in late 1940. One of the committee's tasks was to accumulate relief supplies for the eventual liberation of Europe. This committee handed over its work in 1941 to an Inter-Allied Committee on Post War Requirements which was based in London and which made projections of the anticipated number of refugees. In the United States, meanwhile, the Roosevelt Administration sponsored a President's Advisory Committee on Political Refugees to look into the problem of refugee movements during the war and to consider the possible postwar situation. This body remained in place throughout the war.

Realising that post-war relief would require much more than informal Anglo-American co-operation, Washington pressed for a broadly based international relief undertaking. During 1943, Assistant Secretary of State Dean Acheson concluded extensive negotiations with Russia to build a framework for such an organisation. Discussions then widened to include other governments. UNRRA was established as a result in the autumn of 1943 and the agreement was signed by representatives of forty-four allied countries.

Subsequent discussion defined the scope of UNRRA and set its refugee activity within the framework of relief and rehabilitation. UNRRA would operate in liberated territories with the consent of the military and later the approval of national authorities as they emerged after the liberation. All were working in the dark, uncertain of what rehabilitation would mean in practice. Everyone agreed that its operation would be temporary. The general expectation was that refugees would seek repatriation as a matter of course. Enemy nationals were not eligible for UNRRA assistance, a restriction which was later to cause significant difficulties.

It was always assumed that the military would be ultimately responsible for refugee operations. In the SHAEF-UNRRA Agreement, signed on 25 November 1944, UNRRA duly placed itself squarely under military patronage until this was no longer necessary and agreed to work within the SHAEF Command. The United Nations body was to provide the technical staff, and the soldiers (in the first instance) would furnish the logistical and material support.

In mid-1945, after the cessation of hostilities, UNRRA finally entered the fray, despatching several hundred specially-trained field teams to take responsibility for

Above, Thomas Hall views the camp from his office window. The French flag signifies the military occupation of Austrian Tyrol.

Below, Hall, with Lithuanian children after a gathering, summer 1945.
HU 53977 and HU 53976

assembly centres in Austria and Germany. UNRRA's staff was essentially an international civil service employing around 10,000 persons who were drawn from twenty-four nations. Of these nearly half were employed in Central Europe.[3]

Thomas Hall applied to UNRRA for an appointment in refugee work in February 1945. A career civil servant, Hall had been employed in the Glasgow Post Office until the war when his secondment to the Ministry of Supply had led to an appointment as Manager of the Newfoundland Overseas Forestry Unit. Indeed, he had a flair for organisation; his great enthusiasm for walking holidays had led him to found the Wayfaring Association of Great Britain, as well as the Scottish Rambling Association, and he had been responsible for the construction of the first UK Youth Hostel.[4]

Hall's skills were precisely those required to bring order out of the chaos which confronted UNRRA in its refugee work following the German surrender in May 1945. After five weeks of training at the UNRRA Mobilisation Centre in France, Hall was assigned to lead UNRRA Team 199 and run the Displaced Persons Assembly Centre in Kufstein in the

Left, a refugee surrounded by her belongings waits patiently. The hands of a small child can be seen poking out of the blanket on her lap. Malnutrition and other ravages of war caused the refugees to age much more rapidly than would normally have been the case.
EA 61702

Above, these banners, which appeared across the camp roadways, were fairly typical. This one sports both the United States flag and the five pointed communist star with hammer and sickle.
HU 53978

Austrian Tyrol. He arrived in Kufstein with his team of six on 13 June 1945 to take over command of the camp from the United States military authorities which at that time occupied the western regions of Austria. After July 14 the region was designated a French Zone of Occupation, and the camp was duly supplied with a French military guard.

A typical Tyrolean town, Kufstein was situated in the valley of the River Inn, just south of the Austro-German frontier. The mountains rose steeply behind the town which was dominated by a fifteenth century castle built on a wooded bluff overlooking the valley. The camp lay on the outskirts of the town in the castle's shadow.

Kufstein, like most other refugee camps in 1945, suffered from chronic overcrowding. During the Nazi era it had been a Cavalry Camp of some sixty-four stone and brick buildings, complemented by wooden barracks and designed to accommodate between 4,000 and 5,000 soldiers. When Hall took over in June it had a refugee population of some 7,000 persons, and this figure was to rise as high as 11,000 as further refugees were brought in by the military authorities during the summer.

In such overcrowded conditions, the American military authorities had only been able to concern themselves with the tasks of housing and feeding the refugees while also beginning the enormous task of repatriation. Hall's first priority was therefore to organise repatriation on a large scale. On arrival at an Assembly Centre, new groups of refugees would be registered individually to enable UNRRA officials to determine their origin and status. Those eligible for international assistance were officially classed as 'Displaced Personnel' or simply 'DPs'. Some had been brought from the Nazi work camps and factories for which they had been forcibly recruited during the German occupation of Europe; others had been made homeless by the fighting, particularly in Eastern Europe, and had fled west to find themselves behind the Anglo-American lines when Germany surrendered; still others were former prisoners of war who had fought with the Allies. Many of these owed their allegiance to the pre-war monarchist regimes of Eastern Europe and the Balkans and would not, or could not, return to their homelands since they declined to recognise the new left wing republican governments which had seized power after the liberation.

After registration, the refugees were sent for routine delousing and a medical examination. Liberal use of the pesticide DDT was responsible for greatly reducing the spread of disease which in earlier times would have wiped out vast numbers. (As yet the unpleasant side effects of DDT remained undiscovered.) The medical teams found that a large proportion of the refugee population was in poor physical condition. Although those who had been recruited to work on the land survived the war without too much suffering, the same could not be said of those who had been forcibly recruited as labour to work in the mines and factories, many of them displaying serious, often irreversible signs of

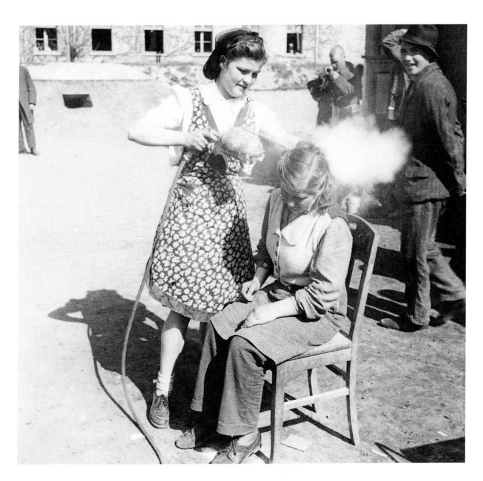

Delousing in progress: the skin
and respiratory infections caused
by the pesticide DDT had not then
been discovered.
BU 3892

malnutrition.[5]

By the beginning of June the Western nationals – French, Belgian, Norwegian and Dutch – had largely been repatriated from Kufstein, and the repatriation of the Russians was in full swing by the time Hall assumed command. One of the first tasks placed before Team 199 was to arrange the repatriation of some 1,000 Russians at just thirty-six hours notice. Hall records in his diary that the great majority who left Kufstein in June 1945 'marched to the station carrying garlands, banners and pictures of Stalin.'[6]

The Hungarians, however, were much more reluctant to accept repatriation. As former enemy nationals, many of whom had fled from the Russian advance, doubtless in fear of the Red Army, they were only too ready to tell UNRRA officials at Kufstein about their anxieties over returning home. A similar, though more complex situation pertained to the Yugoslav contingent. Basically, they fell into two categories. On the one hand there were Royalists, many of whom were former members of the Royal Yugoslav forces who had been captured by the Germans and who did not wish to return to a Yugoslavia where Tito's government no longer recognised the authority of their King. On the other

hand there were those who were prepared to accept post-war conditions in Yugoslavia, including the provisional, communist-dominated government of Marshal Tito which had installed itself in Belgrade earlier in the year. For non-Russians, who were not associated with wartime collaboration or war crimes, repatriation was not forcible. 'Displaced Persons' not wishing to return home were given the option of resettlement elsewhere. In the case of the Yugoslavs, Hall held a plebiscite in the middle of August to give the Yugoslavs at Kufstein an opportunity to state their preferences concerning resettlement. Of the one thousand in the camp at that time, only 164 opted for repatriation to Yugoslavia; 799 wished to join the Royal Forces, which effectively precluded their return home, while 50 requested resettlement in the United States. Serious fighting subsequently broke out between the factions before those eligible for repatriation left for Belgrade.[7].

As the pressure of numbers was reduced, Hall instituted a variety of social services and organisations designed to improve the quality of life within the camp. It was in any case UNRRA's practice to alleviate problems of communication and personnel shortages by recruiting helpers from among the refugees as they were brought into the camps.

Yugoslav refugees, holding the Partisan flag, probably on their departure from the camp in August. HU 51551

A voluntary working party making improvements to the camp under the shadow of Kufstein Castle, summer 1945. HU 51547

Some would be employed doing routine tasks such as construction, while others with professional qualifications would be recruited as doctors, nurses or clerks. Hall ran Kufstein by a committee which he personally supervised through weekly meetings. The Camp Committee was composed of national leaders representing the various ethnic groups within the camp. Barrack Leaders and Block Leaders were also chosen, and a Camp Work Office was set up encompassing plumbers, electricians, carpenters, painters and sanitary workers.

By the end of the year, Kufstein boasted six national schools and a kindergarten, churches and a hospital. A series of shops had been set up, including a tailors, bootmakers, a toyshop and a hairdresser. For recreational purposes, a sports department was created where both indoor and outdoor sports were organised, while special activities were arranged for Boy Scouts and Girl Guides. During the third week of October, the camp theatre director agreed to hold weekly performances for the people of Kufstein for which a charge would be levied. Many of the refugees who operated these services were placed on the Burgomaster's payroll, but those working in the theatre or shops were paid a percentage of the takings. The balance of the monies received was placed in the Camp Fund and administered by the Camp Committee. In order to give camp life some cohesion, *Kamp Kufstein*, a weekly newspaper, was produced. It was circulated to all DP Camps in Austria and included a tracing service which proved invaluable to refugees in the location of relatives.

The emphasis at Kufstein was clearly on self-government, and it is a measure of the extent to which this was successful that Hall was able to establish a Camp Police Force recruited from the refugees. It was also a necessary measure, however, since looting and brawling between different sections of the refugee community were not uncommon. Indeed, there was a dark, sometimes sinister side to camp life. Apart from the inevitable black markets which were brought

to Hall's attention from time to time, it was also a well established fact that former members of the German SS and Wehrmacht, many of whom would be prosecuted as war criminals if caught, were hiding among the genuine refugees. In September, a tighter control was placed on the registration of refugees as they entered Kufstein in the hope that those of dubious status might be picked up. This was not foolproof, however, as many slipped through. Early in the morning of 15 October, Kufstein Camp was sealed by the French military to enable the *gendarmerie* to carry out a comprehensive search for former SS personnel. By midday, thirty suspects had been rounded up and were duly taken for interrogation.[8]

Nevertheless, in the conditons of economic ruin that prevailed in Central Europe after the German surrender, camps such as Kufstein provided a welcome haven for millions who had been uprooted from their native soil, as well as the first step towards their rehabilitation. It is a tribute to Hall as a Director, and a measure of the gratitude felt towards UNRRA generally, that the Kufstein refugees recognised his birthday by the presentation of a commemorative photograph album reflecting life within the camp, together with numerous hand-painted greetings cards from the various national groups.

After a spell of leave at the end of the year, Hall returned to Kufstein early in 1946, but was promoted in February to the post of Assistant Director of Finance and Administration in the US Zone of Austria. During his time at Kufstein, he kept a daily diary together with copies of significant correspondence and memoranda. He was already a published author and it is clear from his papers that he intended to set down his experiences at Kufstein for publication. At the time, however, the publishing fraternity considered that such a subject was only of very short-term interest, and the pressure of existing commitments apparently prevented Hall from completing it, but his personal papers form an important record of an unusual experience of war.

**Drawings done by Lithuanian children, and presented to Thomas Hall.
COL 52 and COL 53**

**Cover of a presentation booklet given to the Director on his forty-fifth
birthday by Lithuanian refugees. The artwork was prepared from the
limited materials then available by the inmates of the camp. COL 51**

Notes

1. Michael R Marrus, *The Unwanted.
European Refugees in the Twentieth Century*,
Oxford University Press, New York, 1985,
p 309; Eugene Kulischer, *Europe on the
Move: War and Population Changes, 1917–47*,
Columbia University Press, New York,
1948, p 305.
2. For a more detailed account of wartime
planning, see Michael Marrus, op cit,
Chapter 5, pp 295–345.
3. UNRRA: Reports of the Director-
General, 1944–45; Reports of The Director
General to the Council, April 1945–30
June 1945, 1 July 1945–30 September
1945.
4. Department of Documents, papers of
Thomas Hall, Public Relations and
Information Office, US Zone Austria, Press
Release, 28 February 1946.
5. Dr Keith Ball, 'Mothering Europe's
Wandering Millions', *Illustrated*, 8
September 1945.
6. Hall, op cit, miscellaneous notes.
7. Ibid, diary entries for 7, 15 and 17
August 1945.
8. Ibid, 21 September and 15 October
1945.

Further Reading

Robert Johnson, 'International Politics
and the Structure of International
Organisation: The Case of UNRRA',
World Politics, No 3, 1950/51.
Eugene Kulischer, *Europe on the Move: War
and Population Changes, 1917–47*. Columbia
University Press, New York, 1948.
Michael Marrus, *The Unwanted: European
Refugees in the Twentieth Century*, Oxford
University Press, New York & Oxford,
1985.
Joseph Schechtman, *Postwar Population
Transfers in Europe 1945–55*, University of
Pennsylvania Press, Philadelphia, 1962.
Malcolm Proudfoot, *European Refugees,
1939–42: A study in Forced Population
Movement*, London, 1956.
George Woodbridge, *UNRRA: The History
of the United Nations Relief and Rehabilitation
Administration*, 2 Vols, Columbia University
Press, New York, 1950.

'Vive La Nation!' French Revolutionary Themes in the Posters & Prints of the First World War

Michael Moody

Michael Moody is a research
assistant and exhibitions organiser
in the Department of Art.

And, as the alarm guns thundered from the Pont Neuf and the Arsenal, municipal officials, wearing tricolour sashes over their shoulders and escorted by troops of cavalry, marched from street to street and square to square to spread abroad the Assembly's proclamation, *'La Patrie en danger'*.[1]

From that midnight onwards through the fifteen days of mobilisation, the French nation took up arms . . . In men's rifles were stuck flowers, officers took nosegays as they rode, cannons rolled garlanded and wreathed with laurel. The *Marseillaise* and Méhul's noble *Chant du Départ*[2] sounded down the Paris boulevards.[3]

A gap of one hundred and twenty-two years separates the two scenes described above. The first passage describes the recruitment of volunteers on 11 July 1792 to face a pressing Austrian and Prussian invasion of a France in the throes of revolution: the second, the Third Republic's mobilisation for war against Germany in August 1914. The times and circumstances differ but the scenes are virtually identical. It is France at bay, France the entrenched camp, the national energy expressed in terms of territorial defence against reactionary forces. It is the spirit of the Great Revolution of 1789, firmly imprinted on the popular memory of the France of 1914.

With the mobilisation order of 1 August 1914, the French people resigned themselves yet again to fighting a

Edouard-Garcia Benito
*Union sacrée La Marquise –
Etonnant ! Je ne distingue le mien
du vôtre.* **Lithograph 1915
32.3 × 25cms
The royalist marquise and** 'Marianne' (wearing a Lorrainer cap) make common cause in the name of national unity.
**Department of Art, Bute
Collection 4162**

defensive war. The need to present a totally united nation to the German threat was expressed in President Raymond Poincaré's *union sacrée*, a call designed to reconcile all the conflicting elements in French society which had so characterised the Third Republic prior to 1914. It must be remembered that France had been governed by a succession of different regimes since 1789; the houses of Bourbon and Orléans, of the Bonapartes and three republics. The country had witnessed three revolutions, the fall of two empires, its most disastrous military defeat in recent history (the Franco-Prussian War 1870–1871), a tide of social reform and the disestablishment of the Church. The social divisions and contrasting colours of political opinion inherent in such a legacy were all too plain.

Nevertheless, France entered the war as one nation and Poincaré's appeal, however ideologically pretentious or cosmetic, met with universal acceptance, at least for the time being.

Royalists, Bonapartists, Clericals and Anti-Clericals, Republicans and Socialists were now regarded as French only; in the words of the patriotic poet, politician and *revanchiste* Paul Déroulède: 'All those names are forenames, the surname is Frenchman'. Likewise, his contemporary, the nationalist writer Maurice Barrès commented: 'We have ceased dividing ourselves into Catholics, Protestants, Socialists and Jews. Suddenly something more basic has emerged, something all of us share: we are Frenchmen.'

Both these men represented that part of French society which was unable to accept the débâcle of 1870 and the subsequent cession of the provinces of Alsace-Lorraine to a newly unified and victorious Germany: 'war to perpetuity under the mask of peace!' The idea of *revanche* (revenge) and the regaining of these occupied territories was central to their particular brand of patriotism, and would later become one of the foremost objectives of stated French war aims.

The extreme left, convinced that France would be involved in a war which it had little power to prevent, came round to lending its unequivocal support. Gustave Hervé, pre-war anti-militarist editor of *La Guerre Sociale* was to perform a complete *volte-face* and rename his paper *La Victoire* by 1916. The aged deputy Edouard Vaillant, veteran communard of 1871 and a lifelong pacifist, considered that it was the duty of all socialists to answer the call of *La Patrie*. In doing so he echoed the Jacobin virtues as preached by his political predecessor, the revolutionary agitator and patriot Auguste Blanqui in the latter's publication of 1870–1871 *La Patrie en danger*.

Henri Barbusse, the novelist already struggling towards communism in 1914 and author of *Le Feu* (1916), his most famous work, recorded his own affirmation of the ideals of 1789 and 1792:

Below, Guy Arnoux 1886–1951
GRENADIERS de FRANCE Vers la Victoire 1792–1915
Lithograph, hand-coloured 1915
70.3 × 51.5cms
Shaking hands across the centuries; a modern grenadier, in the newly introduced 'horizon blue' uniform, acknowledges his eighteenth-century predecessor, a republican *bleu* of 1792.
Department of Art, Bute Collection 82262

Above, Léon-Adolphe Willette 1857–1926
Pour que la France soit victorieuse comme à Valmy! Pour la libération du territoire!
Lithograph 1918 119.2 × 79.4cms
Poster for the Fourth National War Loan. Willette, a staunch patriot, was fanatically anti-German, having lost two sons during the course of the war.
Department of Art, PST 0497

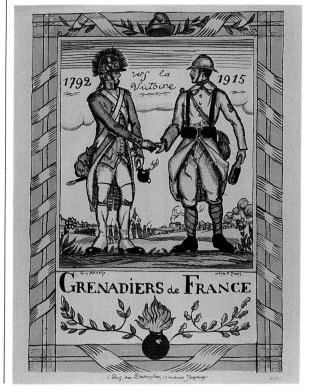

Above, Hermann-Paul 1874–1940
La Tradition
Woodcut, hand-coloured 1916
32 × 28.1cms
A *Hommage des anciens*, published
in an edition of 1000 by Librairie
Lutetia, Paris.
Department of Art, Bute
Collection 6021

Below, Herouard
La Marseillaise
Lithograph c.1918
49.7 × 31cms
The anthem and the army; officers
of 1792 and 1918. The decorative
device of the Gallic swords is
similar to that used in the portrait
of the Revolutionary martyr
*Lepelletier de Saint-Fargeau après
David* (1793) by Anatole Devosge
(1770–1850).
Department of Art, Bute
Collection 6098

The war is directed against our old notorious enemies of the past: militarism and imperialism, the sabre, the jackboot and the crown. Our victory will result in the destruction of the stronghold of Emperors, crown princes, noblemen and mercenaries, the forces that keep our nation in prison and would like to imprison the others. The world can only liberate itself from them by fighting them.[4]

At the same time Albert Sarraut, minister for education, enjoined teachers to present lessons in a patriotic light. Geography classes would follow the course of military operations, the teaching of literature was concerned only with the work of patriotic writers such as Déroulède or Maurice Barrès. History lessons aimed at 'creating patriotic feelings and explaining the real meaning of current events' making particular references to the great French heroes of the past 'from Vercingétorix to Barra.'[5]

In the field of visual propaganda *La Gloire* of former times was a constant theme. Appeals to history and patriotism promoted successive defence loans and charity organisations, while at the same time attempting to raise national morale. The consistent and generous public response to war loan and charity appeals was a measure of the nation's commitment. In one *département* alone, that of Charente, an anonymous schoolteacher made the following observations: 'no appeal falls on deaf ears'; 'magnificent spirit of solidarity when it comes to war charities'; 'everyone makes an offering, even those who are not very well off'. It is also recorded that there was little public reference to the *union sacrée*. The nation silently recognised the need for national unity at least for the duration of hostilities.

The saints Louis, Denis and Geneviève all became subjects for posters and popular prints, while the recently beatified Jeanne d'Arc featured strongly in devotional *imagerie*. In addition *Le Grand Siècle* of Louis XIV and the First Empire of Napoleon Bonaparte enjoyed a marked revival as themes for the patriotic appeal.

It was from the Revolution of 1789, however, that much of French propaganda drew its visual inspiration. The Revolution had provided the French national consciousness with a recognisable pictorial vocabulary of republicanism. Its symbols and rituals had developed in the course of the revolutionary decade of 1789–1799 and they continue to inform the repertoire of political heraldry and iconography familiar to us all.

It is the aim of this article to examine briefly this aspect of French pictorial propaganda and in particular three main themes; the celebration of the army, the *Marseillaise*, and the personification of Liberty. All the illustrations are of

Image de HENRY DE GROUX tirée à 1000 exemplaires et éditée par le " NOUVEL ESSOR ". 40, rue des Saints-Péres. — PARIS

Henry de Groux 1867–1930
La Marseillaise
Lithograph, hand-coloured 1915
40 × 26cms
Frontispiece from a portfolio of

allied national anthems, *Les
***Hymnes Alliés*, published by**
'Nouvel Essor', Paris.
Department of Art, Bute
Collection 6072

posters and prints held by the Museum's Department of Art.

An obvious concern of many artists of the time was the French army, its traditions, successes, heroes and most importantly its *élan vital*, the will to victory. Graphic juxtapositions of the antique and modern were countless, highlighting the camaraderie of republican soldiery – the *hommage des anciens* of the Revolution to those of 1914.

The leading exponent of this genre was Guy Arnoux, a noted poster designer, print-maker and illustrator, and member of the *Salon des Humoristes*. He called for the creation of a new popular art which he helped propagate through his poster and print designs. They encompass a mixture of both the archaic and the modern, using a deceptively simple, almost 'fairground' style which owes much to the nineteenth century tradition· of the *Images d'Epinal*, popular prints and illustrated broadsheets originating at Epinal in the Vosges. Arnoux's output devoted to this particular historical theme was prolific almost to the point of parody. A typical example is the print issued in an unlimited edition, *GRENADIERS de FRANCE. Vers la Victoire 1792–1915*. The year 1792 had particular significance in the history of the Revolution. It had seen war declared on Austria and Prussia, the overthrow of the monarchy, the institution of the Revolutionary calendar and, on 20 September, the Cannonade of Valmy. This French victory over Prussian arms marked a turning point in the fortunes of the national army after an initial series of reversals and defeats. As such, this new success was added to the catalogue of the great *journées*[6] of the Revolution and subsequently of modern French history. Adolphe Willette's poster, *Valmy*, produced for the 4th National War Loan of 1918 celebrates this French military triumph of the past, (although inaccurately – for the battle was won by artillery and musket fire, not through hand-to-hand combat.) An allegory of victory, the poster portrays General Kellerman (both he and Dumouriez faced the Prussians at Valmy), his expression intense and redolent with moral purpose, adopting a protective attitude to a coyly pubescent Liberty (as indeed she was; the monarchy was not officially abolished until the day following the battle, 21 September).

The poster illustrates that *élan vital* so manifest at Valmy which was rekindled in 1918, when, after the crisis of the previous year, France sought to recover her fighting spirit. Once more, the image portrayed is of France the entrenched camp, France invaded, with the parallel of history drawn to remind us that beyond the boundaries of Liberty, the zone of the armies was also French – 'Pour la libération du territoire.'

The year of Valmy was significant for one other reason; it was the year in which the *Marseillaise*[7] had been composed. In the summer of 1915, after almost a year of war, the familiar complexion of Paris was changed. In an atmo-

sphere of restricted gaiety, a certain *esprit parisien* continued although tempered by curfew, air-raid precautions, dramatically reduced public transport, the onset of rationing and the increasingly familiar sight of women in mourning. These were hardly the conditions for a *Fête Nationale*; 'no dancing in the street under swinging paper lanterns to the blare of improvised orchestras.'

However on 14 July, the first *Fête Nationale* of the war (Bastille Day), the remains of Rouget de Lisle, composer of *La Marseillaise* were transferred with great pomp from his suburban grave at Choisy-le-Roi (Seine-et-Oise, and as the crow flies some eight kilometres from the city centre) to Paris, and, via the Arc de Triomphe, to the Hôtel des Invalides. It was a splendid *coup de théâtre*:

. . . first resting place amongst the heroes of the revolutionary wars for him who inspired them and their ragged soldiery with the inflammatory eloquence of the *Marseillaise*. Even dead and turned to clay he is still at the service of his country; his body is carried on a Revolutionary gun-carriage at the front of troops and politicians with their scarves of office shimmering on white shirt fronts . . . No, there are no fireworks today, but the flame of an eternal faith shines in the eyes of France . . .[8]

This *Journée de Paris* was also designated *Journée des Grands Blessés* (War Disabled) and was commemorated as such by the 'striking' of charity tokens in the form of paper medals. After the ceremony at the Invalides, the participants were later treated to a charity concert at the Palais du Trocadero:

> It was crowded with victims of the war, men permanently disabled and disfigured. The national song had never been sung, perhaps, in more affecting conditions.[9]

The wartime veneration for one of the Revolution's most illustrious sons was accompanied by signs of a long-growing religious revival. The Church was eager to subscribe to patriotic ardour. At Saint-Denis, during a memorial service for the fallen of 1915, it was proclaimed from the pulpit:

> And what is the song of those who have died in battle? It is the *Marseillaise*. It is to the strains of the *Marseillaise* that they knock at the door of the basilica. Open it for them, admit them to immortality.

As might be expected the *Marseillaise* was a popular theme for the myriad postcards, artists' prints and crudely coloured newsprint broadsheets produced at this time. In some cases the lyrics were accompanied by the musical notation, in some by verses from the national anthems of France's allies. Others were more light-hearted; on several occasions the spirit of the *café concert* went into combat as illustrated by prints of Liberty attired as either a topical *poilu* or republican general of the Revolutionary wars.

The figure of Rouget de Lisle was central to the theme of these representations, an example being Jacques Carlu's poster of 1918, *LA MARSEILLAISE* where the artist's ineptly drawn portrait is a direct copy from Isidore Pils's romanticised painting of 1849,[10] *Rouget de Lisle chantant pour la première fois la marseillaise chez Dietrich maire de Strasbourg*. An image popularised through numerous lithographs and

Jacques Carlu
'LA MARSEILLAISE', lithograph 1918
119.8 × 80cms
Department of Art, PST 3983

engravings throughout the later nineteenth century, its iconographic status would have been secure in the French national consciousness.

The text is a reminder that Rouget's anthem has returned victoriously to occupied Strasbourg at the head of the Allied armies. Prime Minister Georges Clemenceau, popularly known as '*le Père la Victoire*' adds the rider, the first line of which is an adaptation of Rouget's original words:

> 'Allons donc enfants de la Patrie
> allons achever de libérer les peuples . . .'

Although concerned with the imminent liberation of Alsace-Lorraine, Clemenceau's sentiments recall the crusading spirit of the Revolutionary armies in their conquest of the Europe of the *Ancien Régime*.

It was the personification of Liberty, however, which achieved the most widespread use, a visual convention

Lucien-Hector Jonas b.1880
Emprunt de la Liberation.
Souscrivez
Lithograph 1918 117.6 × 79.2cms
Poster for the Victory Loan. It is
possible that Jonas's choice of

design may have been dictated by
the Bank's address at the bottom
of the poster.
Department of Art, PST 0504

Jules-Abel Faivre 1867–1945
On les aura!
Lithograph 1916 113.1 × 78.8cms
Poster for the Second National
Defence Loan.
A homage to François Rude's

Marseillaise sculptured relief on
the Arc de Triomphe, the original
drawing for this paper is held by
the Musée des Deux Guerres
Mondiales, Paris.
Department of Art, PST 0544

of paramount importance to the repertoire of French political imagery. A descendant of the idealized republics of classical Greece and Rome, Liberty is the embodiment of all virtue: 'Amazonian virginity and independence'.[11] Elevated to the status of a national symbol – *La République*, 'Marianne'[12] as she was popularly known to the collective memory – underwent a variety of representations during the war.

The open *coquetterie* of *Mlle Victoire* and the Atalantean strides of *La Victoire de la Marne* contrast sharply with poster versions of Dalou's lofty monument *Le Triomphe de la République*;[13] likewise with Lucien Jonas's poster of 1918, *Emprunt de la Libération*. Here, Jonas resurrected the *Winged Victory of Samothrace* as a background to his composition, adding both arms, and a head complete with victor's laurels, Phrygian cap[14] and tricolour *cocade*.[15] The poster is a later, more finished version of his 1915 lithograph *La Marne –*

Anniversaire! in which the Nike is shown in her original state as exhibited in the Louvre.

In the foreground of the composition are posed three French soldiers, one *chasseur alpin*, two *poilus*. The *poilu* at the centre raises his arms in a gesture not unlike that of the *poilu* pictured in Abel Faivre's famous poster for the 2nd National Defence Loan *On les aura* (1916). The figure's stance is also very similar to the Georges Scott poster of 1917 *Pour le Drapeau! Pour la Victoire!*

The gestures share one common source; that of François Rude's sculptured relief *La Marseillaise* created for the Arc de Triomphe 1831–34. Commissioned by Louis-Philippe's July Monarchy in the aftermath of *les trois glorieuses*[16] (the revolution of 27–29 July 1830), the original title of the work is *The Departure of the Volunteers of 1792*. Above an animated group of antique figures, romanticised refugees

Georges Bertin Scott (called Scott de Plagnolles) b.1873
Pour le Drapeau! Pour la Victoire!
Lithograph 1917 120 × 79.7cms
Poster for the Third National War Loan. Scott's reputation rests mainly on his prolific output of military scenes, the greatest exponent of which was his master, the distinguished battle painter, Edouard Detaille (1848–1912).
Department of Art, PST 4400

Louis-Oscar Roty 1846–1911
La Semeuse on the reverse of two-
franc piece of 1978
First issued 1897–98.

Lucien-Hector Jonas b.1880
La Semeuse
Lithograph 1916 62 × 41.5cms
Department of Art, Bute
Collection 6046.

from the Enlightenment, soars the ferocious *amalgame* of both Liberty and Nike (the goddess of victories), about to transform those below into all-conquering legionaries. Of the three posters mentioned above, the Scott design is the most faithful to Rude both in spirit and emotive power. The poster was produced during 1917 – the disastrous year which saw the failure of the Nivelle offensive, the army mutinies and a severe crisis in public morale. In the face of these crushing events, Scott's Marianne remains steadfast and defiant, standing on a field of laurel, rallying behind her the massed armies of the Republic. She grasps in her left hand a tricolour, more rag than flag, but which flies bravely, fully visible. Her sword and scabbard pattern are identical to Rude's original, as is the angle of her head and facial expression although the latter is more humanised. Below, the 'slipped chiton' exposes her left breast. What is normally regarded as a classical convention, in this case admits to a France assaulted, yet again, 'France at bay'. It is worth noting that the background of assembled banners recalls the popular engravings of the revolutionary period depicting the ceremonies of the National Fêtes.[17]

Georges Scott was only one of many artists who interpreted Rude's design; the cartoonist Sem (called de Goursat), Théophile Steinlen and Raoul Dufy also drew on the image. However, the Scott adaptation is one of the most successful. It towers above a collection of similarly inspired designs as Rude's original relief towers above ourselves.

In Lucien Jonas's lithograph *La Semeuse* the allegory of Liberty takes another, perhaps unexpected form. An exercise in understatement, it displays, despite faults in the drawing, a profoundly moving image of Liberty as the farm-worker. The figure is a direct reinterpretation of Louis Oscar Roty's[18] original design for the reverse of the one and two-franc piece (1897–98), still in use today. Roty's *La Semeuse*, upon which his reputation rests, is the obligatory classically-garbed figure, whose origin can be traced to Roman republican coinage. On her appearance when first minted in 1897 she was described as 'the most human of our Mariannes'. Jonas's lithograph extends the humanisation process, substituting peasant garb for the archaic republican dress, although retaining the stoical and detached expression which so typifies her classical antecedents. This wartime pastoral portrays the sower as both the symbol of an agrarian economy and the soul of France: *la République* preparing the succour of her children, her soldiers, *les poilus* pictured in the foreground. The overall effect recalls the earthy realism of Jean-François Millet's[19] *Sowers* (1849 and 1850) and *Going to Work* (1851) 'using the trivial to express the sublime ...' An anonymously written text accompanies the print reflecting the themes described above:

This is the French Woman, the mother of the *poilu*, who in courageously taking up the tools left by the husband or father, continues his task untiringly. Her energy redoubles at the vision of soldiers passing, their voices carried by the wind of victory, sounding to her ears like songs of deliverance. 'Sow, sow, woman of France, and we shall reap the harvest.'

As in 1792, France, the birth place of European liberty had again been the victim of foreign aggression and as such had to be defended. In its war of words and images the Third Republic chose to employ the iconography of the First and recalled the observations of the revolutionary cleric, Abbé Henri Grégoire (1750–1831) on the significance of republican symbols in 1796:

> Soon the soul is penetrated by the objects reproduced constantly in front of its eyes; and this combination, this collection of principles, of facts, of emblems, which retraces without cease for the citizen his rights and his duties, this collection forms, in a manner of speaking, the republican mould which gives him a national character and the demeanour of a free man.[20]

'If only they can hold out.' This catchphrase, a frequent theme in popular prints of wartime France encapsulated the country's anxious faith in an eventual victory. At the end of 1918, France emerged from the full brunt of the struggle with Germany a united society and with her national life intact. The *union sacreé*, 'this goddess child, *enfant de la balle* cradled in the crash of arms and in the promiscuity of the trenches,' had served a practical although ultimately temporary purpose. The bitter divisions which were to emerge in French society during the post-war period rendered the *union sacrée* an empty concept. Similarly within the context of the propaganda war, *La Liberté* and her attendant themes had served their purpose. This particular *union sacrée* was consecrated by a marriage of the symbolism of the past to the expediency of the present.

Notes

1. Christopher Hibbert, *The French Revolution*, Allen Lowe, London, 1980, p 151.
2. Etienne Nicolas Méhul (1763–1817). French composer whose style reflected the ideals of the French Revolution. A writer of patriotic works to mark the many Revolutionary Fêtes, his most famous compositions include *Hymne à la Raison* (1793) and *Chant du Depart* (1794).
3. Laurence Jerrold, *France Today*, John Murray, London, 1916, pp 3–4.
4. Henri Barbusse, *Paroles d'un combattant*, Paris, 1920, pp 7–8. The writer echoes Robespierre's sentiments:
'Europe kneels before the shadows of the tyrants we are punishing. . . . Europe cannot conceive that one could live without kings, without nobles; and we, that one could live with them. Europe spills its blood to rivet the chains of humanity; and we spill ours to break them.'
Oeuvres de Maximilien Robespierre (Discours: 27 juillet 1793–27 juillet 1794) Paris, 1967, p 455.
5. Joseph Barra (1780–1793). Revolutionary martyr and hero of the war in the Vendée. Immortalised in Jacques Louis David's painting *The Death of Barra* (1794) Musée Calvet, Avignon.
6. *Journée*, a term originating with the Revolution denoting a day of national importance. During the First World War *journées* were days officially sanctioned by the government for the purpose of charity collections.
7. The *Marseillaise*. Composed 24 April 1792, four days after the French declaration of war on Austria, by a captain of engineers, Claude Joseph Rouget de Lisle (1760–1836). Originally entitled *Chant de guerre pour l'armée du Rhin*, it was popularised by the Marseilles volunteers on their march to Paris. The French national anthem from 1795, it was banned under Napoleon, Louis XVIII and Napoleon III and was not reinstated until 1879.
8. Charles Dawbarn, *France at Bay*, Mills and Boon, London, 1915, p 160.
9. Ibid, p 162.
10. Isidore Alexandre Augustin Pils (1813–1875). History painter and watercolourist, he is most well known for his *Marseillaise* painting, which now hangs in the Louvre.
11. Marina Warner, *Monuments and Maidens. The Allegory of the Female Form*, Weidenfeld and Nicolson, London, 1985, p 280.
12. 'Marianne', the sobriquet originally given to Liberty, *La République*, by the Revolution's detractors. The term was eventually to enter the national vocabulary as one of affection.
13. Jules-Aimé Dalou (1828–1902). Sculptor famed for *Le Triomphe de la République* (1889–1899) standing in the Place de la Nation, Paris.
14. The Phrygian cap or *pilleus* of classical antiquity signifying the freed slave; as the *bonnet rouge* the popular symbol of the Revolution.
15. The colours of the *tricolor* and the national cockade date from the constitutional period of the revolution (1789–1792). Red and blue denote the colours of the city of Paris, the white symbolising the Bourbon Monarchy.
16. The revolution of 1830, which resulted in the abdication of Charles X and the accession of the Duc d'Orléans, Louis-Philippe, 'the citizen king'.
17. See anonymous engraving *Vue de la montagne élevée au Champ de la Réunion pour la fête qui y été célébrée en l'honneur de l'Être Suprème*, published by Chéreau, 1794, Cabinet des Estampes, Bibliothèque Nationale, Paris.
18. Louis-Oscar Roty (1846–1911), responsible for reviving the art of the medal in France during the latter half of the nineteenth century.
19. Jean-François Millet (1814–1875). The two versions of *Le Semeur* (The Sower) were amongst the artist's finest work under the Second Republic (1848–1851).
20. Henri Grégoire, *Rapport fait au Conseil des Cinq-Cents, sur les sceaux de la République* (31 January 1796). As quoted in Lynn Hunt, *Politics, Culture and Class in the French Revolution*, Methuen, London, 1986, pp 91–92.

Further Reading

Maurice Agulhon, *Marianne au combat*, Paris, 1979. Trans. Janet Lloyd, Cambridge, 1981.
Jean-Jacques Becker, *The Great War and the French People*, Berg, Leamington Spa, 1985.
T J Clark, *The Absolute Bourgeois: Artists and Politics in France 1848–1851*, Thames and Hudson, London, 1973.
Hugh Honor, *Neo-Classicism*, Penguin Books, London, 1968.
Lynn Hunt, *Politics, Culture and Class in the French Revolution*, Methuen, London, 1986.
Charles Dawbarn, *France at Bay*, Mills and Boon, London, 1915.
Laurence Jerrold, *France To-day*, John Murray, London, 1916.
Mona Ozouf, *Festivals and the French Revolution*, Gallimard, Paris, 1976. Trans. Alan Sheridan, Harvard University Press, Massachusetts, 1988.
Robert Philippe, *Political Graphics. Art as a Weapon*, Phaidon Press, Oxford, 1982.
Marina Warner, *Monuments and Maidens: The Allegory of the Female Form*, Weidenfeld and Nicolson, London, 1985.
John Williams, *The Home Fronts 1914–1918*, Constable, London, 1972.

Night For Day: the Symbolic Value of Light in the Painting of the Second World War

Angela Weight

The coming of war is traditionally perceived as the descent of darkness or the onset of an endless night. Many poets writing in 1939–1940 in a mood that was half anguished, half defiant, used this kind of imagery:

> One half the map is shaded as if by night
> Or an eclipse . . .[1]

> Defenceless under the night
> Our world in stupor lies . . .[2]

These writers shared the premonition of Sir Edward Grey twenty-five years earlier, on the eve of the Great War: 'The lights are going out all over Europe. They will not be lit again in our lifetime.' His remark was a deeply pessimistic one, as if he sensed the profound geo-political upheavals that world war would bring about, among them the crumbling of the old order, of which he himself was a member, and the unleashing of forces of revolution and social unrest which would stretch from Glasgow to St Petersburg.

In Paul Nash's painting *We are Making a New World* a red sun rises over a ravaged, silent and deserted landscape. Like Sir William Orpen's end-of-war paintings of sunlight and shadows passing over old German trenches, the impression is painful and ironic. Most large-scale fighting took place between dawn and sunset, and it is daylight broken by cloud and shadow rather than darkness pierced by light, which constitutes the visible atmosphere of the First World War. One reason for this, in painterly terms, was the

William Ware b.1915, *Fired City 1942*, Oil.
Department of Art, LD 2635

Angela Weight is Keeper of the Department of Art, and formerly held the post of Keeper of Art at Aberdeen Art Gallery and Museums.

John Armstrong RA 1893–1973
Building Mosquitoes 1943
Tempera on panel
Department of Art, LD 3359

Below, Frank Dobson RA 1888–1960
*An Underground Room in the BBC
Building 1943*
Ink and watercolour
Department of Art, LD 3580

A M Weston
A Wrecked Barrage Balloon at
Dulwich Station, London SE21 1941
Watercolour and bodycolour
Department of Art, LD 3000

Joan Connew 1915–1976
Blackout in Bromley High Street
1942
Oil
Department of Art, LD 2913

Eric Ravilious 1903–1942
Wall Maps 1940
Watercolour
Department of Art, LD 1194

William Scott ARA b.1913
Night Convoy 1943
Oil
Department of Art, LD 6514

Graham Sutherland O M 1903–1980
The City. A Fallen Lift-shaft 1941
Gouache, pen and ink
Department of Art, LD 893

Below, Henry Carr RA 1894–1970
Searchlight on L.C.I.s, North Africa 1943
Oil
Department of Art, LD 3102

persistence in British art of the *plein air*, naturalistic style of the late nineteenth century. Another was that the technological developments that made darkness and light so important in the Second World War were still only in their infancy in 1914–1918. Night bombing of cities by massed squadrons of aeroplanes was still a thing of the future and electric power, although rapidly superseding steam and gas as a source of energy, was not universally available.

Electric streetlamps and lights in private (well-to-do) homes had existed in Britain since the early 1880s and the demands of wartime production accelerated the use of electric power in industry. However, the electricity industry itself, like coal and the railways, was still in private hands. Neither generation nor distribution was standardised with the result that sometimes there was inconsistency in the supply and incompatibility of product. The lessons of war were that the means of production should not be left in the hands of private individuals and from 1919 onwards there were repeated calls in the press for the nationalisation of coal, steel and electricity. A Labour Government tried to establish a Central Electricity Board in 1923 but was defeated by the power of vested interests in Parliament. The succeeding Conservative Government carried through the legislation and the Central Electricity Board was finally established in December 1926. Work started on the National Grid almost immediately and by 1933 it had 'laced the country.'[3] 'When war came in 1939 this national system, though designed for other ends, was of incalculable value.'[4]

Now not only the big cities but towns, villages and rural areas had access to the electricity supply. Electricity became the staff of civilised life and the power behind the technological revolution of the 1930s. Yet there was little evidence that electric light, which had excited the Italian Futurists as early as 1909, had infiltrated the subject matter or the working methods of British painters. The exceptions are Edward Burra's scenes of Twenties low-life in cafes, bars, dance halls and cinema auditoriums, in which cheap lampshades are a keynote of the decor and artificial light creates a particular *ambience*.

Most people over thirty remembered the Zeppelins and Gothas during the First World War, when over 1000 British people had been killed by bombs. Following the Spanish Civil War and the destruction of the town of Guernica by German bombers in 1937, public fear of a German bombing campaign in Britain was greatly intensified. Consequently plans for a universal black-out in the event of war had already been prepared, and this was the first wartime regulation to be imposed. Streetlamps all over Britain were extinguished on 1 September 1939. With the black-out all forms of light assumed a vital importance. The specific depiction of mundane light sources in innumerable paintings and drawings of the period is evidence of this. Joan Connew's painting *Black-out, Bromley High Street* conveys the disorientation of a pedestrian when the night is only sporadically illuminated by torches, dimmed streetlamps and car headlamps.

In Ruskin Spear's *Black-out* almost nothing can be seen, but it is clear no lady would walk these streets at night, peopled by the looming figures of strange men. The black-out's principal effect was to make all forms of transport more difficult and dangerous. Railway carriages were notoriously unpleasant, with their mix of bulky soldiery and weary, under-nourished civilians, unable to read and even more disinclined to talk than usual under the dim blue night light. The carriage windows were blacked-out too, with only a small screened circle in the middle through which you could look to see if you had reached your destination. James Boswell's *Crewe, 2.00am*, Henry Carr's *Familiar Silhouettes* and Edwin La Dell's *Railway Carriage at Night* have an almost palpable feeling of the chronic boredom of long journeys at night and the dislocation of human relationships in wartime. William Scott's *Night Convoy 1943* is about his personal nightmare as a soldier of being driven away in a lorry at an unearthly hour, along a vanishing perspective of tenement houses with blank black windows, going he knew not where or why.

To a nation blacked-out and blitzed, electric light was a symbol that the world had not dissolved into chaos. Not only did it light homes and places of entertainment but it was the power that enabled work to go on around the clock in factories, offices and basements, underground stores and transport systems. The demands of wartime production enforced constant overtime and regular nightshifts. This relentless industry, particularly on the part of women workers, was a constant theme of official war art. Now, thrust by the war into situations which they would otherwise never have penetrated, artists began to show an awareness of the modern technology that was born in the 1930s. Laura Knight's *Ruby Loftus* screws a breech ring by the light of a green industrial spotlight; Frank Dobson made vivid pastels of underground production, including an escalator carrying descending streams of workers, *Metropolis* fashion, and a mysterious underground control room in the BBC building. In all these drawings, long fluorescent tubes, their suspension wires and each radiant burr of light, are treated as important elements in the picture. Similarly, in John Armstrong's paintings of aircraft production the serried ranks of green-shaded electric light bulbs are given equivalent value in the formal design with the shapes of the aircraft themselves.

The offices of bureaucrats, planners and administrators became legitimate subjects for such artists as Eric Ravilious, Barnett Freedman, Meredith Frampton and John Piper. In paintings such as *The Teleprinter Room, Headquarters*

Edwin La Dell ARA 1914–1970
Night Train, Brussels, 1944

Watercolour, pen and ink
Department of Art, IWM ART 15849

Room, The Passage to the Control Room at S.W. Regional Head-quarters and Meredith Frampton's portrait of *Sir Ernest Gowers, Lt-Col Child and K A L Parker in the London Region Civil Defence Control Room* we see ample evidence that order, stability and control are being maintained. In these paintings the ubiquitous green-shaded bulb emits a steady glow, illuminating for us wall charts with coloured pins, large numerals and directional signs, tidy women clerks and busy confident men. Such paintings were a subtle form of propaganda, contributing to morale at home and abroad by convincing their audience that Britain could and would carry on – even alone.

These paintings of administrative *sang-froid*, of people and things embalmed in the glare of an electric light bulb, can be contrasted with other paintings of the chaos, darkness, discomfort, and even death, that reigned outside. Certainly the night was pierced by some spectacular light effects. Searchlights were used by AA batteries and coastal defence stations to probe the sky and sea, to provide light for nightwork at the docks (the black-out notwithstanding) and even in the countryside, as in Bernard Casson's *Land Drainage – overtime*. Burning barrage balloons created mesmerising aerial bonfires – both Frank Dobson and A M Weston painted these, the latter at East Dulwich Station. Perhaps here, in the category of portents and supernatural fireworks, should come Henry Carr's painting of *Vesuvius in Eruption*. He recorded the scene in March 1944 as Army hospital staff prepared to evacuate from the foot of the mountain. The violence and scale of the eruption dwarfed the man-made destruction in and around Naples as the battle for Southern Italy was waged by the Allies. Henry Carr's large wartime output contains many paintings of night scenes and strange light effects, such as the one entitled *Infantry Landing Craft Landing Troops* in which the troops look like ants in the beam of a low-level

searchlight, while the purple sky is illuminated by curly green streamers of phosphorescent smoke from flares.

But the real fires began with the bombing of London. In his perceptive introduction to *Air Raids*, one of a series of illustrated booklets on the official war art published by OUP during the war, Stephen Spender remarked that 'The background to this war, corresponding to the Western Front in the last war, is the bombed city; and the artist of this war is the Civilian Defence Artist.'[5] The aerial bombing of civilian targets produced apocalyptic imagery: the bombers of the RAF and the Luftwaffe were the new Riders of the Apocalypse. Stephen Spender felt that the fires they started had a revelatory effect on cultural attitudes – a view that might not have been appreciated by the citizens of Coventry, Dresden or Cologne. With the hindsight of one who had known Europe in the Thirties he wrote that 'For years before the war, European cities were unreal, with the unreality of a landscape sunlit and unspeakably silent before a storm. Some artists expressed this violent sense of disorder in surrealism, others by withdrawing into the search for an abstract and integrating symbol. The war is the fulfilment of the prophetic visions of art, and in a sense it means a return to reality by artists who found the peace too unreal to be accepted at its face value.' For Spender, 'the artists of the war' were clearly Sutherland, Piper and Moore: 'There is an unearthly glory about Graham Sutherland's study of *Devastation in an East End Street*; and his pictures of twisted girders have something in them of twisted humanity. John Piper makes us more directly aware of a great architectural tradition burning up with a sunset fire which our civilisation has neglected. Henry Moore's figures of people sleeping in the Underground shelters have acquired something of the quality of stone buildings. We feel that these people are the guardians and even the foundations of the streets above them.' Piper, Moore and Sutherland were the 'visionary' artists who rose above the naturalism of most of the official war artists. There was, however, one other visionary painter, William Ware, whose small painting *Fired City 1942* is a universal image of a world devouring itself. The poisoned-looking landscape might be the Western Front in 1918; the fired tracery of walls might be Dresden.

A quite different kind of picture came from the artists who served in the Auxiliary Fire Service or who were in some other branch of civil defence. W S Haines's *Fire Blitz on Bath* – a holocaust of orange light against which church spires, trees and rooftops are silhouetted – A R Thomson's *A High Explosive Bomb in High Street, Kensington*, Bernard Hailstone's *An Evening in the City* – a routine title for routine destruction – Henry Carr's *Incendiaries in a Suburb* and *St Clement Dane's Church on Fire after being Bombed* and Matvyn Wright's *A Parachute Bomb* are examples of straightforward English painting that everyone could understand. But Leonard Rosoman's *House Collapsing on Two Firemen, Shoe Lane* is possibly the only painting that hints that people were actually killed in the Blitz. At issue in many of these paintings of London burning is the artists' fascination with spectacle, their tendency to construct pictures which look like a bonfire party that has got badly out of control.

Just as in the First World War the ruins of Ypres and Albert were endlessly fascinating to every passing artist, so the bomb-shattered urban landscape of British cities, especially London, caused a flood of submissions to the War Artists Advisory Committee. These ranged from the architectural precision of Muirhead Bone's *St Brides and the City after the Fire* to the picturesque melodrama of F T W Cook's *St Nicholas Cole Abbey*. However the WAAC[6] had its own plans to record the effect of the Blitz, at least where property was concerned. A committee minute coolly remarks, 'It is our experience that damage by bombing is most spectacular when seen soon after the event'[7], and the committee matched the abilities of John Piper and Graham Sutherland to the task. In fact the emotions aroused by the spectacle of the Blitz were often ambivalent. Stephen Spender's 'great architectural tradition burning up with a sunset fire' acknowledges the historical loss and at the same time implies a feeling of release from the old

Establishment order which that tradition enshrined. John Piper's studies of bomb damage in Bath and at the Houses of Parliament embody that sense of *fin d'époque* which both world wars brought about.

Graham Sutherland's experience of the Blitz was different. In the City of London his imagination was stirred by the suddenly exposed entrails of office buildings and factories. But the East End was another country. The East End was 'much more tragic.'[8] There he was aware of the damage to people and to their livelihoods. The horror he felt then remained fresh in his memory forty years later, when he described in an interview 'the shells of long terraces of houses ... great – surprisingly wide – perspectives of destruction seeming to recede into infinity and the windowless blocks were like sightless eyes.'[9] (Sutherland, one suspects, was suffering from culture shock as much as from the shock of destruction on this scale.) His description is close to William Scott's quoted earlier in connection with his painting *Night Convoy*. The difference between the latter and Sutherland's *Devastation, 1941 : an East End Street*[10] – surreally deserted except for a queer curled 'monster' shape at the end of the vista – is that Sutherland, for all his imaginative engagement with the scenes of devastation in the East End, was nevertheless able to distance himself from the war when he was not working

Meredith Frampton RA 1894–1984
Sir Ernest Gowers KCB KBE, Senior Regional Commissioner for London, Lt. Col. A J Child OBE MC Director of Operations and Intelligence and K A L Parker, Deputy Chief Administrative Officer in the London Regional Control Room 1943
Oil
Department of Art, LD 2905

for the War Artists Advisory Committee. Although the amount of time he could devote to it was limited, he continued to do his own work while a salaried war artist. Scott, on the other hand, spent the war as a soldier in the Royal Engineers, mainly at Ruabon in North Wales, an experience which for him was little better than a term of imprisonment. Metaphorically speaking, Scott was travelling down his endless black perspective, not seeing any light at the end of the tunnel, while Sutherland's perspective represented an abyss from which he could always draw back.

There are more vanishing perspectives – and a multitude of eerie light effects – in the neglected work of Alan Sorrell, remembered by those of a certain age as the illustrator of school history books on Roman Britain. His pastel, pen and ink drawings of requisitioned country houses and far-flung RAF encampments are immersed in the chill of winter. The bare branches of trees cast spidery shadows by the light of the moon and stars, and when the wind is up, thick bubbling smoke from barrack stoves is blown horizontally across the turbulent sky. Sorrell is also fond of the bleak light of early morning, when men emerge from warm lighted doorways and march to the parade ground for the 8 am roll call. A sliver of moon still hangs in the sky, but now plumes of smoke drift painlessly upward in the still air of dawn, making dirty streaks across the brightening horizon. In *FIDO in Operation* the values are reversed: a plane comes in to land under a flesh pink tunnel of smoke from the flarepath. More planes circle above this mock inferno while the moon, rarely absent from Sorrell's work, is reduced to peering through a gap in the clouds. In a large painting dated 1946, *Construction of a runway at an aerodrome*, the landscape has been ravaged by two runways like gigantic Roman roads driving straight into the distance. Dark, rolling clouds are rapidly overtaking what remains of the evening sunlight. The nuclear age is on the horizon.

Notes

1. Ruthven Todd, 'It was easier', *Poets of Tomorrow I*, Hogarth Press, London, 1939.
2. W H Auden, 'September 1, 1939' *Poetry of the Thirties*, Penguin, London, 1964.
3. C L Mowat, *Britain between the Wars*, London, 1955, p 342.
4. C L Mowat, op cit p 343.
5. Stephen Spender, *War Pictures by British Artists*, Second Series: *Air Raids*, Oxford University Press, 1943.
6. The War Artists Advisory Committee was set up in September 1939 at the instigation of Sir Kenneth Clark, then Director of the National Gallery. The War Artists Advisory Committee operated under the auspices of the Ministry of Information and met 197 times between 1939 and 1945. Chaired by Clark, it was administered by a Secretary and contained representatives from the Ministry of Information, the War Office, the Air Ministry and the Admiralty. The Committee acquired 5,570 works of art through its commissions or as the result of direct purchases from artists and exhibitions.
7. Department of Art, War Artists Archive, Dickey/Schwabe, 17 November 1940.
8. Edwin Mullins, 'Images wrought from destruction', *The Daily Telegraph Magazine*, no 359, September 1971.
9. Edwin Mullins, op cit.
10. Tate Gallery 5736
Note: A shorter version of this article appeared under the title 'The Wartime Nocturne in British Painting, 1940–45' in the catalogue of the exhibition *A Paradise Lost: the Neo-Romantic Imagination in Britain 1935–55*, published by Lund Humphries in association with the Barbican Art Gallery, 1987.

JW.53: Convoy to Russia

Paul Kemp

Paul Kemp is a research assistant in the Department of Photographs, and was formerly Schools Officer onboard HMS *Belfast* 1981–1983.

'It is a grim and bitter effort amid fearful gales and ceaseless perils'

– Winston Churchill.

The decision to send supplies of war material to the Soviet Union following the German invasion in June 1941 by the northern route through the Arctic Ocean to north Russia presented the Royal Navy with what appeared to be an impossible task. In order to reach their destination the convoys had to pass along hundreds of miles of enemy held coastline over which the Luftwaffe held complete air superiority and where the surviving portion of the German surface fleet was based together with a large number of U-boats.

But it is the physical conditions in which these convoys fought their way to Russia which give them a unique place in the history of naval operations during the Second World War. After assembling in a remote Scottish loch or in the bleak harbour of Hvalfjord in Iceland the convoys were routed through the Arctic Ocean to Russia's only ice-free port, Murmansk, at the mouth of the Kola Inlet. In summer months the ports of Archangel and Molotovsk were used. These waters were renowned for their bad weather and conditions which tested human endurance to the limits. Spray turned to ice on the rigging, masts and superstructure so that it became a constant struggle to keep equipment in working order. The northern latitudes produced winters of perpetual darkness followed by summers of almost continuous daylight. A glance at the map will show that the route the convoys could follow was restricted to the north by the seasonal movement of the polar ice pack and to the south by the threat posed

Arctic Convoy Routes

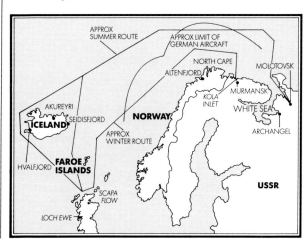

by German aircraft in northern Norway. The mixing of the warm waters of the Gulf Stream and the cold water of the Arctic produced fog and poor SONAR conditions, thus favouring U-boat operations. Such were the conditions under which men of the Royal and United States Navies, together with their respective merchant fleets, laboured to bring supplies to Russia.

JW.53[1] was one of forty[2] such convoys which travelled the northern route to Russia between August 1941 and May 1945. The convoy was assembled in Loch Ewe throughout early February 1943 under the command of the convoy's commodore, Rear Admiral E W Leir DSO. Difficulties in assembling and loading the ships meant that the sailing date was put back to 15 February and only 25 of the planned 30 ships were ready to sail.

Since by the middle of February there would be approximately seven hours of daylight in the latitude of the North Cape it was decided that the convoy should be accompanied by a strong escort whose composition reflected the multitude of threats to which the merchant ships would be exposed. The Close Escort, which would go all the way to Murmansk, was under the command of Commander H G A Lewis RN in the minesweeper HMS *Jason* and consisted of three Hunt class destroyers, three corvettes, one minesweeper and two trawlers. Off Iceland the convoy would be joined by the Ocean Escort under the command of Captain I M R Campbell RN in the destroyer HMS *Milne* and consisting of the anti-aircraft cruiser HMS *Scylla*, the escort carrier HMS *Dasher* (with two Hunt class destroyers for rescue purposes), and thirteen destroyers of the 3rd and 8th Destroyer Flotillas. To guard against the threat of attack by German capital ships the 10th Cruiser Squadron consisting of HMS *Belfast*, *Cumberland* and *Sheffield* (known as Force 'R'), under the command of Rear Admiral Robert Burnett in *Belfast*, would screen the convoy from 5°E to 35°E and then proceed direct to the Kola Inlet. To provide distant cover there were the battleships HMS *King George V* and *Howe* together with the cruiser HMS *Norfolk* under the command of the Commander-in-Chief of the Home Fleet, Admiral Sir John Tovey, which would cruise as far as 32°E depending on the fuel states of their escorting destroyers. Finally, although not strictly part of the escort, the submarines *Truculent*, *Sportsman*, *Simoom* and *Sea Nymph* were ordered to patrol off the Norwegian coast to intercept any German surface units tempted to leave harbour.

The pre-sailing conference for the Commanding Officers of the ships in the Close Escort and the Masters of the merchant ships was held on 14 February at Loch Ewe and was attended by Admiral Burnett, who had intended to sail for Seidisfjord on the east coast of Iceland immediately afterwards to rendez-vous with the other two cruisers of his squadron and the destroyers of the Ocean Escort which were

sailing from Scapa. At Seidisfjord the warships would top up with fuel too before joining the convoy. However problems with a recalcitrant capstan engine delayed *Belfast*'s departure until 16 February.

The convoy sailed on 15 February and as the heavily laden merchant ships rounded the Butt of Lewis and lost the shelter of the Hebrides they met the full force of an Atlantic gale. Many ships carried heavy deck cargo such as railway locomotives and tanks and two ships had to return to resecure cargo which had come adrift. On 17 February the Russian merchant ship *Komiles* reported that the lashings securing her deck cargo were broken and that she was proceeding to the Faroe Islands to make good the damage, but on the nineteenth her Master reported that the ship was breaking up and sinking; a search was organised but no wreckage or survivors were found. Under the buffeting of the gale the merchant ships quickly lost formation and the convoy became scattered. Commander Lewis reported:

> Heavy seas and swell from the NW ... visual communication with escorts difficult due to low visibility and height of waves. Convoy somewhat scattered and escorts out of position.[3]

The various components of the Ocean Escort fared no better in the gale as they made their way to the rendezvous. The escort carrier *Dasher* was forced to return with storm damage and a subsequent inspection of the American built carrier revealed that:

> ... no attempt had been made to fit ship for Arctic service. Few if any of the exposed essential hydraulic fittings required for the operation of aircraft are fitted with heating ... consider her operational value has been prejudiced by these omissions.[4]

The cruiser *Sheffield*, proceeding to Iceland from Scapa, was another casualty of the storm. On 19 February she was struck by a wave which tore away a third of the armoured roof of 'A' turret and did much other damage on the upper deck.[5] On arriving at Seidisfjord it was decided to substitute HMS *Glasgow* for *Sheffield*, but *Glasgow* had been driven aground by high winds so HMS *Norfolk* was detached from the Home Fleet, her place being taken by HMS *Berwick*.

The bad weather severely disrupted the arrangements for the Ocean Escort to join the convoy. Admiral Burnett in *Belfast*, having finally got away from Loch Ewe on 16 February, described the weather encountered during the voyage to Iceland;

All this time the wind and sea were increasing . . . the wind was force 9, the sea state 7 and *Belfast* was rolling heavily. The average height of the waves was 40 feet, the maximum 45F5 and the distance between the crests 500′ to 600′[6]

Belfast arrived off Seidisfjord in the afternoon of 18 February, but the weather was so bad that she could not enter the fjord to fuel. The cruisers *Scylla* and *Cumberland* together with the destroyers *Intrepid, Fury, Eclipse, Impulsive* and the Polish *Orkan* were also in the same predicament, so Burnett took all the ships under his command and headed for Akureyri on the north coast of Iceland where they arrived on the twentieth. The remaining destroyers of the Ocean Escort, consisting of *Milne, Faulknor, Boadicea, Obedient, Opportune, Orwell, Obdurate* and *Inglefield* had sailed from Scapa on 14 February and had arrived at Seidisfjord on the fifteenth, but the appalling weather prevented them from fuelling until the nineteenth.

By 20 February fuelling was complete. *Milne* and her seven destroyers sailed from Seidisfjord on the morning of 20 February and joined the convoy on the following day while *Scylla* sailed from Akureyri with her destroyers in the evening of 20 February and joined the convoy on the twenty-second. Finally Burnett's cruisers got under way on the twenty-first, although in doing so *Belfast* nearly suffered the same fate as the luckless *Glasgow*:

> It was a day of ill omen for *Belfast* . . . the capstan engine failed to respond to treatment, the cable of the port anchor took a complete turn around the fluke of the starboard anchor, thus providing an interesting seamanship problem. A strong squall arose just as the cable had been cleared and the ship was anchored with two shackles in 24 fathoms and the engine room reported no steam on the main engines due to water in the fuel oil.[7]

The problems were overcome and by the twenty-third Burnett's cruisers were steaming in position eight miles ahead of the convoy.

After nearly four days the gale blew itself out and the escorts began the task of shepherding the scattered merchant ships back into formation. In the course of the night of 19/20 February the battle fleet came within radar range of the convoy enabling the *King George V* to plot the positions of the merchant ships on her radar and pass the information to the escorts.

One advantage of the appalling weather was that the Luftwaffe could not undertake air reconnaissance of the convoy. But as the skies began to clear from 22 February

onwards, it became clear that this fortunate state of affairs could not continue. An additional factor favouring the Germans was that the southern edge of the polar ice cap extended unusually far south so that the convoy was only 250 miles from the German base at Altenfjord. It was only a matter of time before the Luftwaffe found JW.53.

Two Blohm and Voss 138 reconnaissance aircraft sighted the convoy on 23 February and the next day shadowing aircraft were sighted at 11.35 and 13.15, both of which were heard transmitting homing signals presumably intended for U-boats lying in wait for the convoy. Between 18.00 and 21.30 the convoy was repeatedly harassed by two or three U-boats, but each contact was rigorously prosecuted by the escorts with apparent success for no attack developed.

The major alarm of the day came at 17.30 when the destroyer HMS *Obedient* obtained a radar contact which was classified as a large surface ship. The destroyer immediately broadcast the code word STRIKE indicating that an attack by German surface units was imminent. On receipt of this codeword, Admiral Burnett's cruisers, which were steaming ahead of the convoy, altered course to the south west with *Belfast* leading *Cumberland* and *Norfolk*. Burnett later wrote of this incident that:

> I had the greatest doubts as to the truth that enemy surface forces were in contact with the convoy. The Germans must have been well aware of the composition of the escort and I could not believe that even Admiral Dönitz could throw heavy surface ships in the dark on such a force. Neither was I prepared to plunge with Force R into a melee of our own fighting destroyers. My intention was to steam to the southwards towards the Norwegian coast and get between any enemy, who might have been foolish enough to take such a great risk, and his home port, getting in touch with Captain (D)3 by signal so that he could track the retiring enemy for my benefit and then get out of the way before I went in to destroy him.[8]

Burnett clearly relished the prospect of a night action with the enemy but his hopes were to be frustrated for at 17.45 *Obedient* signalled that the STRIKE signal had been a false alarm. The contact had probably been a U-boat caught beam-on by the destroyer's radar.

The shadowing aircraft returned at daybreak on 25 February and at 11.15 a signal was received from the Senior British Naval Officer in North Russia that a force of Ju.88 and Me.109 aircraft had been observed crossing the coast. Fifteen minutes later 14 Ju.88s were detected astern of the convoy at a height of 13,000 feet. The aircraft made a shallow glide attack which

> ... was not well pressed home and few aircraft rendered a clean dive. It was an inspiring sight to see *Scylla* steering across the convoy listing heavily under wheel and helm with every gun spitting skywards.[9]

A few bombs fell near the tanker *British Governor*, but no hits were scored. Subsequently two Ju.88s returned and made a high altitude bombing attack without effect.

The aircraft which had been shadowing the convoy remained in contact until darkness fell. During the night there was considerable U-boat activity. The value of the HF/DF[10] apparatus was amply demonstrated: time after time a U-boat unwise enough to have given her position away by transmitting a homing signal would find herself illuminated by starshell and attacked by the escorts. Several alterations of course had to be made during the night because of reported U-boat contacts, but the aggressive tactics of the escorts once again denied the U-boats any success.

On 26 February the shadowing aircraft returned and circled the convoy at a range of 20 to 30 miles transmitting homing signals all the while. At 12.25, without warning, German aircraft approached the convoy from all directions: a tactic possibly intended to make the escort think that the attackers were merely the usual reconnaissance aircraft. The Germans grouped at a distance of 12 miles from the convoy and then made a high level bombing attack from above the cloud base. A heavy and varied blind barrage was put up by the escorts and merchant ships with such success that soon intercepted German R/T was heard ordering the pilots to fly higher, drop their bombs as quickly as possible and return to Petsamo. At no time were any of the attacking aircraft observed, but it was thought that twelve Ju.88s were involved: like the first air attack it was unsuccessful.

Early on the morning of 27 February the convoy divided: fifteen of the merchant ships and the majority of the escort proceeded to Murmansk where they arrived later that day. The remaining seven merchant ships escorted by *Inglefield*, *Intrepid*, *Fury* and *Bluebell* proceeded to the White Sea port of Archangel where they arrived on 29 February. JW.53 had arrived safely without loss: sadly the freighter *Ocean Freedom* was sunk and the *Doverhill*, *British Governor* and *Empire Kinsman* were damaged while they lay at anchor at Murmansk in air attacks launched by Ju.87 dive bombers.

Such was the story of JW.53. It is not perhaps the best known of the Arctic convoys but its story is fairly typical. The effort made by the Royal Navy to escort convoys such as JW.53 was considerable; practically the whole of the Home Fleet had been marshalled to ensure the safe passage of the merchant ships and their valuable cargoes. The need to keep large numbers of warships in the Arctic for convoy escort duty placed a great strain on the Home Fleet and naturally meant that other theatres of operations, notably the Mediterranean and the Far East, were deprived, often at critical times in the war. But throughout the Second World War, given the adverse strategic circumstances in which these operations took place, the maintenance of the Arctic supply route was 'amazingly successful'[11] as is shown by the statistics given in the Appendix.

But the price of this success was high. Eighteen allied warships were sunk while escorting convoys to Russia and 1,944 naval personnel lost their lives together with 829 merchant seamen. When considered in the light of overall Allied aid to Russia the question must be asked whether the Arctic route was worth the effort and sacrifice needed to maintain it. The quantities of material supplied to the Soviet Union by Britain and the United States from 1941 to 1945 were enormous[12] but only 22.7% of it was sent via the Arctic route; the remaining 77.3% went via the Persian Gulf and short-sea Pacific routes. Of the goods carried by the Arctic route some 7.5% were lost in transit, the highest of any convoy route, as compared with a loss rate of 0.7% for Atlantic convoys. There were, of course, drawbacks to each of the three routes, but the strategic disadvantages of the Arctic route were so obvious that it is difficult to understand why so much effort was expended upon it.

Undoubtedly the failure of the Germans to interdict the passage of the early convoys in 1941/42 caused unfounded optimism as to the amount of supplies that could be safely delivered by this route. A more important factor is that Soviet reluctance to see the establishment of an Anglo-American presence in Iran, a necessary consequence of the development of the Persian Gulf route, caused the Russians to insist on the Arctic route. It took the disaster that befell convoy PQ.17 in July 1942 to convince Stalin, who had a Canute-like view of maritime strategy, that a steady trickle of supplies through the Persian Gulf was better than occasional deliveries by the Arctic route.

In conclusion, while accepting the fact that it was imperative to maintain the supply of material aid to the Soviet Union, it is difficult to comprehend the continued use of the route with the most disadvantages. The use of the Arctic route was justifiable while Russian fortunes were at their lowest ebb in 1941/42 but once the Russians had surmounted their early difficulties the British and American governments were wrong in not pressing ahead with the expansion of the Persian Gulf route. That Russian convoys like JW.53 were so successful is due in part to the mistakes and ineptitude shown by the German High Command, but above all it is due to the courage and tenacity of the men of the Royal and Merchant Navies.

Notes

1. From 1941 to September 1942 outward bound convoys were coded PQ and homeward ones QP. After Convoy PQ 18 in September 1942 the codes were changed to JW for outward convoys and RA for the return convoy.

2. This figure excludes JW.61A in November 1944 which was a special fast convoy in which 11,000 Russian PoWs were forcibly repatriated to the USSR.

3. Report of Proceedings of Commander H G A Lewis RN of HMS *Jason*, 18 February 1943. PRO ADM 199/73.

4. C in C Home Fleet to Admiralty, 15 February 1943. Signal reprinted in Home Fleet War Diary, 15 February 1943. Typescript copy held by Naval Staff Duties Division, Ministry of Defence.

5. Log of HMS *Sheffield*, 19 February 1943, PRO ADM 53/118525.

6. Report of Proceedings of Rear Admiral commanding the 10th Cruiser Squadron, 17 February 1943. PRO ADM 199/73.

7. Ibid, 20 February 1943.

8. Ibid, 24 February 1943.

9. Report of Proceedings of Captain I M R Campbell RN of HMS *Milne*, 25 February 1943. PRO ADM 199/73.

10. HF/DF: High Frequency Direction Finding.

11. Roskill, Captain Stephen, *The War at Sea*, Vol 3 Part 2, HMSO, London 1954–61, 262.

12. See Schofield, Vice Admiral B B, *The Russian Convoys*, Batsford, 1964, pp 213–214 for details of allied aid to the USSR.

Further Reading

Admiralty, *The War at Sea 1939–45*, typescript account prepared by Historical Section of the Naval Staff Duties Division. Copy held by IWM Library.

Kemp, Paul, *The Russian Convoys 1941–45*, Arms and Armour Press, London, 1987.

Roskill, Captain S W, *The War at Sea*, Vol 3 Part 2, HMSO, London, 1954–61.

Schofield, Vice Admiral B B, *The Arctic Convoys*, MacDonald and Janes, London, 1977.

Schofield, Vice Admiral B B, *The Russian Convoys*, Batsford, London, 1964.

Appendix

Analysis of Russian Convoys

	1941	1942	1943	1944	1945	Total
No. of Convoys to N. Russia:	8	13	6	9	4	40
No. of ships in Convoy to N. Russia:	64	256	112	284	95	811
No. of convoys from N. Russia:	4	13	6	9	5	37
No. of ships in convoy from N. Russia:	49	188	93	249	136	715
Ships obliged to return as a result of weather damage:	45	21	8	6	1	40
Ships sunk by U-boat:	1	24	4	7	5	41
Ships sunk by aircraft:	..	36	..	..	1	37
Ships sunk by surface vessels:	..	3	..	..	..	3
Ships sunk at Kola after arrival:						5
Foundered in a gale:						1
Sunk in a British minefield:						5
Sunk while sailing independently:						6
Total No. of ships sunk:						98

The Photographic Record

The selection of photographs accompanying this article represent the work of the three Admiralty Official Photographers who recorded the passage of JW.53. Lieutenant F Davies RNVR sailed in HMS *King George V* and recorded the operations of the Battle Fleet. Lieutenant F A Hudson RNVR was in HMS *Inglefield* and his photographs graphically portray the violence of the storm which battered the convoy. Finally, Lieutenant J A Hampton RNVR in HMS *Scylla* took photographs which remain the most enduring images of the Arctic Convoys.

The negative numbers covering the work of each of the three photographers are as follows:

Lt Davies: A 15422 to A 15431.

Lt Hudson: A 15385 to A 15421.

Lt Hampton: A 15348 to A 15357.

Where appropriate the name of each photographer is given in parentheses after the negative number.

The cruiser HMS *Scylla* on the Clyde on completion in June 1942. *Scylla* was known as the 'Toothless Terror' because her main armament consisted of eight 4.5″ guns on four Mk.III mountings instead of the five 5.25″ twin turrets usually fitted in ships of this class. FL 2392

The Battle Fleet at sea. Taken from HMS *King George V*, the photograph shows the County class cruiser HMS *Berwick* (left) and the King George V class battleship HMS *Howe* (right). A 15429 (Davies)

The view from the bridge of HMS *Sheffield* during the voyage to Iceland. The two forward turrets have been trained on the beam to prevent damage to the canvas blast screens of the 6″ guns: even so, the ship suffered severe weather damage. A 14892

The destroyer HMS *Opportune* in heavy weather. If life on larger warships was bad then life onboard a destroyer in such conditions must have pushed men to the limits of their endurance. A 15389 (Hudson)

A view down *Inglefield*'s starboard side as the ship rolls heavily to port. The HF/DF apparatus, the aerial for which can be seen on top of the mainmast, proved invaluable in locating U-boats. A 15394 (Hudson)

Waves break over *Inglefield*'s bow during the gale. A 15393 (Hudson)

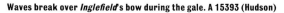

The view looking forward along the starboard side of HMS *Scylla* showing how ice quickly accumulated on the superstructure. A 15352 (Hampton)

Seamen using steam hoses to clear ice and snow from *Scylla*'s forecastle. A 15365 (Hampton)

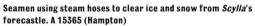

Rear Admiral Robert Burnett commanding the 10th Cruiser Squadron and one of the outstanding tactical commanders produced by the Royal Navy during the Second World War. A 10318

Commander A G West RN, commanding officer of the destroyer HMS *Inglefield*, in arctic clothing on the bridge of his ship. A 15401 (Hudson)

JW.53 under attack on 25 February. Bombs are falling around the tanker *British Governor*. A 15362 (Hampton)

The convoy passes through pancake ice early in the morning of 26 February. A 15359 (Hampton)

Merchant ships of the White Sea section at anchor at Archangel after their arrival on 29 February. The photograph taken from the after end of the bridge of HMS *Inglefield*. Note the bleak nature of the surroundings. A 15421 (Hudson)

Escorts at anchor at Vanega Bay in the Kola Inlet before the departure of the homeward bound convoy RA.63. From left to right: HMS *Cumberland*, HMS *Obdurate*, an unidentified O class destroyer and HMS *Belfast* with HMS *Faulknor* alongside. The escorts had a respite of only 48 hours at Murmansk before sailing with the homeward convoy RA.53. A 15419 (Hudson)

'The Dead Man's Penny': A History of the Next of Kin Memorial Plaque

Philip Dutton

I t is a commonplace to remark on the widespread enthusiasm with which the declaration of war was greeted in Britain in August 1914. The images are familiar: cheering crowds outside Buckingham Palace and provincial Town Halls; long queues of recalled reservists and eager volunteers at the military depots. Much of the writing of the time, popular and serious, spoke of war in terms of a glorious opportunity; as a noble and generous cause; an honourable duty. C E Montague, an elderly and eloquent volunteer, wrote of these early days:

> All the air was ringing with rousing assurances, France to be saved, Belgium righted, freedom and civilization re-won, a sour soiled and crooked old world to be rid of bullies and reclaimed for straightness and decency, good nature, the ways of common men dealing with common men.[1]

But the experience of nearly two years of fighting, with the prospect of victory none the nearer, revealed the 'undisguisedly mechanical and inhuman'[2] face of modern war. A grim readjustment of vision was effected. The theme of a perceived change in the nature of the war was one which, by 1916, was shared by many contemporary writers and observers.[3] Edmund Blunden's comments on the introduction of steel helmets for use by his unit, 11th Battalion Royal Sussex Regiment, just prior to its involvement in the Somme offensive indicate, in typically restrained and oblique language, how the scale and fundamental character of the war was changing:

> Steel helmets now became the rule; their ugly useful discomfort supplanting our friendly soft caps. . . . The dethronement of the soft cap clearly symbolized the change that was coming over the war, the induration from a personal crusade into a vast machine of violence.[4]

Blunden's intimations of disquiet proved well founded. Posterity has come to regard the offensive, and especially its calamitous opening day, as symbolic of the wastefulness and 'futility'[5] of British First World War combat experience. Recorded photographically, the appalling conditions in which much of the later winter fighting took place have become seminal images of the nature of Western Front trench warfare. The grotesque contrast between effort expended, in terms of casualties, and effective achievement, territorial gains, has made the campaign highly contentious. Conceived, in part, as an attempt to distract German atten-

Philip Dutton is a cataloguer in the Department of Information Retrieval. He formerly held the post of Assistant Curator at the Towner Art Gallery, Eastbourne, 1975–1977.

tion from the French at Verdun, the British effort on the Somme resulted in losses in manpower on a scale unimaginable in 1914. The disquieting image of a gruesome leering skeleton, personification of Death, vigorously pumping the lifeblood of Europe's manhood into a scorched and ruined earth, used by Walther Eberbach in his satirical medallion 'Verdun die Weltblutpumpe,' was as relevant to British military experience in the summer of 1916 as it was to the ordeals of the massive conscript armies of France and Germany. The British failure to breach the German lines on 1 July inevitably led to the strategy of attrition. A vital aspect of the change in the nature of the war was, from the British perspective, the pledging of an alliance by the deliberate trading of losses:

Walther Eberbach:
'VERDUN.DIE.WELTBLUTPUMPE.', obverse design. A grim reference to the drawn out tragedy of the battles for Verdun and ghastly comment on the scale of casualties incurred on the Western Front during 1916. A leering skeleton pumps the lifeblood out of Europe and leaves a scarred and ruined earth. Bronze, 70 mm, catalogue number MED/733.
HU53984

> The exact proportion of the losses stemming from 1 July is not often appreciated. Eighty per cent of Britain's casualties occurred after the opening of the Battle of the Somme. Most of Britain's losses were on the Western Front; 522,206 casualties were sustained there up to the end of June 1916; 2,183,930 afterwards.[6]

Despite the optimistic public claims made on behalf of the offensive its real achievement was to bring mourning into nearly every household in Britain. The experience of receiving the fateful War Office letter, Army Form B104-82A, or the fearful scanning of the newspapers' crammed columns of casualties could not but place wearying strain on the spirits.

The year 1916 was a turning point in the soldier's and civilian's perception of the war and it was perhaps appropriate that in October, when fighting on the Somme had reached the slogging matches of the Transloy Ridges and Ancre Heights, a Government Committee should have been set up by Secretary of State for War David Lloyd George to consider what form of memorial should be made available to the next of kin. Although weighted with tragic overtones the memorial scheme manifested the existence, among the Committee members at least, of a grim spirit of optimism. For the belief that at some future time the British Government would have the means and will to put it into effect, a belief held despite the disappointments on land and sea, implied a strong but hardly reassuring faith in victory.

The scheme was first made public in *The Times* for Tuesday 7 November 1916. Under the headline 'Memento for the Fallen. State Gift for Relatives' the committee's form and function were precisely defined:

> A General Committee, representative of both Houses of Parliament and of the Government Departments most concerned has been appointed to consider the question of a memorial to be distributed to the relatives of soldiers and sailors who fall in the war . . .

The Committee was composed of two peers, six MPs, two of whom held military rank, and representatives for the Dominions, the India Office, the Colonial Office and the Admiralty.[7] Sir Reginald Brade, Secretary of the War Office and Army Council, was appointed Chairman and Mr W Hutchinson, also of the War Office, was made Secretary. As Sir Reginald was, from that same month, also a member of the War Office Cinematograph Committee it is tempting to agree with Nicholas Reeves's assessment of his priorities[8] and suggest that it must have been 'very difficult for him to devote much time' to the work of either Committee. Nonetheless his wide political experience and understanding of the importance of good public relations stood the work of the other members in good stead. Additionally a specialist subcommittee was subsequently set up to assist the General Committee on the more arcane points of artistic and technical detail. It included the Directors of the National Gallery and the Victoria and Albert Museum, Sir Cecil Harcourt-Smith and Sir Charles Holmes, and the Keeper (since 1912) of the Department of Coins and Medals at the British Museum, George Francis Hill.

Already, by 7 November, as *The Times* informed its readers, the decision had been made that the cost of the memorial was to be borne by the State. The precise form it was to take was a matter for much longer consideration. The initially accepted idea was that it should be '. . . a small metal plate recording the man's name and services.'[9]

After the announcement of 7 November 1916 the Committee's deliberations disappeared for many months from public view. It was not until August 1917, in the midst of the Third Battle of Ypres, that the memorial 'plate' project resurfaced in the General Committee's decision that the commemoration should now take the form of a bronze plaque. The announcement was reported in *The Times* for Monday 13 August 1917 and the competition for appropriate designs described in extravagant detail:

> The Government are offering prizes, amounting in all to not less than £500 (in proportions to be subsequently decided) for a limited number of the most successful models for a small memorial plaque in bronze to be given to the next of kin of those members of His Majesty's naval and military forces who have fallen in the war. The plaque must have an area of as near as possible 18 square inches. It may be a circle of $4\frac{3}{4}$ inches in diameter, or a square of $4\frac{1}{4}$ inches, or a rectangle of 5 inches by 3 to $3\frac{1}{2}$ inches, and it should be so produced by casting from a mould, which should be finished with precision. All designs submitted must be actual models in relief in wax or plaster of the size indicated. No models on a larger scale will be considered, and no competitor may submit more than two models. The design should comprehend a subject and a brief inscription. It is suggested that some symbolical figure subject should be chosen but the following inscription has been decided upon: 'HE DIED FOR FREEDOM AND HONOUR' and this must form part of the design.

There followed instructions relating to the need to leave space for the deceased person's name and the reminder 'that the design should be essentially simple and easily intelligible'. The final paragraph informed readers that all competitors 'must be British born subjects' and that the model 'should be packed in a small box and delivered to the National Gallery not later than 1 November'. In an effort to avoid all forms of discrimination the designers were requested not to sign their works; instead they were to be marked on the back with a motto or pseudonym 'which should also be written on a sealed envelope containing the competitor's name and address'. The prize-winning models would become the property of the Government and arrangements were to be made for the artist's signature or initials to appear on the finished plaque. The detailed instructions for the scheme, itself the consequence of the casualty lists, ignore the grave crises of 1917 in their bureaucratic self-absorption and illustrate the bland confidence of the members of British government institutions in the eventual outcome of the war. The competition's rules also gave rise to various questions. The size restrictions, precisely quantified, were clearly included as part of a considered endeavour to avoid the unnecessary consumption of precious raw materials. As early as December 1915 the steeply rising costs of bronze had delayed the execution of Sir George Frampton's memorial to Edith Cavell. The originally proposed bronze was not in fact employed: Carrara marble, which necessitated a long wait, was preferred to the vital metal.[10] Indeed it might be argued that the plaque could, without offence, have been made slightly smaller although an additional concern of the General Committee was that it should be of such a size and character as not to be mistaken for a medal. The stipulation that the piece should be cast has been seen as the direct contribution of G F Hill, Keeper of the Coins and Medals Department at the British Museum and an active member of the advisory artistic sub-committee. His commitment to the traditional cast medallion, a product of his profound knowledge and appreciation of the magnificent cast works of the Renaissance, did not ease the problem of the mass production of the finished model and was perhaps inappropriate to the needs of the time. The decision to obtain a design through an open competition was probably a good one and may have been influenced by the success of the Jutland medal competition, inspired by Sir Arthur Evans, of the previous year. It was surely reasonable that a memorial to the nation's dead should be the concern of as wide a section of the population as possible.[11] Even if the final product met with criticism it could be claimed as the culmination of a wide-ranging process of consultation and cooperation. More cynical interpretations may suggest that the competition provided a busy distraction from the terrible mismanagement of the war which made sure that the demand for plaques, when once available, would be a large one. Finally, the advertised mandatory inscription obscured the fact that the memorial was equally applicable to women.[12]

The competition aroused enormous interest, especially from overseas entrants and, for the sake of fairness, the Committee extended the closing date for submissions to 31 December 1917. An announcement to this effect appeared in the 10 September issue of *The Times*. The following month, on Thursday 18 October, the same paper printed a reference to the good progress of the scheme and repeated the information that the closing date had been extended to the end of the year. The article also added that:

> . . . In addition to the plaque, a scroll with a suitable inscription will be given. This is being designed at the present moment and it is hoped that it will be possible to put printing in hand in less than a fortnight.

This last sentence expressed a hope indicative of a powerful optimism. The stated timescale was not fulfilled; the production of the scroll was to prove something of a textual problem.

By the revised closing date over 800 entries had been received from all over the Empire, from the Western

Front, the Balkan and Middle Eastern theatres of war and from many artists based at home in Britain.

Assisted by its specialist 'artistic' sub-committee the ninth meeting of the General Committee arrived, not without difficulty, at a decision on 24 January 1918. Its recommendations were now considered by the Admiralty and War Office. A short notice to this effect was inserted in *The Times* for 30 January 1918; it was also stated that the Committee sought to obtain the King's approval for the winning design. (Lloyd George's commendation of the plaque was communicated to the General Committee by a telephone message from his secretary, Frances Stevenson, on 27 February.) At the same time the design of the memorial scroll and its text were being considered in detail. The minds of the contemporary literary world were ransacked in an effort to obtain a satisfactory formula. The elderly stay-at-home poets in England singularly failed: suggestions from Kipling,[13] Newbolt, Binyon (an exception insomuch that he had served in France with the Red Cross in 1916) and even the Poet Laureate himself, Robert Bridges, were received and judged inadequate. According to Rose Coombs, former librarian at the Imperial War Museum, the solution came via the good offices of Sir Vincent Baddeley, the Admiralty representative on the General Committee, who sought permission to consult the Provost of King's College, Cambridge (and foremost exponent of the ghost story genre) Dr Montague Rhodes James. Sir Vincent remembered that he was supplied with a draft wording by return of post.[14] Subsequent discussion in Committee produced two small changes and the introduction of a new final sentence from the pen of the historian and novelist Charles P Keary. The tardy alteration in the first sentence of the original draft was a consequence of King George V's wish that the Sovereign be specifically mentioned. Sir Cecil Harcourt-Smith could hardly control his irritation with the amendment but Dr James willingly agreed to the suggested rewording.

After a flurry of activity following the *Daily Mail*'s premature disclosure of a photograph of the prize-winning medal the results of the competition were officially announced in *The Times* for Wednesday 20 March 1918. This was the day before the beginning of the German *Kaiserschlacht* offensive against British positions on the Western Front, an attack which so narrowly missed making the memorial plaques an interesting irrelevance.

The first prize of £250, for two model designs, was awarded to 'Pyramus' – E Carter Preston of the Sandon Studios Society, Liverpool. The second prize of £100 went to 'Moolie' – Charles Wheeler of Chelsea. Third prizes of £50 each went to 'Sculpengro' – William McMillan (who later was responsible for the reverse design of the British War Medal and the obverse of the Victory Medal), 'Weary' – Sap-

per G D MacDougald and 'Zero' – Miss H F Whiteside. Another nineteen competitors[15] were considered 'worthy of honourable mention'. The announcement also stated that 'The King has approved the design'. As a postscript competitors were requested to reclaim their models from the National Gallery. It is difficult, given the large numbers of entries, not to consider the irony that many who sent in model designs might have themselves 'finally passed out of the sight of men' in the 1918 fighting to be recorded as names on the piece designed by the victorious 'Pyramus'. Again it would be interesting to know what became of the unclaimed models left at the National Gallery.[16]

Edward Carter Preston's prize-winning design (the Museum holds an original model in plaster, catalogue number MEDP/3) comprises the figure of Britannia, classically helmeted and robed, standing facing right, holding a modest laurel wreath crown in her extended left hand and supporting a trident by her right side with her right hand. In the foreground a male lion stands facing right; the animal

The problematic 'Next of Kin Memorial Scroll'. Design and production were supervised by the LCC Central School of Arts and Crafts. The hand-cut wood blocks used in the printing process (the printer's name is not known) were presented to the Museum in 1933 by the Central School's Principal, Mr F H Burridge.
HU53979

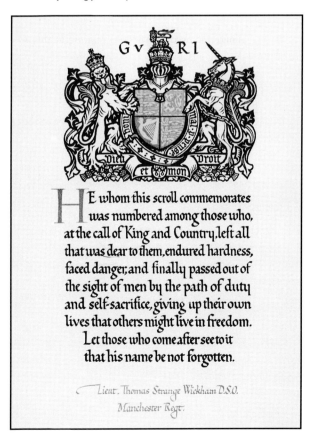

Gᵛ Rᴵ

HE whom this scroll commemorates was numbered among those who, at the call of King and Country, left all that was dear to them, endured hardness, faced danger, and finally passed out of the sight of men by the path of duty and self-sacrifice, giving up their own lives that others might live in freedom. Let those who come after see to it that his name be not forgotten.

Lieut. Thomas Strange Wickham D.S.O.
Manchester Regt.

was originally described as 'striding forward in a menacing attitude' which may explain its unusually low profile. 'Menacing' or otherwise, the proportions of the beast, earlier queried by Sir Frederick Ponsonby (on behalf of the King), deeply upset officials at Bristol's Clifton Zoo.[17] Above the lion's head was a blank rectangular panel, in which the name of the deceased would 'by an ingenious method of casting' be inserted.[18] To the right of Britannia's head and by the side of her right arm is a small sinuous dolphin, a reference to British seapower and one that recalls the use of that same animal (in the singular) by Pegram in his prize-winning Jutland medallion. At the lower right edge is a branch of oak leaves and acorns. The standard text is arranged around the edge of the piece: 'HE + DIED + FOR + FREEDOM + + AND + HONOUR'. Within the exergue, in symbolic confrontation, a lion pounces on an eagle: a reference to the desired destruction of the Central Powers. Incorporated from Carter Preston's second model entry the exergue's contents had necessitated a personal interview between Sir Charles Holmes and the artist in London in January 1918.[19] The original concern of Sir Charles Henry at the last meeting of the General Committee was that the German eagle should not appear too hopelessly humiliated. He argued that the imagery was anticipatory and potentially unhelpful with regard to future, post-war relations – admirable sentiments which were reiterated by Charles Marriott in the April 1918 issue of *Land and Water*. On the mass-produced plaques made available for distribution E Carter Preston's initials were embossed above the lion's right forepaw and a number (possibly an operative's or Ministry of Munitions' factory number) was impressed by the animal's right rear paw.

The appropriateness of this design for its sensitive commemorative task is the matter for some debate. The stipulation that the design be 'essentially simple and easily intelligible' and the fact that the winning entry would need royal approval, no doubt acted as a constraint upon entrants to the competition, who very likely foresaw the unhappy consequences of employing a controversial or unfamiliar image in their work. Acknowledging these limitations which the competition's rules applied, some criticism of the carefully wrought prize-winning model is permissible. The subject of sacrifice, death and loss, the essence of the memorial, is dealt with very indirectly by the artist. In common with designers of many later large scale memorials, and perhaps reflecting a refined sense of consideration, a desire not to offend, Carter Preston (unlike three of the runners up, Miss Whiteside, McMillan and Wheeler) deliberately avoided the depiction of a dead warrior even in an idealised classical form. In an interview conducted with the artist at the time of the award Carter Preston made clear his opposition to the depiction of 'death':

'I believe in making such medals quite impersonal and keeping them free from morbid sentimentality such as might appear in the presentation of dead heroes. I believe we should not have the maudlin element in art.'[20]

The guidelines for the competition did not preclude such themes but realistic representations of battlefield death were widely regarded as negative and distasteful. Representations of soldiers' corpses on British war memorials are quite rare; one tops Lutyens's cenotaph erected in Manchester in 1924[21] – it is so high one hardly notices it – and Jagger belatedly included a dead gunner in his Royal Artillery Memorial at Hyde Park Corner (1925); the head and upper portions of the body are covered by a greatcoat.[22] Instead Carter Preston opted for the distancing tactic of the allegorical female figure and all the associated dangers of misinterpretation that entailed. As James Stevens Curl put it when discussing the Royal Artillery Memorial:

Allegorical figures mean little to the average person, while lugubrious angels, naked heroes in classical poses, and mock heroic images of war can attract ridicule or induce a sense of outrage in those who have taken part in the deadly, numbing dehumanising horrors of battle.[23]

Britannia's sword, an accessory fitting for her stirring poses in recruiting posters, has been replaced by the crown of laurel. Perhaps deliberately there is no soothing Christian symbolism (nor disturbing invocations of God in terms of a tribal deity), but Britannia's head is only very slightly lowered; she is not bent in distress. It is merely the text, amplified by the message on the decorative scroll,[24] which makes clear that the plaque is in fact a tribute to the dead. Without its inscription the image might easily be interpreted as the celebration of some sporting rather than military achievement. The body and soul relationship of the piece, the image and motto, are disparate; the latter explains rather than complements the former. Again it may be argued that there is no suggestion of timescale, no hint of the nature of the war, which was 'more than ever a war of machinery'[25], that the plaque is a polite allegory which renders little assistance in formulating 'the unspoken questions as to the meaning and purpose and fruit of all that daring, all that endurance and all that suffering'.[26] But this is to misunderstand Carter Preston's conception of his commemorative task. His design was entirely in accordance with the principle of the consolatory memorial. The aim was to perpetuate the name of the deceased within the context of a healing and comforting national symbolism. The criticism that the plaque hardly conveys an adequate sense of loss or grief misses the point that the reawakening of grief was precisely the object that the artist was seeking to avoid. It was perhaps, given the scale of losses, an impossible task. If Carter Preston sought to console the living by discreet commemoration of the dead it was left to another Liverpool based sculptor, G H Tyson Smith, to commemorate the sorrows of the survivors, recipients of the plaque. In a remarkable thirty-one feet long bronze relief, supplied for Lionel Budden's cenotaph which was unveiled outside Liverpool's St George's Hall, the survivors, racked by their sense of loss and fighting to master it, file tragically towards a centrally placed coffin. Their sad progress is accompanied, at the frieze's base, by the inscription:

AND THE VICTORY THAT DAY WAS TURNED INTO MOURNING UNTO ALL THE PEOPLE

Postscript

The prize-winning designs were exhibited for a time during the spring and early summer of 1918 at the Victoria and Albert Museum. The large scale production of the plaques was delayed by a whole series of problems relating to the refinement and unsuccessful modification of Carter Preston's winning model. These difficulties form the basis for detailed correspondence between G F Hill and the artist through the months of October to December 1918.[27] It is clear that at times both became exasperated by the conflicting demands of standardisation for mass production and the claims for artistic integrity of the original piece. In December Hill, clearly annoyed, wrote:

> The more I compare the electrotype which I sent back to you yesterday . . . with the earlier version, the more puzzled I am at the modification. You have made it much harder and preciser, but by flattening the tops of the letters and generally taking out the roundness and softness of the forms. You have made it quite a different thing, and it is no longer the model as we passed it . . . I propose therefore to use the old electrotype. . . . The result of the alteration is to make the model look like a cast that has been very much worked up.[28]

It was typical of Carter Preston's temperament that no lasting damage to the relationship was done (throughout his career associates praised his ability to withstand 'constructive advice') and production of the plaques began that same month. Difficulties continued to beset the project. A disused laundry in Acton, grandly called 'The Memorial Plaque Factory' was the first centre of production. It was managed by an eccentric American engineer and entrepreneur,

"FOR FREEDOM AND HONOUR": PRIZE DESIGNS FOR A MEMORIAL PLAQUE.

AWARDED PRIZES IN THE COMPETITION FOR A MEMORIAL PLAQUE TO THOSE FALLEN IN THE WAR: THE SIX DESIGNS ADJUDGED NEXT IN MERIT TO THAT SELECTED.

The runners-up: prize-winning designs by Charles Wheeler, William McMillan, Sapper G D MacDougald and Miss H F Whiteside, as published by the *Illustrated London News*, 20 April 1918, p 469. HU53987

Manning Pike, and staffed principally by women. Hill had been impressed by Pike's solution to the problem of incorporating the names of the deceased on the plaque in a manner which was in harmony with Carter Preston's chosen script.[29] Despite his technical expertise Pike's monopoly was later brusquely terminated by the War Office and work transferred to Woolwich Arsenal and, later, other former munitions factories. The whole process of production was a slow and 'weary business'[30] and Hill's unhappy intimations with regard to the transfer were communicated to Carter Preston in a letter dated 30 November 1920:

> There is an attempt by the War Office to take the production of the Plaque out of the hands of Pike and transfer it to Woolwich. There will be a row about it; and I may have to ask you to help us prevent the reproduction being turned into a mere engineering job.

At Woolwich the project foundered and Manning Pike was recalled to save the situation. The work was completed but not without the decline in standards of output which Hill had predicted:

> I have asked the War Office to let you have a copy of the plaque. I fear that you will find the quality of recent castings very much deteriorated. Woolwich is no good even with all that Pike does to bring it up to the mark.[31]

Hill originally postulated a total number of '800,000' plaques to be produced; later estimates have put the total figure at some 1,150,000 specimens. In either case the figure is staggering and the memorial plaque represented 'the most universally distributed numismatic work ever cast or struck – excluding money'.[32] The plaques issued commemorated those who died between 4 August 1914 and 10 January 1920, for Home Establishments, Western Europe and the Dominions. The final date for other theatres of war (including Russia) or for those who died subsequently from attributable causes was 30 April 1920.

The scrolls started to be manufactured in January 1919 (the original estimate for the scrolls by the Central School was 'about 970,000') and were sent out in seven and a quarter inch long cardboard tubes with a standard covering letter which bore the facsimile signature of King George V. The letter read as follows:

> I join with my grateful people in sending you this

memorial of a brave life given for others in the Great War.

The plaques themselves were despatched under separate cover in stiff card wrapping enclosed within white envelopes bearing the Royal Arms.

The memorial plaques and scrolls, sometimes additionally embellished by the deceased's war medals, were proudly displayed in thousands of homes after the First War. In that more deferential and less sophisticated age it was not felt out of place to honour the memory of one who had made the ultimate sacrifice by the establishment of small domestic 'shrines'. Commercially made frames, produced by a variety of manufacturers, provided assistance for such household displays. The frames did not please Hill:

> As to the frames, anyone who pleases can put on the market . . . such things. Of course if we had a proper 'Committee of Taste' such things could not happen.[33]

Many plaques were further honoured by regular and vigorous cleaning, an obliterating fate, especially for the impoverished later casts, which Hill had gloomily foreseen:

> All the poor people will scrub the plaque to keep it bright like soldiers' buttons (doesn't the thought make you shiver?)[34]

Plaque sent to the relatives of Nurse Winifred Coates. Serving in Malta she contracted a serious illness and was invalided home. She died in hospital in London on 8 February 1916, five days before her twenty-seventh birthday. The Museum also possesses the badge of the Royal Red Cross, 2nd class, awarded to Winifred's sister, Miss Edith Coates.
HU53981

Plaque presented to the relatives of poet and painter Isaac Rosenberg (1890–1918). First encouraged to write poetry by Laurence Binyon (who later proffered text for the memorial scroll) Rosenberg enlisted in the King's Own Royal Lancaster Regiment in 1915 and was killed in action near Arras on 1 April 1918. His body was never found.
HU53982

Obverse of Edward Carter Preston's prize-winning model in plaster. 126 mm, catalogue number MEDP/3.
HU53985

The apparatus for official recognition of the ultimate sacrifice – letter of tribute from King George V, the Memorial Plaque enclosed in its protective card folder, together with the HMSO envelope bearing the address of Manning Pike's 'Memorial Plaque Factory', the converted laundry in Acton. HU53986

'Of course if we had a proper "Committee of Taste" such things could not happen': two commercially produced frames for the plaque, one in Bakelite, the other metal. HU53980

Notes

1. C E Montague, *Disenchantment*, Chatto and Windus, London, 1922, p 3.
2. Siegfried Sassoon, *Memoirs of an Infantry Officer*, Faber and Faber, London, first illustrated edition, 1931, p 143.
3. 'The third Christmas of the war and the gloomiest. To wish each other "Merry Christmas" is a mockery', M MacDonagh, *In London during the Great War*, London, 1935, p 64. Quoted by Nicholas Reeves, *Official British Film Propaganda during the First World War*, Croom Helm, 1986, p 22. Writing of his experiences home on leave in the early spring of 1917 Captain J C Dunn of the 2nd Battalion, Royal Welch Fusiliers corroborates MacDonagh's response: 'At home the political air was sharpened by the contrasted privation of many and the vastness with which war-wealth had been created for others; by the effect on many minds of the two-months old German naval policy of sinking every ship at sight; and by the losses, disappointment, and disillusion of the battles of the Somme.' *The War the Infantry Knew*, Jane's edition, 1987,

p 305.
4. Edmund Blunden, *Undertones of War*, Cobden and Sanderson, London, 1928, p 74. Using the daily 'sick parade' as an index of 'morale' on active service Captain J C Dunn made some interesting comparisons. Writing after the Somme battles he observed: 'The daily sick parade had become a serious affair by this date in the war. A year ago it was very exceptional to see a dozen "sick"; now nothing was too trivial to be a pretext for "going sick", and 60 was the daily average.' op cit, pp 288–289.
5. Correlli Barnett, 'Of Horrors and Scapegoats. Ending World War I Legends', published in *Encounter*, vol 50, no 5, May 1978, p 67.
6. Martin Middlebrook, *The First Day on the Somme*, Fontana edition, London 1975, p 275. His figures are taken from *Statistics of the Military Effort of the British Empire*. Despite the enormous casualties on the Somme the minutes of the War Committee as late as October 1916 reveal an undismayed optimism. See Minutes of the War Committee, October 3 1916 (PRO/

CAB 22, 81–82).
7. The members of the General Committee were as follows: 'Lord Lincolnshire, Lord Plymouth, Colonel Norton Griffiths MP, Mr G N Barnes MP, Mr G R Thorne MP, Captain Stephen Gwynn MP, Sir Charles Henry MP and Mr Donald MacMaster MP (representing the Dominions), the Assistant Military Secretary, Colonel M D Graham CB, Colonel Selwyn (India Office), Mr C W Johnson, CMG (Colonial Office), a representative of the Admiralty, and Mr W Hutchinson (War Office), secretary.' As reported in *The Times*, 7 November 1916. The Admiralty representative was subsequently identified as Sir Vincent Baddeley.
8. Nicholas Reeves, op cit, p 62.
9. *The Times*, 7 November 1916.
10. The Carrara marble for Frampton's Cavell memorial did not reach England until the end of the war.
11. The sentiment of public involvement in the design of war memorials in general was given vigorous support by the Civic Arts Association: 'we shall not succeed in expressing ourselves either as individuals or

as a community, unless we discover for ourselves what we want and ask our artists to make it for us.' A Clutton-Brock, *On War Memorials*, Civic Arts Association, n.d. (circa 1919), p 6.
12. There was in fact no anti-feminist conspiracy; arrangements were made in the production process for both plaque and scroll to incorporate the female personal pronoun, 'SHE', when appropriate. As would be expected far fewer plaques were named to women than men. The Museum has only one example. Herbert G Smith in his detailed account of the memorial plaque and scroll (*For Freedom and Honour*, 1983, unpublished thesis held at the IWM) quotes from the regulations governing the issue plaques and scrolls to women published by the War Office in December 1919:
'Women. The only classes of women for which the memorials will be issued will be those serving under direct contract with the War Office (eg QAIMNS), (QMAAC), as defined in AO 206 of 1919, which lays down the classes of women eligible for the King's Certificate of

Discharge.'

13. In his short poem 'Common Form' Kipling displayed a guilt-laden bitterness which was entirely absent from his efforts with regard to the plaque and, later, the War Graves Commission:
'If any question why we died
Tell them, because our fathers lied.'
His son, an officer in the Irish Guards, had been killed in action at the Battle of Loos, 1915.

14. Dr James's original draft was as follows: 'He whom this scroll commemorates was numbered among the sons of the British Empire who at the bidding of their country left all that was dear to them, endured hardness, faced danger, and finally passed out of the sight of men by the path of duty and self-sacrifice giving up their own lives that others might live in freedom.'

15. The work of the following nineteen candidates were considered worthy of honourable mention: 'Astra Castra', 'Athenian', 'Bec', 'Canada', 'Casual', 'Cross', 'Desiree', 'Fluvius', 'Gaza', 'Intrepidus', 'Litigation', 'Nomen est Omen', 'Oneiros', 'Pink', 'Red Shield', 'Rex Royal', 'Sun A', 'Sun B' and 'Wattle Blossom' (the last nickname almost certainly denoted an Australian).

16. By 1917–18 many of the National Gallery's paintings had been dispersed for safe-keeping and many rooms of the building had been requisitioned for Government offices; the Ministry of Munitions, Public Works, Census Office and Admiralty at one time or another claimed former gallery space. An examination of the Board files for the period yielded no reference to the competition nor the supposed accumulation of entries.

17. *The Times* several days after its published description of the prize-winning model design (23 March 1918) printed a letter from irate officials at Clifton Zoo, Bristol. The Honourable Chairman, Mr Alfred J Harrison and the Head Keeper, Mr J F Morgan vigorously attacked E Carter Preston's portrayal of the lion 'as a meagre-big-dog size presentation' and as 'a lion which almost a hare might insult.' They concluded that Carter Preston's lion could not have been modelled from life, and certainly not from the 'fine male specimen in Clifton Zoo!'. Consolation was offered to the artist in the post-script of a letter he received from G F Hill, dated 3 April 1918:
'Don't mind what the naturalists and cat-fanciers say about your lion (eg that letter in the *Times*). Doubtless the poulterers object to your eagle and the fishmongers to your dolphins as not sufficiently "naturalistic".'
Hill's sympathy for the artist appears to have declined by the summer. Writing to

Carter Preston he allies himself with the 'naturalists':
'By the way, two or three people criticise the hind leg of your lion . . . they dislike the lump that projects on the hock (if that's the right word). When the pattern is finally ready for casting to begin I think you ought to go over it carefully to see whether you want to make any alterations' (dated 8 July 1918, Carter Preston papers, 730 PRE 4/25/15a–15b).
A photograph of the winning entry was published in the *Illustrated London News*, 6 April 1918, p 402. The same journal printed a photograph of the other six prize-winning designs, 20 April 1918, p 469.

18. *The Times*, 23 March 1918. The process for incorporating the name of the deceased on the plaque is described in detail in the fragment of G F Hill's autobiography published in *The Medal*, No 8, Summer 1986, p 25.

19. Letter from C J Holmes, at the National Gallery, to Carter Preston, 24 January 1918.

20. *Liverpool Echo*, 20 March 1918.

21. A similar memorial by Lutyens is in Derby.

22. 'It was only very late in the day that the dead soldier was proposed for the north end of the memorial. It was decided that this figure gave the design a "proper finish" and made the memorial a monument to the dead as well as to the living although there were voices raised against the "gruesomeness" of the recumbent figure. One critic . . . noted that Jagger regarded a "war memorial as a means of forcing home on the minds of the public the horror and terror of war" and felt the figure was inappropriate.' James Stevens Curl, 'The Royal Artillery Memorial at Hyde Park Corner', p 92 of *Charles Sargeant Jagger. War and Peace Sculpture*, edited by Ann Compton, IWM, 1985.

23. Ibid, p 98.

24. The scroll was to be produced on good quality paper, sized 11 inches by 7 inches, but due to the exigencies of war production the design was not ready until late summer 1918. The cutting of the wood block from which it would be printed was made the responsibility of a group of artists attached to the Central School of Arts and Crafts (LCC), under the supervision of the principal Mr F H Burridge. Again, delays in production were encountered in the form of severe difficulties in obtaining supplies of suitable paper and ink.

25. Charles Sargeant Jagger, quoted by Nicholas Penny, 'English Sculpture and the First World War', *The Oxford Art Journal*, November 1981, p 41.

26. Quoted by Nicholas Penny, op cit, p 42.

27. See Carter Preston papers, Liverpool Record Office, Liverpool City Library.

28. Letter, Hill to Carter Preston, 18

December 1918.

29. See also *The Medal*, Feb 1988, no 12, p 43.

30. Letter, Hill to Carter Preston, 18 October 1919.

31. Letter, Hill to Carter Preston, 4 February 1922.

32. *Liverpool Echo*, 20 March 1918.

33. Letter, Hill to Carter Preston, 31 January 1922.

34. Letter, Hill to Carter Preston, 3 April 1918.

Further Reading

Correlli Barnett, 'Of Horrors and Scapegoats. Ending World War I Legends', article in *Encounter*, vol 50, no 5, pp 66–74, May 1978.

Mary Bennett (editor), *The Art Sheds 1894–1905* (catalogue for an exhibition to celebrate the centenary of the University of Liverpool), Merseyside County Council, 1981.

Carter Preston Papers, held in Liverpool Record Office (Liverpool City Libraries).

A Clutton-Brock, *On War Memorials*, Civic Arts Association, n.d.

Ann Compton (editor), *Charles Sargeant Jagger. War and Peace Sculpture*, Imperial War Museum, 1985.

E J Cook, 'Memorial Plaque', article in *Coins and Medals*, pp 26–29, May 1974.

C R M F Cruttwell, *A History of the Great War*, Oxford University Press, 1934.

Design of Plaque and Scroll to be issued as a personal memorial to the relatives of officers and men who fell in the war, Public Record Office (Kew), file W032/4677.

'G F Hill and the Production of the First World War Memorial Plaque', article in *The Medal*, issue no 8, p 25, Summer 1986.

(G F Hill), 'An Autobiographical Fragment', article in *The Medal*, issue no 12, pp 37–48, Spring 1988.

Mark Jones, *The Dance of Death. Medallic Art of the First World War*, British Museum, London, 1979.

P G Konody, *Art and War*, Colour Ltd, n.d.

Liverpool Daily Post and Mercury, 20 March 1918.

Liverpool Echo, 20 March 1918.

L Manton, 'Memorial Suggestion', article in *The Military Chest*, vol 1, no 1, p 4, September 1982.

Nicholas Penny, 'English Sculpture and the First World War', article in *Oxford Art Journal*, pp 36–42, November 1981.

J Schulman, *La Guerre Europeenne 1914–1919. Medailles, Decorations, Medailles Militaires*, Catalogue LXXV, p 28, ref 246, 1919.

Herbert G Smart, 'For Freedom and Honour. A history of the memorial plaques and scrolls given to the next of kin of those who fell in the Great War of 1914–1918', unpublished typescript, 1983 (copies held by the IWM and PRO).

The Japanese 'Long Lance' Torpedo and its Place in Naval History

John Bullen

John Bullen is a research assistant in the Department of Exhibits and Firearms.

In Hangar 3 at Duxford Airfield, the Imperial War Museum's outstation in Cambridgeshire, is displayed one of the most dramatic items in the collections of the Department of Exhibits and Firearms. It is the Japanese 24-inch Type 93 Long Lance torpedo which, when first introduced into the Imperial Japanese Navy in the 1930s, was the *ne plus ultra* in torpedo technology. The successes and failures of Long Lance during the Pacific naval campaigns of 1941–45 mirrored the rise and fall of the Imperial Japanese Navy, and the latter's failure to maintain Japan's Asian and Pacific possessions – the Greater East Asian Co-Prosperity Sphere – conceived as an autarkic empire capable of withstanding all potential aggressors and of maintaining Imperial Japan's Great Power status.

The first effective torpedo prototype had been developed in 1868 by an English expatriate, Robert Whitehead, who managed an engineering factory in Fiume, and the weapon's development continued throughout the nineteenth century. The French were enthusiastic champions of the torpedo and evolved a philosophy of naval warfare which advocated its use, principally against Great Britain.

During the winter of 1884–85 Gabriel Charmes expounded his theory that steam propulsion and the torpedo had revolutionised naval warfare in the *Revue des Deux Mondes*. In 1886, encouraged by the Minister of Marine, Captain Hyacinth Aube, Charmes published his *Jeune Ecole* theory more fully in his book *La Reforme de la Marine*. In this Charmes urged that France should deploy small, cheap and fast torpedo boats *en masse* against Great Britain's merchant shipping, sink the Royal Navy's numerous ironclads, and bring about the ruin of the British Empire.[1] The torpedo, while still not proven in war, was already espoused as an essential weapon of the inferior naval power.

By the 1890s Imperial Japan was an emerging industrial nation[2] and a growing rival to the European colonial powers. Japan's Asian ambitions were longstanding. During the sixteenth century Hideyoshi Toyotomi had believed that Japan's destiny was to conquer Korea and subsequently China, an expansionist theme that was taken up in the mid-nineteenth century by the nationalist poet Shoin Yoshida.[3] The two agents that were to secure Japan's 'place in the sun' were the Imperial Japanese Army and the Imperial Japanese Navy.

As early as 1870 British naval instructors, the representatives of the premier naval power, were active in Japan and by 1894, on the eve of the Sino-Japanese War, Imperial Japan possessed eleven battleships.[4] Yet Japan's enthusiasm for her navy was not just the result of her island geography.

Before the turn of the century the internationally acclaimed works of the American, Captain Alfred Thayer Mahan,[5] were translated into Japanese. Mahan expounded his theme of an historically-based pattern of sea power relating to the importance of navies in international affairs; and he emphasised the climactic battle for 'command of the seas'.[6]

His works were published at a time when European naval rivalries were intensifying, and his ideas were enthusiastically accepted by the leading naval powers.[7] In Japan, Vice-Admiral Akiyami Saneyuki, 'the father of Japanese naval strategy', who actually met Mahan, introduced staff planning and table-top manoeuvres at the Japanese Naval War College, and absorbed Mahan's philosophy of naval history.[8] Japanese experiences in wars with China (1894–95) and Russia (1904–05) seemed to confirm Mahan's doctrines. A Japanese fleet under Admiral Ito destroyed the main Chinese fleet in the Battle of the Yangtze. On the night of 8/9 February 1904 Japanese torpedo boats attacked and disabled two Russian battleships and a cruiser in Port Arthur, which was then blockaded. Desperate land battles raged, culminating in Russian defeats, and on 27/28 May 1905 the Russian Baltic Fleet was annihilated by Admiral Togo at Tsushima, the most decisive sea battle since Trafalgar in 1805.

In both wars, especially the conflict with Russia, the Japanese had achieved their limited objectives. Overwhelming naval supremacy, obtained by a combination of the torpedo, the mine, and the set-piece 'big battle', had enabled Japan to localise the conflicts, maintain the initiative by a concentration of force, and fight successful land battles of attrition. The Imperial Japanese Navy, using light units armed with torpedoes and mines, had worn down opposing forces by inflicting disproportionate losses. As a last resort the precious main battlefleet had been committed to the struggle, decisively so at the Yangtze and Tsushima. This concept was to be the mainstay of Japanese strategy during the 1919–1941 period, slowly becoming untenable in the relentless struggles with the United States Navy in the Pacific during 1942.

The Anglo-Japanese Alliance of 1902 and the Treaty of Portsmouth, of 5 September 1905, which ended the Russo-Japanese War, confirmed Japan's position as a leading Asian power. Equally important, Japan's ability to absorb Western technology and ideas, including the naval philosophies of the *Jeune Ecole* and Mahan, had vindicated the enormous investments made in building the Imperial Japanese Navy. Naval supremacy, albeit on a localised scale, had underpinned Japan's territorial gains, including Formosa (Taiwan) from China and Port Arthur from Russia. In 1907 Russia and Japan divided Manchuria into spheres of influence, and in 1910 Japan annexed Korea.[9] The First World War acted as a catalyst to stimulate Japan's expansionist foreign policy. In 1914, Japan entered the conflict as Great Britain's ally and, while contributing little to the defeat of the Central Powers, gained the German concession of Tsingtao on the Shantung Peninsula; and in the Pacific she obtained the German colonies of the Mariana, Caroline, and Marshall Islands, the latter gains being confirmed by the Peace Conference of 1919.[10]

Japan's expanding Imperial frontiers were matched by the growth of her warship industry. Originally Great Britain had supplied most of Japan's warships, but in 1902 Japan began manufacturing armour plate, and the Vickers-built battlecruiser *Kongo*, ordered in 1910, was the last major Japanese warship built abroad.[11] It was also the first warship to be equipped with 14-inch guns and was followed by the Japanese-built *Nagato*-class, which were the first capital ships mounting 16-inch guns.[12]

Yet it was in the development of torpedoes, in turn heavily influenced by the naval lessons of the First World War and the Washington Naval Conference and Treaty (1921–22), that Japanese technological innovation was most marked. Japanese staff studies accepted that at Jutland (31 May/1 June 1916), the greatest naval battle of the First World War, the torpedo had proved relatively ineffective. Destroyers and lighter torpedo boats had been forced to close to unacceptably short ranges to launch torpedoes. One British battleship, HMS *Marlborough*, had been hit, but not crippled, by a torpedo, and only one German pre-dreadnought, the *Pommern*, had been sunk by this weapon. The staff's analysis was disquieting for the Imperial Japanese Navy. Japanese success with the torpedo during the Russo-Japanese War had led to great emphasis being placed on its tactical use as the weapon able to negate the dreadnought superiority of potential adversaries.[13] To maintain the effectiveness of the doctrine the Japanese began to develop powerful, long-range torpedoes which could be launched in massed cruiser and destroyer attacks at night beyond effective range of enemy gunfire.

The Washington Naval Treaty of 1922 provided further impetus to Japanese torpedo development and evolving naval doctrine. By 1921, for various strategic and political reasons, Great Britain, the United States, and Japan had embarked on a massive programme of capital ship construction. To avoid the ruinous expense and to redefine other aspects of inter-power relations, the victorious Allies of the First World War assembled in Washington in 1921. The Washington Naval Treaty, among other decisions emerging from these meetings, allowed Great Britain a battlefleet of 581,000 tons, the United States 501,000, and Japan 301,000 tons. The 5:5:3 ratio, (so-called after agreements on other warship classes) was not an erosion of Imperial Japan's naval power, since her maritime responsibilities were less than those of the other two major naval powers, and her capital ship strength was concentrated in home waters. Yet Japan was affronted and believed that she had been forced to accept a position of permanent capital ship inferiority. Japanese pride was further mortified when Great Britain, under American and Dominion pressure, failed to renew the Anglo-Japanese Alliance.

Imperial Japan now increasingly viewed Great Britain and the United States, especially the latter, as her main potential naval adversaries in the Pacific. The Japanese Naval Staff devised a doctrine which would utilise the advantageous strategic position of her newly-acquired Central Pacific island possessions, while accepting the numerical inferiority of the Japanese battlefleet. The Japanese strategy had two parts: the attritional; and the 'decisive battle' stage.

In the event of war with the United States, Japanese submarines would be stationed off the American west coast and attack the United States' Pacific Fleet. American naval forces, when within range of Japan's Central Pacific islands, would be attacked by land- and carrier-based aircraft. The final stage of the campaign would evolve when the United States' Fleet reached the Philippines. Japanese cruisers and destroyers would carry out night torpedo attacks. The next day the Japanese battlefleet would engage the surviving American forces – the climactic Mahanian battle – and achieve a decisive victory.[14] To ensure the success of this plan the Japanese relied on the traditional bravery and skills of their naval crews; on their excellent training; and on the superiority of Japanese naval weaponry. Nowhere was this superiority more emphasised than in Japanese torpedo technology.

During 1920–21 the Japanese began introducing the massive 24-inch 8th Year Type (1919) torpedo into some destroyers and light cruisers. The largest British and American torpedoes used on destroyers and cruisers were of 21-inch calibre. In 1942 at the Battle of Guadalcanal the light cruiser *Nagara* was still equipped with this paraffin and air propelled torpedo. But it was Japan's persistence in experimenting with pure oxygen propellent that led to the technological superiority of the Imperial Japanese Navy's torpedoes over all other types. Pure oxygen propellent eliminated the 77% nitrogen content in air, which did not aid the combustion process and left an obvious bubble wake. Pure oxygen also gave a higher performance.[15]

Japan, like other countries, had investigated the use of oxygen in torpedoes, but experiments were discontinued in 1917 after explosions in generators when the fuel was ignited. The Royal Navy, too, had also tried both oxygen-enriched and purely oxygen propelled models, but the programme was abandoned when the oxygen propellent proved to be either unstable or highly corrosive to air chambers in the torpedoes, causing accidents and explosions.

In 1924 Japan also began work on enriched-oxygen fuelled torpedoes but consecutive accidents led to the programme being dropped. The manifest advantages of utilising oxygen as a torpedo propellent, however, led to the resumption of the programme in 1926. Again, the experiments ended in failure, but in late 1927 Japanese Intelligence reported that the battleships HMS *Rodney* and HMS *Nelson* were equipped with oxygen-fuelled torpedoes and that the Royal Navy was introducing these weapons into general service.

The report was wrong. The torpedoes on *Rodney* and *Nelson* used oxygen-enriched air and not pure oxygen and were, moreover, highly unstable. Any grease in the vicinity of the torpedoes – even hair oil according to one observer[16] – could set off an explosion. But the Japanese Navy Department redoubled its efforts to perfect an oxygen-propelled torpedo.

In 1928 work was restarted at the Torpedo Department, Kure Naval Arsenal under Rear-Admiral Kashimoto Kaneji and Captain Toshida Asakuma. By 1930 a successful torpedo using 50% oxygen had been built, but in constructing a purely oxygen-fuelled torpedo five main problems had to be solved; it was necessary to prevent the oxygen exploding on ignition; to control generator temperatures; to use sea water as a diluent; to increase engine strength and life; and to improve the gyro to achieve superior direction keeping at the longer ranges now required. The most difficult obstacle, which took a year to overcome, was in designing and constructing a durable generator.

Even as these experiments continued, the Imperial Japanese Navy, in keeping with its tactical doctrines, was introducing new and improved torpedoes into its submarine and surface units. The 21-inch Type 89 paraffin and air-propelled torpedo was introduced into submarines in 1931 and was to be widely used during the early part of the Pacific War (1941–45). Another powerful torpedo, the 24-inch Type 90 (also propelled by paraffin and air), was introduced into surface units in 1931. It had a range of 7650 yards at 46 knots, or 10,900 yards at 43 knots, or 16,400 yards at 35 knots. Its overall length was 27ft 10ins and it weighed 5743lbs. The Type 90 had an 827lb warhead. The Type 90 still equipped *Fubuki*-class destroyers in 1941–1942.[17]

These measured advances in the Imperial Japanese Navy's torpedo technology were not unknown to the West, but were discounted. In 1934, Commander Ross, the British Assistant Naval Attaché at Tokyo, discussed torpedo development with Captain Watanabe, the commanding officer of Taura Torpedo School. Ross told Watanabe of the oxygen-enriched air system which propelled the special 24.5 inch torpedoes that had been installed in *Nelson* and *Rodney*, although he did not disclose that the Royal Navy had abandoned the development of this technology. Ross reported the following conversation:

> 'Very interesting' said the Captain (Watanabe), 'but I think our 24-inch torpedoes have long-enough range.'
> 'You could not carry enriched air anyway in a destroyer.'
> 'That is what I mean. The destroyer torpedoes have a long range – I mean of course the new 24-inch.'[18]

Watanabe's enigmatic reply (this conversation took place in 1934) was most probably a reference to the Type 90 24-inch torpedo. He might also have had in mind the experimental oxygen-fuelled torpedoes. Ross observed:

> I had to check this information from another source. Sure enough the Navy (Japanese) was using torpedoes in their destroyers, much larger than ours. But I was not believed – it is impossible, I was told, to handle such a huge torpedo on the deck of a destroyer. The next edition of Confidential Book 1815, which gave particulars of foreign warships, noted 'TORPEDOES 24-inch?' under the chapter on Japanese warships. The truth came out when we captured one during the war but that was rather too late.[19]

By 1935 the team of Japanese naval designers had developed at Kure the 24-inch 'Shiki Sanso Gyorai' Type 93 (so called because it was designed in the Japanese year 2593) torpedo, evocatively named the 'Long Lance'. Long Lance was the most powerful weapon of its kind in the world and was 29ft 6.3ins long, weighed 5952lbs, carried a warhead of 1080lbs, and had a range of 21,900 yards at 48–50 knots, 35,000 yards at 40–42 knots, or 43,700 yards at 36–38 knots. In comparison the American Mk15 torpedo of 1941 vintage was 23ft long, 21in in diameter, weighed 3289lbs, carried a 660lb warhead, and, compressed-air propelled, had a range of 6100 yards at 45 knots, 10,130 yards at 33 knots, or 15,190 yards at 27 knots. Flaws in the torpedo design, especially the magnetic exploder, caused by insufficient testing and lack of co-operation between the Naval Torpedo School, the fleet, and the Bureau of Ordnance, bedevilled American torpedo performance until well into 1943.

The Imperial Japanese Navy officially adopted Long Lance in 1935.[20] It was manufactured at Kure Naval Arsenal and approximately 2600 Long Lances were made, 1350 of them by the end of 1941. The Imperial Japanese Navy kept Long Lance's performance a close secret, although some details of a Japanese oxygen-fuelled torpedo filtered through

to the West. Commander Masataka Chihaya wrote:

> 'When we made mention of this torpedo in the documents of the Navy, we always discounted 10 knots on the speed and one-half on the range, and nobody ever seemed to doubt the veracity of such reports.'[21]

Long Lance fulfilled the Japanese design requirement of a very fast, almost wakeless, long-range, extremely powerful torpedo which, when used by cruisers and destroyers in night actions, could counter a potential adversary's superiority in capital ships. Apart from aircraft carriers and battleships, Japanese warship design emphasised the lavish equipment and use of torpedoes, and the deployment of Long Lance enhanced the considerable striking power of the Imperial Japanese Navy. By the outbreak of the Pacific War the Imperial Japanese Navy had equipped all its 18 heavy cruisers with Long Lance, (American heavy cruisers did not carry torpedoes); selected light cruisers, including the *Oi* and *Kitakami*, flagships of destroyer squadrons, which carried the exceptional total of 40 torpedoes each in 10 quadruple tubes; and the latest destroyers from the *Hatsuhara* class (1931–1935) on. Destroyers so equipped generally carried 16 Long Lances, including reloads, and cruisers from 16 to 24.[22]

The excellence of the Imperial Japanese Navy's *matériel*, of which torpedoes were only one aspect,[23] was matched by the realism of its training. After the Washington Conference, and especially after 1936, when Japan withdrew from the London Naval Conference and rejected the limiting capital ship ratios accepted at Washington, war training became more rigorous. The training year started on 1 December with single-ship and squadron training. Combined Fleet manoeuvres began in May and intensified until after October. Training was carried out in secrecy and conditions were often severe. The Combined Fleet sortied from bases in the Kurile Islands and exercised in appalling weather. Sometimes up to a hundred men were lost overboard in a single exercise. Allied to this careful preparation was the Imperial Japanese Navy's emphasis on the Japanese 'fighting spirit' which had overcome superior Chinese and Russian forces and would prevail again, it was believed, in combat with the untried United States Navy.[24]

In particular, the Imperial Japanese Navy practised night fighting more assiduously than the United States Navy. Standard Japanese night-fighting doctrine was to launch the torpedoes first, to use gunfire only when necessary, and searchlights as little as possible.[25] Special range-finders, illumination devices, and binoculars were developed, and reloading facilities for Long Lances were incorporated on cruisers and destroyers. Most of the destroyers carried their reloads in deck lockers fitted with hinged lids. By rotating the empty torpedo tubes until they were in line with the re-load lockers, the spare Long Lances could be pushed from the lockers directly into the tubes. The area used for torpedo tubes and torpedo stowage was served by a special rail track, along which the torpedo-handling bogie was pushed by Japanese ratings.[26] (See photograph of Japanese destroyer *Shiranui*.)

In the last Combined Fleet manoeuvres carried out off Tokyo Bay in the late summer of 1941, numerous Long Lances, without their warheads, were fired by all the cruisers and destroyers so equipped and at high speed.[27] As events transpired in the Pacific War, the decisive planned surface battle with the United States Navy was a carrier battle, Midway, but during the period 1942–43 Long Lance's performance was to justify both its lengthy and expensive development and the Imperial Japanese Navy's emphasis on the doctrine of the night torpedo attack.

The Pacific War is often seen as a carrier war but most of the battles fought during 1942–1943 were night surface actions and took place around the Solomon Islands. Superior Japanese techniques in night fighting, and the excellence of Long Lance, enabled the Imperial Japanese Navy to win or draw most of these battles. Such victories are all the more remarkable since the Japanese forces – the superbly trained cruiser and destroyer forces – often fought at a tactical disadvantage, sometimes against heavy odds, and always facing superior United States Navy radar.

In spite of the loss of four carriers and other units at Midway Japanese expansion in the South Pacific continued. Imperial General Headquarters planned to conquer New Guinea and the Solomon Islands, either to add further bastions to Japan's oceanic empire, or as a springboard to invade Australia. The United States Joint Chiefs of Staff were aware through cryptanalysis[28] that the Japanese were building an airfield on Guadalcanal. Operation 'Watchtower', planned to forestall Japanese consolidation in the Solomons and as the first stage of a counter-offensive to recover the Philippines, began on 7 August 1942 when United States Marines assaulted Guadalcanal and Tulagi off Florida Island. As the Marines fought to establish themselves onshore, and to protect the captured airfield on Guadalcanal – soon called Henderson Field – the US Navy and its Allies struggled to prevent the Imperial Japanese Navy from reinforcing the defenders.[29]

The Japanese reacted quickly to the American offensive. On 7 August Vice Admiral Gunichi Mikawa sailed from Rabaul, New Britain, leading a powerful squadron of 7 cruisers and 1 destroyer against Guadalcanal. Mikawa's battle plan emphasised the use of the torpedo:

On the rush-in we will go from S. of Savo Island

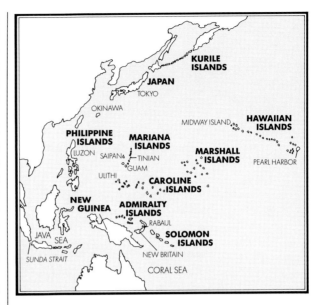

The Pacific Theatre

and torpedo the enemy main force in front of the Guadalcanal anchorage; after which we will turn toward the Tulagi forward area to shell and torpedo the enemy. We will then withdraw north of Savo I.[30]

Five Allied heavy cruisers and five destroyers patrolled the western end of the Sound between Florida Island and Guadalcanal. Two destroyers, *Blue* and *Ralph Talbot*, equipped with radar, guarded the approaches to Savo Island. Mikawa achieved total surprise, eluding American radar, and with torpedoes and gunfire sank four heavy cruisers, *Astoria*, *Quincy*, *Vincennes*, and HMAS *Canberra*, and damaged another cruiser and two destroyers.[31] It was the worst American naval defeat since the War of 1812.

Unlike the Battle of the Java Sea, 27 February–1 March 1942, when American warships were part of a larger heterogeneous Allied force under the command of the Dutch Rear-Admiral Karel Doorman, the battle of Savo Island was fought by a predominantly United States Navy force under American command. The United States Navy had been at war for eight months, was operating in a combat zone, and faced an enemy who was little superior in strength, and who lacked radar. The only comfort that the Americans could draw from this fight was the sinking, by the US submarine S-44, of the Japanese heavy cruiser *Kako* as she returned to Rabaul.

Savo Island was an outstanding Japanese success and gave the Imperial Japanese Navy local command of the sea. But before the Japanese could adequately reinforce their troops on Guadalcanal the establishment of American aircraft at Henderson Field wrested from the Imperial Japanese Navy command of the sea by day. The battles of the Coral Sea, 7/8 May 1942, and Midway, 4/5 June 1942, had weakened the Imperial Japanese Navy's carrier strength and offensive air power and the most powerful, supporting Japanese airbase was at Rabaul, nearly 700 miles distant on New Britain. The Japanese were thus faced with the alternative of operating at sea by day within range of land-based American aircraft or confining their supply operations to night time. The Imperial Japanese Navy's continuing victories at night were Pyrrhic, since its losses were less easily borne than those inflicted on the United States Navy.

Imperial Japan faced a destiny which had been brutally prophesised in 1941 by the United States Navy's Chief of Naval Operations, Admiral Harold Stark. Stark told the Japanese ambassador in Washington, Kishisaburo Nomura, before Imperial Japan's attack on Pearl Harbor:

> If you attack us we will break your empire before we are through with you. While you may have initial success due to timing and surprise, the time will come when you too will have your losses but there will be this great difference. You not only will be unable to make up your losses but will grow weaker as time goes on; while on the other hand we not only will make up our losses but will grow stronger as time goes on. It is inevitable that we shall crush you before we are through with you.

Nomura, it is recorded, made no reply.[32]

Japanese ships from Rabaul ran ammunition, fresh troops and food into Guadalcanal. These fast convoys were known as the 'Tokyo Express'. Their mainstay was Rear-Admiral Raizo Tanaka's Transport Group. The Japanese Admiral's resilience and audacity in fighting his destroyer-transports through to Guadalcanal were to earn him the sobriquet 'Tenacious' Tanaka. The Americans sent equivalent convoys to supply the Marines on Guadalcanal.[33]

The struggle between the United States Navy and the Imperial Japanese Navy continued at the battles of Cape Esperance, (11–12 October 1942), Guadacanal I (12–13 November 1942), and Guadalcanal II (14–15 November 1942), with both sides losing many ships. A classic night action, the Battle of Tassafaronga, was fought on 30 November/1 December 1942. The Americans expected a Japanese force of eight destroyers and six transports to supply Guadalcanal. The information was erroneous. After the heavy losses of the previous weeks the Japanese now ran high speed destroyers to Guadalcanal, and jettisoned floating drums of provisions, oil, etc, which could be recovered by small craft operating from the beaches. The Americans sent Task Force 67, under Rear Admiral Carleton H Wright, to intercept the convoy. Task Force 67 comprised 1 light and 4 heavy cruisers and 6 destroyers. The Japanese convoy which sailed for Guadalcanal was commanded by the formidable Rear Admiral Tanaka and composed of a Striking Force of two destroyers, and a Transport Force of 6 destroyers, encumbered with supply drums and some troops. The Americans planned to pin-point the Japanese ships with radar, launch a massive torpedo attack from the destroyers, and then open fire with the cruisers' 8-inch and 6-inch guns. The battle did not go according to plan.

The Americans had complete radar superiority but near Tassafaronga Point the Japanese destroyer *Nanagami* spotted the US vessels and warned Tanaka who prepared for battle. Admiral Wright, although the Japanese vessels were clearly defined on his ships' radars, was slow in ordering his destroyers to launch their torpedoes. When the torpedoes were launched it was from the tactically unfavourable position of astern the Japanese convoy. The US cruisers opened fire.

Thus far the Americans had the advantage. The Japanese responded with superb discipline and with tactics that were well-rehearsed in accordance with naval doctrine. Tanaka ordered a massed torpedo attack. The screening destroyer *Takanami* was the nearest target to the US force and, after firing her torpedoes, was heavily engaged by gunfire and sunk. Although encumbered by supplies and troops the Japanese destroyers complied with Tanaka's instructions and nearly 50 Long Lances were launched against Task Force 67. Three heavy cruisers the *Minneapolis*, the *New Orleans* and the *Pensacola* were crippled. The heavy cruiser *Northampton* was sunk. Of the heavy units only the light cruiser *Honolulu* escaped damage or sinking.[34]

Tanaka's victory was outstanding. Outgunned by the US Navy cruisers, facing American radar superiority, and with six of the eight destroyers carrying 200 cargo drums each and troops, he had decisively defeated the American force by the use of his devastating Long Lances. Tassafaronga, nevertheless, was the last major sea battle for the Southern Solomons. The Imperial Japanese Navy had lost 24 combat ships: 2 battleships, 1 light carrier, 3 heavy cruisers, 1 light cruiser, 11 destroyers and 6 submarines. The Allies, but principally the United States Navy, had also lost 24 combat ships: 2 aircraft carriers, 6 heavy cruisers, 2 light cruisers, and 14 destroyers. The majority of them were sunk by Long Lance.[35] Yet the United States Navy could bear these losses, however grievous, better than the Imperial Japanese Navy. Accordingly, between 1–9 February 1943, the Japanese evacuated Guadalcanal. Not since the Anglo-Dutch Wars of the seventeenth century had there been such a continuing series of heavily contested naval battles.

Japanese expansion in the South Pacific had been blunted, but the fighting for the Solomon Islands continued. Two naval battles in the space of a week centred around the Tokyo Express, at Kula Gulf 5/6 July, and Kolombangara 13/14 July, again demonstrated the superior night-fighting skills of the Japanese. The Tokyo Express lost a light cruiser and a destroyer. The Long Lances sank a light cruiser, a destroyer and damaged three cruisers.[36]

To a marked extent the Japanese had replaced the gun by the torpedo as the primary offensive weapon of their cruiser and destroyer forces. In five battles of the Pacific War during the period 1942–43 – the Java Sea, Sunda Strait, Tassafaronga, Kula Gulf and Kolombangara – the primary duel was between Allied gunpower and the Japanese Long Lances. Nearly all the Japanese losses in these five engagements were by gunfire and the Long Lances were responsible for most of the Allied sinkings. At Tassafaronga, Kula Gulf and Kolombangara, the Long Lances were launched about the same time as the Allies opened gunfire. In the first two battles, Java Sea and Sunda Strait, the Long Lances were not fired until the guns had been in action for some time.[37]

The effectiveness of Japanese naval gunfire should not, however, be underestimated. At the battle of Savo Island HMAS *Canberra* was hit by two Long Lances but also by twenty-four shells from devastating Japanese cruiser gunfire. The heavy cruisers USS *Chicago*, USS *Quincy*, and USS *Vincennes* were hammered by both gunfire and torpedoes, while the USS *Astoria* was ravaged by the Japanese cruiser *Chokai*'s 8-inch gunfire.[38]

Nevertheless, the Imperial Japanese Navy demonstrated, during 1942–43, the effectiveness of its night-fighting and torpedo doctrines. The Japanese use of the torpedo showed that if this weapon was properly handled it was more than a match for good gunnery, although the losses inflicted by US radar-directed gunfire at Kula Gulf and Kolombangara were a portent of things to come. Yet few ships could withstand the destructive power of Long Lance's 1080lb warhead, and in these five battles the tactical decision was in favour of the Japanese, and Allied forces suffered over four times the losses inflicted on the Imperial Japanese Navy.[39]

Long Lance's safety record in service was good. The main danger was that shell splinters could pierce the torpedo oxygen vessel and the heat of the impact could then detonate the powerful warhead. In surface ships, since a derivative of the Type 93 Long Lance, the Type 95, was developed for use in submarines, a number of men were detailed for duties with water hoses and an emergency tank by the torpedo mountings. If the situation was too dangerous then the Long Lances were jettisoned. The sides of the torpedo tubes were also armoured to impede splinter penetration.[40]

The torpedoes were launched by compressed air from tubes located on deck amidships in the destroyers, or in the heavy cruisers on mounts placed on the port and starboard side of the ship. On entering the water the Long Lances used complex mechanisms to run at a pre-selected depth. The torpedoes were unguided. They were aimed by director control and the torpedo tubes trained automatically. The speeds of enemy vessels were estimated and the directors used deflection aiming to launch the torpedoes at the targets. The Long Lances were fired in salvoes or individually. In an emergency, local firing could be initiated. Long Lance's powerful offensive capability was doubled by the reloading capacity. A Japanese destroyer carried eight Long Lances in two quadruple tubes. All the Long Lances could be launched at two-second intervals.[41] In excellent conditions the tubes could be reloaded in ten minutes. In combat this replenishing could take longer. At Kula Gulf the Japanese destroyers took an hour to reload. At Kolombangara the Japanese destroyers took eighteen minutes.[42]

The excellent performance of the oxygen-propelled Long Lance mitigated the operational dangers it might present. Two examples will suffice. During the battle of the Java Sea the heavy cruiser *Haguro*, at 16.22, launched 8 Long Lances at Allied forces at a range of $12\frac{1}{2}$ miles. At 16.40 the Dutch destroyer *Kortenaer* was hit by a torpedo and blew up.[43] The Allied force believed *Kortenaer* had been mined or sunk by submarine. The first major Allied offensive in the Solomons began on 21 June 1943. In a destroyer fight off Vila on 5 July Japanese destroyers directed by the radar-equipped *Niizuki* launched Long Lances at a range of 11 miles at bombarding US forces. One Long Lance hit the US destroyer *Strong* which later sank. The Americans were mystified by the sinking since they could not accept it was caused by a torpedo launched by the ships detected on their radars.[44]

The Americans, like the British, arrogantly discounted the sophistication of Japanese torpedo technology and the potency of Long Lance. The distinguished naval historian Samuel Eliot Morison, who took part in some of the Solomons battles, discusses this attitude at some length.[45] Even more damning, however, is the statement by Rear Admiral A H McCollum, former Head of the Far Eastern Section of the Office of Naval Intelligence US Navy. Information on Long Lance came to the US Navy several years before the Pacific War, and reports on its performance were sent to the Bureau of Ordnance. McCollum states:

> The Bureau of Ordnance came back and said that, in the first place, a 1200-lb warhead would be so long that its centre of gravity, which is the origin of the burst, would be so far back that it

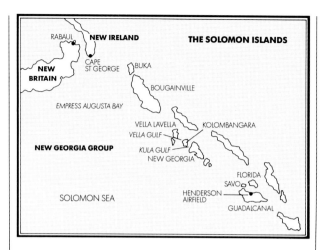

The Solomon Islands

would have a not materially different effect from our own torpedo which, at that time, carried 800lbs of TNT, that the speeds were completely ridiculous, that no torpedo could go that far so fast. . . . They only came round to our point of view when the Japanese started blowing the tails off our cruisers down in the Solomon Islands.[46]

Yet by late summer 1943, Long Lance's heyday was over. American superiority in radar, and more skilful night fighting techniques, began to overcome the advantages enjoyed by the Japanese. On the night of the 6/7 August 1943 four Japanese destroyers, three of them carrying troops and supplies, were sailing towards Kolombangara. Six US destroyers were sent to intercept. The Japanese squadron was detected by radar and the engagement took place in Vella Gulf, which separates the islands of Vella Lavella and Kolombangara. Three of the American destroyers launched 24 torpedoes at the Japanese vessels, three minutes before the destroyer *Shigure* sighted the warships and launched eight Long Lances. Three Japanese destroyers were hit, but the Long Lances missed. The American destroyers opened fire with 5-inch guns and launched further torpedoes. Only *Shigure* escaped. Three Japanese destroyers and over a thousand men were lost.[47] Vella Gulf showed that US destroyers could also win night actions.

On 1 November 1943 US Marines invaded Bougainville at Empress Augusta Bay. The capture of Bougainville would threaten the powerful Japanese base of Rabaul. On 2 November the US and Japanese Navies clashed at Empress Augusta Bay when the Japanese attempted to sink Allied transports. In another confused night action the Imperial Japanese Navy failed to sink the transports and lost a cruiser and a destroyer. As the Americans consolidated their

grip on Bougainville the Japanese attempted to strengthen Buka airfield, on Buka Island just to the north of Bougainville.

The Buka Reinforcement Unit was composed of three troop-carrying destroyers and two escorting destroyers. It was to be the last Tokyo Express. Five American destroyers, alerted by air intelligence, were sent to intercept on 24 November 1943. Two Japanese screening destroyers were detected by US radar, in the early morning of 25 November in St George's Channel off New Ireland. In the ensuing battle of Cape St George the Imperial Japanese Navy lost three destroyers.[48] This was to be the last surface battle for the Solomon Islands.

By the end of 1943 the defensive perimeter of Imperial Japan's oceanic empire was contracting as the Allies invaded New Guinea, the Admiralties, and the Central Pacific which the Imperial Japanese Navy could not withstand. Imperial Japan faced a resurgent United States Navy backed by American industrial might. More specifically, on 31 December 1942, the fleet carrier *Essex* was commissioned. She displaced 34,881 tons (full load) and could operate nearly 100 aircraft. By the end of 1943 6 sister-ships had been commissioned, as had 9 *Independence*-class light carriers, which carried 30 aircraft each, displaced 14,751 tons (full load), and could also operate with the Fast Carrier Task Forces. In February 1943 the new 58,000 tons (full load) 16-inch gunned fast battleship *Iowa* was commissioned, followed by her sister-ship *New Jersey* in May 1943. Their speed and massive anti-aircraft firepower substantially aided the Fast Carrier Task Forces, centred on the *Essex*-class carriers. During 1943, moreover, nearly 400 destroyers and destroyer escorts were launched.[49] This torrent of warships, including scores of submarines and new generations of naval aircraft, such as the Grumman Hellcat, improved Grumman Avenger, and Chance Vought Corsair, spearheaded America's reconquest of the Pacific.

As Imperial Japan's strategic position deteriorated, tactical necessity forced the Japanese leaders to utilise the abundant but outstanding courage of Japanese combatants. One expedient, the Kamikaze pilots, who deliberately flew their aircraft into Allied warships, was to inflict severe damage on the United States Navy, particularly in the struggle for Okinawa during April–June 1945. Another utilisation was the manned Kaiten I, an adaptation of Long Lance, now rendered tactically superfluous by American carrier power and radar technology. The most numerous was the Type I Modification I of which 330 were constructed. It was 48ft 4.3ins long, weighed 18,300lb, had an explosive charge of 3420lb, and had a performance of 25,000 yards at 30 knots, 47,000 yards at 20 knots, and 85,000 yards at 12 knots.[50] It was launched from a submarine, although some were carried by warships. Only two successes are recorded,

Japanese destroyer *Shiranui* damaged by torpedo from a US submarine off the Aleutian Islands, in Maizuru Dock. Sunk by Task Force 77 off Panay, 27 October 1944. 2490 tons, 35 knots, 6 × 5in (3 × 2), 4 × 25mm AA (later augmented) 8 × 24in torpedo tubes (2 × 4), 16 depth charges. (Notice the rails and other reloading facilities for the Long Lance) MH 6229

Japanese destroyer *Kiyoshimo*, off Uraga, 15 May 1944. *Yugumo*-class destroyer launched in February 1944 and sunk by American PT-boats and aircraft in December 1944. 2520 tons, 35 knots, 6 × 5in guns (3 × 2), 4 × 25mm AA (later augmented) 8 × 24in torpedo tubes (2 × 4), 36 depth charges. MH 6237

Japanese destroyer *Isokaze*, off Sasebo, November 1940. *Kagero*-class destroyer, launched June 1939, and sunk by air attack April 1945. 2450 tons, 35 knots, 6 × 5in guns (3 × 2), 4 × 25mm AA (later augmented) 8 × 24in torpedo tubes (2 × 4), 16 depth charges. MH 6231

Japanese cruiser *Furutaka* after reconstruction, off Ukuru Island 9 June 1939. *Furutaka*-class cruiser (sister ship *Kako*), the first Japanese heavy cruiser type built to Washington Treaty restrictions. Launched February 1925, and sunk by gunfire and a torpedo from US cruisers in the Battle of Cape Esperance, October 1942. 10,341 tons, 33 knots, 6 × 8in guns (3 × 2 after armament revised) 4 × 4.7in AA (4 × 1), smaller AA, 8 × 24in torpedo tubes (2 × 4). MH 6199

Japanese heavy cruiser *Chokai*, Yokosuka, 18 June 1938. Close-up view of bridge, showing recessed torpedo tubes. The massive bridge structure was a characteristic of the *Takao*-class heavy cruisers. *Chokai* was launched in April 1931 and sunk in the battle of Samar, October 1944, by air- and destroyer attack. She had a high reputation, always being assigned to the Combined Fleet.
14,838 tons, 34.2 knots, 10 × 8in guns (5 × 2), 8 × 5in AA (4 × 2), smaller AA, 16 × 24in torpedo tubes (4 × 4). MH 6206

Japanese Kaiten (Human torpedo) Type I. Launching experiment from Japanese cruiser *Kitakami*, near Kure, 26 February 1945. MH 6529

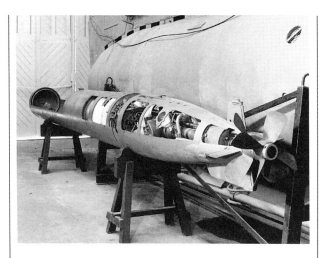

The Long Lance torpedo on display in one of Duxford Airfield's First World War hangars. In the background is X51, HMS *Stickleback*

the sinking of the fleet oil tanker *Mississinewa* at Ulithi in November 1944, and the destroyer escort *Underhill* off Luzon in July 1945.[51]

Imperial Japan had been able to localise her conflicts with China and Russia but this ability to fight limited wars ended when Admiral Nagumo's[52] carrier aircraft attacked Pearl Harbor. Imperial Japan no longer faced a weak China led by the palsied Manchu dynasty and already being carved up by the Western Powers: or Romanov Russia, fighting a war at the end of attenuated communications and facing rising internal discontent. Now Imperial Japan faced the United States, a nation of both continental proportions and also the greatest industrial power in the world. Within the frontiers of the American land mass of over three and a half million square miles was a self-sufficiency of oil, coal. iron ore and other minerals – the jewels in the industrial crown – and food. The United States was, in effect, the autarkic power that Imperial Japan strove to be. War with such a power could not be limited.

As the Pacific War expanded in area and intensity, cherished Japanese weapons – Long Lance, the battleship, the Zero fighter – and hallowed Japanese strategic doctrines – the 'decisive' naval battle, the protective glacis of island redoubts – were swept aside by the juggernaut of American industrial power. The mobility of land – and carrier-based air power conquered the immense distances of the Pacific, the largest single theatre of operations in which war had ever been fought, greater than the Mongol campaigns waged in the twelfth and thirteenth centuries over the vast Eurasian land mass; and surpassed only by the campaigns fought simultaneously in Canada, Europe, and India by Great Britain in the Seven Years' War (1756–1763): or by Great Britain and the United States in Europe, Africa,

and Asia in the Second World War.

By June and July 1944, the Americans had captured the Mariana Islands in the Western Pacific. From Tinian, Guam, and Saipan, the B-29 Superfortresses[53] were to burn the heart out of Japanese cities, complementing the United States Navy's fast carrier operations, and devastating submarine attrition of Japan's merchant shipping: while the United States Army and United States Marines continued their inexorable 'island-hopping' campaign ever closer to metropolitan Japan. Long Lance had become irrelevant in a technological war that culminated in the first nuclear strikes on Hiroshima and Nagasaki in August 1945, which forestalled a massive Allied amphibious assault on the Japanese home islands, and were a chilling *dénouement* to the whole Pacific tragedy. Imperial Japan's terrible defeat was a crushing indictment of her flawed foreign policy and military strategy.

The decline of the European powers after the Second World War led to the emergence, for a time, of a bi-polar world. The rivalry of the extra-European super-powers, the United States and the Soviet Union achieved *de jure* legitimacy with the creation of the North Atlantic Treaty Organisation and the Warsaw Pact. The antagonistic ideological blocs confronted each other in a state of rivalry which stopped short of open hostilities. The Cold War was conditioned by the mutual possession of nuclear weapons. Both blocs built up large conventional forces to achieve tactical and strategic flexibility and to avoid a nuclear confrontation and mutual annihilation.

In particular, NATO and the Warsaw Pact maintained large naval forces and at the present time the nuclear-powered submarine with its warload of missiles and torpedoes is the capital ship of the world's major navies. The torpedo remains a powerful weapon. The Soviet Union, which has a conventional – and nuclear-powered submarine force almost as big as the world's combined submarine fleets, is deploying a torpedo of 25.6ins calibre, with a 1980lb warhead, over $29\frac{1}{2}$ft long, and with a range of 27 nautical miles at 50 knots. It has an improved propulsion system and contains sensors to home on to a ship's wake. It is being fitted into the *Akula*, *Sierra* and *Victor III* classes of fleet submarines.[54]

The progenitor of this torpedo and its NATO equivalents is the Japanese 24-inch Type 93 Long Lance torpedo, which inflicted such great losses on Allied ships during 1942–43. Long Lance was the most powerful torpedo in the world, the most famous to emerge from the Second World War, and its place in naval history is assured.

Notes

1. Alan Coupe, 'The Royal Navy and the Whitehead torpedo', *Technical Change and British Naval Policy 1860–1939*, B Ranft (Ed), Hodder and Stoughton, London 1977, pp 23–26.

2. For a straightforward account of Japan's emergence from feudal seclusion in the nineteenth century see M E Cameron, T H D Mahoney, and G E McReynolds, *China, Japan and the Powers: A History of the Modern Far East*, The Ronald Press Company, New York, 1960, pp 238–275.

3. H P Willmott, *Empires in the Balance: Japanese and Allied Pacific Strategies to April 1942*, Orbis, London, 1982, p 17. Hideyoshi Toyotami was one of the unifiers of Japan during the sixteenth century.

4. For a brief account of early Anglo-Japanese relations see A J Marder, *Old Friends, New Enemies: The Royal Navy and the Imperial Japanese Navy: Strategic Illusions 1936–1941*, Clarendon Press, Oxford, 1981, pp 3–5.

5. A T Mahan, *The Influence of Sea Power upon History*, Sampson Low, Marston and Co Ltd, London, 1890, *The Influence of Sea Power upon the French Revolution and Empire*, 2 vols, Sampson Low, Marston and Co Ltd, London, 1892, and the later *Sea Power in its Relations to the War of 1812*, 2 vols, Sampson Low, Marston and Co Ltd, London, 1905.

6. For a fuller description of Mahan's life and an exposition of his philosophy see M T Sprout, 'Mahan: Evangelist of Sea Power', *Makers of Modern Strategy*, edited by E M Earle, Princeton University Press, Princeton, 1948, pp 415–445; D N Schurman, *The Education of a Navy: The Development of British naval strategic thought 1867–1914*, Cassell, London, 1965, pp 60–82.

7. Earle, op cit, pp 440–445.

8. M R Peattie, 'Akiyama Saneyuki and the Emergence of Modern Japanese Naval Doctrine', *US Naval Institute Proceedings*, Vol 103, January 1977, pp 62–65.

9. A D Coox, *Nomonhan: Japan Against Russia, 1939*, Vol 1, Stanford University Press, Stanford, 1985, pp 1–4.

10. S E Morison, *History of United States Naval Operations in World War II, Vol III, The Rising Sun in the Pacific 1931 – April 1942*, Little, Brown and Company, Boston, 1948, pp 6–7.

11. Marder, op cit, p 5.

12. H Jentschura, D Jung, P Mickel, *Warships of the Imperial Japanese Navy 1869–1945*, Arms and Armour Press, London, 1977, p 28. When *Nagato* and *Mutsu* were launched in 1919/1920, they were the most powerful capital ships in the world.

13. H P Willmott, *The Barrier and the Javelin, Japanese and Allied Pacific Strategies February to June 1942*, Naval Institute Press, Annapolis, 1983, p 23.

14. S E Pelz, *Race to Pearl Harbor*, Harvard University Press, Cambridge, Mass, 1974, pp 35–39. Also S E Morison, op cit, p 82.

15. The information on Japanese torpedoes is taken from Marder, *Old Friends New Enemies*, pp 309–310 and J. Campbell, *Naval Weapons of World War II*, Conway Maritime Press, London, 1985, pp 202–208.

16. Commander G Ross, Typewritten copy of Report to Naval Intelligence Division, p 237, Department of Documents, Imperial War Museum. Ross (later Rear Admiral George Ross CB CEng) was Assistant Naval Attaché to the British Embassy in Tokyo, 1934.

17. Campbell, op cit, p 203.

18. Ross, op cit, p 237.

19. Ibid.

20. Information on Long Lance and American Mk15 torpedoes taken from H Lengener, S Kobler-Edamatsu, and T Rehm-Takahara 'Kitakami', *Warship 37* January 1986, Conway Maritime Press, p 34, R O'Neill, *Suicide Squads*, Salamander Books Ltd, London, 1981, p 224 and Campbell, op cit, p 207.

21. Marder, op cit, p 310.

22. Lengener, S Kobler Edamatsu and T Rehm-Takahara, op cit, p 35 and Campbell, op cit, p 203.

23. The Japanese built the *Yamato* and *Musashi*, at 72,809 tons full load and with 9 × 18.1 inch guns the largest and most powerful battleships ever built. Both were sunk by air attack. Among other examples is the Mitsubishi A6M Reisen (Zero) fighter, the finest carrier fighter in the world during 1941–1942.

24. R H Spector, *Eagle against the Sun*, The Free Press, New York, 1985, pp 44–45.

25. Paul S Dull, *A Battle History of the Imperial Japanese Navy (1941–1945)*, Patrick Stephens Ltd, Cambridge, 1978, p 60.

26. Constructor Commander N Hancock (RCNC) to Director of Naval Construction, *A Report of Investigations into matters of interest to the Director of Naval Construction*, February 1946. Section Torpedo Arrangements, p 67. Typescript copy held by Naval Historical Branch, MOD.

27. Marder, op cit, p 310.

28. For a stimulating account of the cryptanalysis war in the Pacific see R Lewin, *The Other Ultra*, Hutchinson, London, 1982.

29. S E Morison, *History of United States Naval Operations in World War II, Vol V, The Struggle for Guadalcanal*, Little, Brown and Company, Boston, 1950, pp 12–20.

30. Ibid, p 20.

31. Dull, op cit, pp 187–196, Morison, op cit, pp 40–61.

32. L Morton, *The United States Army in World War II The War in the Pacific: Strategy and Command: The First Two Years*, Department of the Army, Washington, 1962, p 125.

33. Morison, op cit, p 104; Dull, op cit, p 215.

34. Morison, op cit, pp 288–315; Dull, op cit, pp 255–260.

35. Morison, op cit, p 372.

36. Dull, op cit, pp 274–277, S E Morison, *History of United States Naval Operations in World War II, Volume VI, Breaking the Bismarck's Barrier*, Oxford University Press, London, 1950, pp 160–175.

37. Directorate of Naval Operational Studies, *Report No 36/45, Surface Action in the Pacific 9 July 1945*, ADM 219/239. PRO

38. Dull, op cit, pp 187–193. Morison, *Guadalcanal*, op cit, pp 17–64, *Battle Summary No 21, Naval Operations in the Campaign for Guadalcanal August 1942– February 1943*, Admiralty, 1949, pp 15–30.

39. Directorate of Naval Operational Studies.

40. Campbell, op cit, p 203.

41. Marder, op cit, p 301.

42. Morison, *Breaking the Bismarck's Barrier*, op cit, p 172, p 187.

43. Dull, op cit, p 78.

44. Ibid, p 274.

45. Morison, op cit, pp 194–197.

46. Marder, op cit, pp 353–354.

47. Dull, op cit, pp 278–279; Morison, op cit, pp 212–221.

48. Dull, op cit, pp 294–295.

49. R Chesnau (ed), *Conway's All the World's Fighting Ships, 1922–1946*, Conway Maritime Press, London, 1980.

50. Campbell, op cit, p 211.

51. D C Evans (ed), *The Japanese Navy in World War II*, Naval Institute Press, Annapolis, 1986, pp 442–452.

52. Admiral Chuichi Nagumo led a task force centred on six fleet carriers which devastated Pearl Harbor, 7 December 1941.

53. The most sophisticated operational heavy bomber of the Second World War. Specifications for B-29B
Crew: 10. Power Plant: 4 × 2200 h.p. radial piston engines. Dimensions: span 141ft 3ins; length 99ft; height 29ft 7in. Weight: empty 69,000lb: gross 137,500lb. Performance: Maximum speed 364 m.p.h. at 25,000ft. Cruising speed 228 m.p.h. Range 4200 miles. Armament: 10 × 0.5in and one 20mm cannon, 20,000lb bomb load.

54. Siegfried Breyer, 'The Soviet Submarine Force Today', *International Defence Review*, No 9, Vol 20, 1987, pp 1155–1159.

'Swingmusik ist Verboten': Popular Music Policy and 'Swing Youth' in Nazi Germany

Terry Charman

Terry Charman is a research assistant in the Department of Printed Books.

T he 1930s are rightly considered to have been the 'golden age' of dance band music, not only in Britain and the United States, but also in Europe. Even with the assumption of power by the Nazis on 30 January 1933, and the supposed outlawing of Jewish and Negro music, dance bands remained extremely popular in the Reich. Britain's Jack Hylton and his band, who had recorded frequently in Berlin during the Weimar years, appeared in 1935 at Berlin's Philharmonic Hall. Two years later the Hylton band played at the Foreign Press Club Ball, and both Goering and Dr Goebbels with their respective spouses took to the dance floor during such numbers as 'Dinah' and 'The Organgrinder's Song'.[1] As late as February 1939 Henry Hall and his orchestra, ('der tanz-orchester des London sender' – the dance orchestra of the London radio station), appeared at Berlin's leading music hall, the Scala.[2] It was not only foreign orchestras and bands which received official approval. Dr Robert Ley's Labour Front daily *Der Angriff* reported on 18 August 1936 details of Dr Goebbels's fabulous party held at Peacock Island on the Wannsee near Berlin to commemorate the Olympic Games: 'the enormous dancing area, set amid the majestic groves of trees, filled up with couples who danced to the music of bandleader Oskar Joost of the Femina [night club], Eugen Wolff of the Eden [Hotel] and Emanuel Rambourn of the Kaiserhof [Hotel].'[3]

Throughout the twelve years of the Third Reich's existence there was an ambiguous official stance towards popular dance music in general and swing music in particular. Swing, (a successful blend of traditional Negro jazz and white dance band music whose most famous exponent was Benny Goodman, 'The King of Swing'), was a particular target for Nazi disapproval, especially during the war years. Yet at the same time there were many musicians in the Reich including Willy Berking, Benny de Weille, Freddie Brocksieper, Lutz Templin, Kurt Widman, and perhaps the best of all, Kurt Hohenberger who made Germany the swing capital of Europe, even at the height of the campaign against Anglo-Saxon 'decadent' music. Indeed the Nazis did not allow their antipathy to swing music to blind them to its value as propaganda, and a special band of leading German and other European musicians was recruited to take part in propaganda broadcasts to Britain. This band was known as Charlie and his Orchestra. 'Charlie' was Karl Schwedler, a wartime employee of the German Foreign Office, who wrote and then sang parodies of popular songs – 'The St Louis Blues', 'You're Driving me Crazy' etc – with anti-British lyrics.[4] The BBC replied in kind with Geraldo and his Orchestra and Jack Payne's Band with Payne's wife Peggy Cochrane singing the

REVIEW

IMPERIAL WAR MUSEUM

80

latest Anglo-American 'hits' in German. Later Major Glenn Miller's American Band of the Allied Expeditionary Force joined the propaganda battle with Sergeant Johnny Desmond singing the German versions of such great songs as Jerome Kern's and Ira Gershwin's 'Long Ago and Far Away'.[5] To jazz enthusiasts such as Hans Otto Jung, a member of the Hot Club of Frankfurt, such broadcasts were irresistible: 'I remember having heard Glenn Miller's "Tuxedo Junction" one night, and I immediately sat down and wrote an arrangement for four instruments plus rhythm section ... we regularly listened to the latest hits from London, Switzerland, and even the United States (on short wave) ... we were all united in the desire to play hot music we all enjoyed so much – although it was a music which was frowned upon, even "verboten" '.[6] Indeed a 1976 record of Kurt Hohenberger with such tracks as 'The Sheik of Araby', 'Limehouse Blues' and 'Run Rabbit Run' – the Noel Gay 'hit' from the Crazy Gang's show *The Little Dog Laughed* of 1939 – is entitled 'Swing Tanzen Verboten' – 'Swing Dancing Forbidden', words that often appeared on notices at the entrances to German dance halls during the war.

To what extent German youngsters took notice of such edicts, and what was the official Nazi reaction to the 'swing craze' is examined below, using, as far as possible, contemporary accounts.

> 'Five o'clock tea: this means above all ... dancing! And what kind of dancing! One dances swing – one hears all the latest hits and learns to recognize all the famous dance orchestras. Actually all this would be no more than a harmless waste of time for the "nice young man" if, a few lines further down, this choppy, noisy meaningless squeaking were not described as "good music". We most decisively reject the possibility that, in the Third Reich, a newspaper can still exist and serve as the advocate of the Jewish impulse which has been done away with once and for all, that a spirit against which the Fuehrer, and with him the whole healthy-minded German people, has declared a war to the death, can again be allowed to worm its way into the field of music'.[7]

So fulminated an unknown writer in *Der S A Mann*, 18 September 1937, against a fellow journalist, who, in the popular Berlin daily *12 Uhr Blatt*, had praised the practice of musical five o'clock teas at Berlin hotels. Protests of this sort were uttered with unfailing regularity from 1933 onwards, and even as late as February 1945 the music programme committee of the Reich Radio still had to deal with complaints about the amount of non-German dance music being broadcast.[8] The 'impudent swamp flowers of Negroid pandemonium in German dance-halls regrettably abetted by so-called German dance bands' and 'perverse jazz music,'[9] seemingly abolished in 1933 showed, especially among young people, amazing powers of resilience.

Music policy in Nazi Germany was exercised by the Reich Chamber of Music, whose second president, (the first was Richard Strauss), Dr Peter Raabe, claimed it 'was founded to encourage a study of music, to enhance the standing of the musicians, and to provide an agency through which the needs of the musicians shall be recognised, thus carrying out a task which neither individuals nor earlier organizations had been able to accomplish.'[10] As with the other Reich cultural chambers there was a heavy Nazi ideological slant. Folk music was greatly encouraged and the Chamber was supposed to act as a 'purifying influence' and to bar all 'un-German music'. By 1938 the work of the Chamber was done by four sections. The first was concerned with administration, and included a sub-section which collected evidence of the proper 'Aryan' origins of the Chamber's members. The second section dealt with general affairs, especially looking after all aspects of musical education, and established liaison with institutes for music and training colleges, both public and private. It also co-operated with the Hitler Youth, the Strength through Joy organization and with schools. Section Two also comprised a number of professional units. The Composers' Group dealt with professional questions, the playing of contemporary music and the planning of programmes. A Performers' Group supervised the training of students, discouraged unsuitable performances, and provided facilities for young artists. The Orchestral Group dealt with the salaries and appointments of its musicians, and also had responsibility for the raising of standards of public musical performances, especially at health and recreational resorts. By far the largest group was that of 'Unterhaltungsmusiker', those providing music as an entertainment. It controlled the work, and salaries, of some 60,000 members. Section Two also embraced a number of professional organizations, the music publishers, owners of music shops and even manufacturers of musical instruments. Section Three dealt with choirs, folk music and such organizations as the Association of German Singers, the Reich Association for Mixed German Choirs, and the Association for Protestant Church Music. Section Four was responsible for the organization of concerts, and had sub-sections for concert impresarios, concert managers, and for secretaries of musicians. Finally, there were special offices for arranging concerts for handicapped and blind persons, and an agency STAGMA[11], the approved society for musical copyrights. All German musical publications were controlled by the Chamber. Formidable as the controls of the Chamber may appear, it seems that music, which has fewer overt political implications than the other arts, and despite the Fuehrer's obsession with Wagner and Lehar, not to mention 'The Donkey Serenade', suffered less under the Nazis' system of control.[12] Indeed it has been argued that with orchestras such as the Berlin Philharmonic under Wilhelm Fuertwangler, and the Berlin State Opera 'the excellent music fare did much to make people forget the degradation of the other arts and of so much of life under the Nazis'.[13]

Nevertheless such purveyors of music 'Kulturbolschewismus'[14] as Hindemith, Krenek and Alban Berg were outlawed, and no words were too strong enough to condemn 'nigger jazz and swing'.

'Disgusting things are going on, disguised as "entertainment". We have no sympathy for fools, who want to transplant jungle music to Germany. In Stettin ... one can see people dancing as though they suffer from stomach pains. They call it "swing". This is no joke. I am overcome with anger. These people are mentally retarded. Only niggers in some jungle would stomp like that. Germans have no nigger in them. The pandemonium of swing fever must be stopped. We are not prudes, on the contrary. ... Maybe a boy wants to go out with a girlfriend to dance. Well and good. But there are limits. Impresarios who present swing dancing should be put out of business. Swing orchestras that play hot, scream on their instruments, stand up for solos and other cheap devices are going to disappear. Nigger music must disappear.'[15]

And not just 'nigger music'. The official newspaper of the Sturmabteilungen[16] *Der S A Mann* of 6 January 1939 attacked the Noel Gay hit dance number from Lupino Lane's *Me and My Girl*, which at the time was enjoying worldwide popularity:

'Who wouldn't want to join in! Who isn't tempted by this society dance, which permits one to -er, take arms and whirl round, to go down on one's haunches (hey, who's tumbling over?), to slap one's thighs in a giddy vortex, and finally picking up the tempo again in a thrilling climax to stamp on the floor and – to let out an enthusiastic yell of 'Oi' – the passionate love cry of the noble art of Terpischore. Long live – in a word – the 'Lambeth Walk', the uncrowned king of contemporary fashionable dances. We will not cast up in reproach its murky origin from the slums of London and other harbour districts, even though this dance has already claimed the sacrifice of human lives. In Brighton a 52 year old waiter, called Herbert Brennan, fell dead from heart failure while doing the 'Lambeth Walk'. With the frenzied cry of 'Oi!' on his lips, the cry of the joy of living, he left this world for the eternal dancing ground. He was the first victim of the dance floor. Shall the sense of style of German Society be next? A degenerate dance? – no, degenerate people! And these things go on not only in cheap dance halls and disreputable night clubs. Even high class hotels have opened their revolving doors to this disgusting bit of Jewish apery.'[17]

Nonetheless, the taste for such music among ordinary Germans and especially the young remained, and indeed grew with the war years, leading to the swing movement of mainly upper middle class youngsters. The coming of the war removed to some extent parental restraint, especially if the father was serving in the *Wehrmacht*, and quite early on 'excesses' were being noted by the authorities. The Leipzig S.D.[18] in the Spring of 1940 reported especially heavy frequenting of dance-halls in which about half the clientele danced 'dances of a jazz-like nature despite clearly posted notices prohibiting swing and the "Lambeth Walk" '. About 20 per cent of the visitors were under eighteen, or even under sixteen.[19] A watch was placed on members of the *Wehrmacht* too. William Russell, a US Embassy employee in Berlin noted in November 1939 that soldiers who were caught dancing swing (and during military campaigns all dancing in public was forbidden), were given three days in solitary confinement, while at the same time 'the big Nazi bosses sit in Berlin's Scala Theatre and tap their comfortable feet to the good jazz of Otto Stenzel's orchestra'.[20]

Similarly, in 1941 two US correspondents for CBS noticed a discreet flouting of the rules. Howard K Smith often visited a night club 'because it has a good orchestra which defies Nazi propriety and plays American music. ... As it is also a favourite spot for big shot Nazis, the band doesn't play American jazz bluntly; it sandwiches it in between the opening and closing chords from some German number, salving the consciences of Nazi visitors who might otherwise be reminded that what they were listening to was written by a racial inferior.'[21] Smith's superior, Harry W Flannery, noted that in Garmisch Partenkirchen's exclusive Alpenhof Hotel the visitors

'danced to American music ... and crowded the bar to drink and hear a pianist play such forbidden numbers as "Bei mir bist du schon", those written by American Jewish composers such as Irving Berlin, starting with "Alexander's Ragtime Band", and continuing with such a miscellany as "Remember", "Chloe", "Dinah", "St Louis Blues" and "I Can't Give You Anything but Love Baby".[22]

Even in Berlin during the Summer of 1940, Dr Goebbels, the city's Gauleiter[23] had to order his State Secretary Leopold Gutterer 'to instruct the police to make one or two raids on the Wannsee and the adjacent lakes to confiscate all English gramophone records as well as the gramophones themselves. As for their owners, a check should be made to see whether they are perhaps listed as in "reserved occupations", and, where possible, they are to be employed in labour squads. The Minister (Dr Goebbels) describes it as a scandal that jazz music with English words should be publicly disseminated in the English language during the war. One or two such operations should be sufficient for the news of this action to spread very rapidly among the circles concerned.'[24]

To combat such official measures swing musicians resorted to ingenious ploys. Hans Otto Jung recalls that while playing at Frankfurt's 'Rokoko Diele' a Gestapo agent responsible for 'waifs, strays and hooligans' would make an occasional official visit: 'we had to stop playing hot improvisations and play straight instead. Also we immediately switched to popular tunes such as "Bel Ami" or "Komm Zuruck". Another way to fool the authorities was to announce Anglo-American compositions by fancy German titles: thus "Whispering" becomes "Lass mich dein Badewasser trinken", (literally "let me drink your bath-water"), the "St Louis Blues" became "Sankt Ludwig Serenade" '.[25]

Dr Goebbels, in his capacity as Reich Minister of Propaganda and Public Enlightenment and overall head of the Reich Chamber of Music, was much exercised as to the amount of 'jazz' and 'swing' music that should be allowed to the German public. He had encouraged 'a dehydrated form of syncopated music called "German Jazz" . . . pioneered by Peter Kreuder, Theo Mackeben and Barnabas Von Geczay',[26] but began to realize that this was not fulfilling the needs of young people, many now in uniform. To some extent there was a reversal of the policy previously stated by Heinrich Glasmeier, the Director General of Reichsrundfunkgesellschaft[27] on 10 August 1938 when he had announced that 'hot jazz and swing music' were going to be prevented from 'debasing and corrupting the German listener'.[28] In his diary on 3 February 1942 Dr Goebbels bemoaned the fact that 'radio programmes have deteriorated very much. During the hours set aside for entertainment almost nothing but symphonic

The dust jacket of a 1937 forty pfennig book denouncing 'Jewish-Negro jazz' as being 'entartete' – not in conformity with the pure German character.
Department of Printed Books, 54(4)/5 4 86/153.

music is offered. That's what we get for letting Glasmeier put a musical director, Schulz-Dornburg, in charge of the entertainment programme. People of his type usually sit in an ivory tower and don't know what the common man wants and what he needs most. It is wrong to appoint a musical expert for so difficult a task. Experts are always handicapped in their relation to common people. They lack the necessary instinct for realizing what the people are thinking'.[29] Goebbels returned to this theme in his diary again on 27 February and two days later announced in the *Voelkischer Beobachter*[30] of 1 March a change in direction:

We should like to speak quite freely about whether the German radio ought to broadcast the so-called jazz. If jazz means music which completely disregards or even makes fun of melody, and in which rhythm mainly shows itself in an ugly squeaking of instruments offensive to our ears, we can only answer in the negative. . . . On the other hand, it should not be claimed that the waltzes of our grandmothers and grandfathers must be the end of musical evolution and that everything that goes beyond them is evil. . . . We are not living in the Biedermeier epoch but in a century whose melody is determined by the hum of machines and the roar of motors. . . . The radio must pay due attention to this fact, if it does not want to run the risk of 'sticking to the frock coat' . . . we feel bound to consider the just demands of our fighting and working people.[31]

Accordingly, a considerable amount of swing and jazz music was played, even numbers by Negro composers such as Louis Armstrong and Duke Ellington. The names of the composers of such tunes were, naturally, never given.[32] Hans Otto Jung recalls that swing bands from Sweden, Holland or Belgium were also booked 'by the authorities to keep up the morale at (sic) the "Home Front", and the Gestapo did not interfere.'[33] For some potential listeners the change had come just too late. On 26 January 1942 Reichsfuehrer SS Himmler had written to his deputy Heydrich concerning the subject of swing.

Dear Heydrich,
I enclose a report which Reich Youth Leader Axmann has sent me about the 'swing youth' in Hamburg. I know that the Secret State Police have already intervened once. In my view, however, this mischief must be destroyed root and branch. I am against half measures here.
All the ringleaders, and I mean ringleaders both male and female, and all teachers with enemy views who are encouraging 'swing youth', are to be assigned to a concentration camp. There the youth should first be given thrashings and then put through the severest drill and set to work. I think that any sort of labour camp or youth camp would be inappropriate for these youths and worthless girls. The girls should be put to work weaving and do land work in the summer. The spell these people should spend in a concentration camp must be a fairly long one, 2–3 years. It must be made clear that they will never be allowed to go back to their studies. We must investigate how much encouragement they have had from their parents. If they have encouraged them, then they too should be out in a concentration camp and their property confiscated.
It is only by intervening brutally that we shall be able to prevent the dangerous spread of this Anglophile tendency at a time when Germany is fighting for her existence.
Please send me further reports. I should be grate-

'International exchange of culture. But not for us', read the caption to this cartoon, from *Der S A Mann* of 6 January 1939, which accompanied an article attacking the 'Lambeth Walk' as 'this disgusting bit of Jewish apery'.
Department of Printed Books, 49/4(43) 7(43) 25414.

ful if this action can be conducted in co-operation with the Gauleiter and the senior leader of the SS and police.
Heil Hitler!
Heinrich Himmler[34]

As already has been mentioned these 'swing boys and girls' to whom Himmler had taken such exception came from the upper middle class, in contrast to the 'Edelweiss Pirates' and 'Meuten', gangs of other youthful 'opponents' of the regime almost exclusively of working class background. Hamburg, perhaps because of its international connections as Germany's leading port, seems to have been the main centre of 'swing youth', although Frankfurt too had its 'Ohio Klub' and 'Cotton Klub' of 'degenerate youngsters'.

At first the 'swing youth' did not attract much attention from the authorities, and a number of swing music events were allowed to take place in public. This came to an abrupt halt when Hitler Youth officials reported on a Swing Festival that took place in Hamburg in February 1940 and which was attended by 500–600 young people. In the report 'we can hear all the leitmotifs that recur in the lamentations of the authorities when faced by the jazz and rock cultures of the twentieth century':[35]

The dance music was all English and American. Only swing dancing and jitterbugging took place.

At the entrance to the hall stood a notice on which the words 'Swing prohibited' had been altered to 'Swing requested'.

The dancers were an appalling sight. None of the couples danced normally; there was only swing of the worst sort. Sometimes two boys danced with one girl; sometimes several couples formed a circle, linking arms and jumping, slapping hands, even rubbing the backs of their heads together; and then bent double, with the top half of the body hanging loosely down, long hair flopping into the face, they dragged themselves round practically on their knees. When the band played a rhumba, the dancers went into wild ecstasy. They all leaped around and joined in the chorus in broken English. The band played wilder and wilder items; none of the players was sitting down any longer, they all 'jitterbugged' on the stage like wild creatures. Several boys could be observed dancing together, always with two cigarettes in the mouth, one in each corner.[36]

Eighteen months later in the same city, the S.D. reported that a wild jam session had taken place at the Alsterpavillon when 300 'degenerate and criminally inclined juveniles, some of mixed blood had terrorized the healthy-minded public by their mode of behaviour and undignified music excesses'.[37] Worse still such behaviour had now taken very much an 'unpatriotic form'.

The 'swing youth', with already enough education to be able to speak English, now began to take on the appearance of the Anglo-Saxon enemy: 'the predominant form of dress consisted of long, often checked, English sports jackets, shoes with light crepe soles, showy scarves, Anthony Eden hats, an umbrella on the arm whatever the weather, and, as an insignia, a dress shirt button worn in the button-hole, with a jewelled stone. The girls too favoured a long over-flowing hair style. Their eyebrows were pencilled, they wore lipstick and their nails were lacquered. The bearing and behaviour of the members of the clique resembled their dress.'[38] A cult of 'sleaziness' was established: 'their ideal is the sleazy life' reported the Hitler Youth, a fact cheerfully acknowledged by the 'swing youth' themselves. A member of the Kiel swing club, the 'Plutocrats', (one of the favourite Nazi terms of abuse for the British), wrote to a friend: 'Be a proper spokesman for Kiel, won't you? ie, make sure you're really casual, singing or whistling English hits all the time, absolutely smashed and always surrounded by really amazing women.'[39]

Measures as outlined in Himmler's letter were not slow in coming: wartime conditions had produced inadequate controls and German youth were not displaying, in their Fuehrer's words, the qualities demanded of them, to be 'hard as Krupp steel, tough as leather, and swift as greyhounds.'

The 'rod of discipline' was to be used unsparingly, as in the case of one Hasso Schutzendorf from Hamburg who appeared before the Hanseatic Juvenile Court in October 1942. The Gestapo had put him in a concentration camp on the suspicion of being a 'swing youth'. Here he had his hair shorn, was thrashed with an iron bar, and forced to push earth laden trolleys uphill for a fortnight. The court's medical expert found that Schutzendorf was suffering from general debility and exhaustion.[40]

Despite such barbaric punishments swing would not go away, and still at concerts 'the applause after . . . English hits was extraordinarily loud and in sharp contrast to the applause bestowed on the German numbers.'[41] Newspaper and magazine articles were produced denouncing swing. As late as 29 June 1944, three weeks after D-Day with thousands of Allied troops pouring into France and the Atlantic Wall well and truly breached, the Nazi Party's *Illustrierter Beobachter*[42] devoted a whole page to denouncing the 'King of Swing' the 'Jew Benny Goodman'. Three photographs showing Goodman, Goodman's hands holding his clarinet, and a couple dancing at a concert, carried the following captions:–

(1) The Jew Benny Goodman (Gutmann). With his swing band he not only received the top radio fees, but exerts a positively sinister influence on American youth. 'My music is more immoral than all the courtesans in history put together', he himself boasts.

(2) Hands of a criminal. The hands of the swing Jew Benny Goodman, described as 'definitely a criminal's hands' by a Milwaukee music magazine held in high regard by experts.

(3) No dance floor here. But the boys and girls who have been seduced by the 'immoral' music of the 'Pied Piper of New York' jerk their way between aisles in a cinema.[43]

Such propaganda did little to sway the 'swing youth' or indeed others: a sixteen-year-old girl from the upper middle classes weekending in Pomerania with aristocratic military opponents of the regime danced with her young host to 'hot Benny Goodman music (that) filled the hall'.[44] And to the delight of the 'swing youth' in the Schumann Cafe in Frankfurt, Ernst Hollerhagen, clarinettist with Teddy Stauffer und seinem Teddies, one night in 1942 clicked his heels, raised his right arm, and said in a loud voice (and parody of the 'German greeting'): 'Heil Benny!'[45]

How much weight should be placed on these actions of 'swing youth' as examples of real opposition to the Nazi regime itself, and not just its banal 'moon in June' popular music policy? Certainly the more intelligent of the Nazi leadership, such as Dr Goebbels, saw the inherent danger of

The *Munchner Illustrierte Presse* of 27 March 1941 attacks an American Negro swing version of 'A Midsummer's Night Dream' as an insult to Shakespeare. Department of Printed Books, *Munchner Illustrierte Presse* 18 Jahrgang, Nr 13.

the attitudes of 'swing youth' with too much free time on its hands. For even the outward, individualistic *persona* of the 'swing youth' carried an obvious rejection of the regime's ideal of uniformity and regimentation or 'gleichschaltung'. The boys were far removed from the image of the ideal German boy, 'Hitlerjunge Quex'[46]. And the girls were diametrically opposed to the behaviour patterns set by the 'Bund deutscher Madchen'[47]. There was defiance too in the obvious liking for the proscribed 'nigger jazz and swing', and in setting up of swing clubs (the 'OK Gang', 'Haarlem Klub' etc) in direct opposition to the state youth organizations.

Thus although incapable, by its very nature, of organized resistance, and poorly articulated, 'swing youth' was a symptom of genuine opposition to the Nazi regime. How much so may be gauged by a report which the S.D. sent to Martin Bormann on the subject of 'juvenile demoralization'. In it there was abundant detail to support the view that the 'Anglophile' youngsters entertained an extreme aversion to the state and Nazi party youth organizations, the Hitler Youth, League of German Maidens and the compulsory Labour Service[48] because the organized activities of such organizations encroached on the 'swing youths'' spare time. The youngsters shirked voluntary work and had no taste for military service. They opposed the war, and admired the music and clothes of the Anglo-Saxon enemy. They doubted the truth of the *Wehrmacht* communiqués and the outpourings of the Propaganda Ministry. They greeted each other with 'good morning' rather than 'Heil Hitler'.

In its damning last sentence the S.D. report regretfully concluded that 'Their ideal is democratic freedom and American laxity.'[49]

Notes

1. Richard Grunberger, *A social history of the Third Reich*, Weidenfeld and Nicolson, London, 1971.
2. Mike Zwerin, *La tristesse de Saint Louis : swing under the Nazis*, Quartet Books, London, 1985, pp 54–55.
3. *Der Angriff*, 18 August 1936.
4. *The Mail on Sunday*, 30 August 1987.
5. Geoffrey Butcher, *Next to a letter home. Major Glenn Miller's wartime band*, Sphere Books, London, 1987, p 184 and p 189.
6. Sleeve notes to *Swing under the Nazis : the clandestine recordings of the Frankfurt Hot Club*, Harlequin, HQ 2051, 1986.
7. George L Mosse, *Nazi culture*, W H Allen, London, 1966, p 50.
8. Josef Wulf, *Presse und Funk im Dritten Reich*, Siegbert Mohn, Gutersloh, 1964, p 379.
9. *Der S.A. Mann*, 18 September 1937.
10. Ministry of Economic Warfare Germany : basic handbook Part II, 1944, pp 310–311.
11. *Staatlichgenehmighte gesellschaft zur Verwertung musikailischer Urheberrechte*. The State Society for the Utilization of Musical Copyrights.
12. Ernest K Bramsted, *Goebbels and National Socialist Propaganda 1925–1945*, The Cresset Press, London, 1965, pp 80–81.
13. William L Shirer, *The rise and fall of the Third Reich : a history of Nazi Germany*, Secker and Warburg, London, 1960, p 242.
14. *Cultural Bolshevism*.
15. Zwerin, op cit, pp 13–14.
16. The Stormtroopers or Brownshirts.
17. W G Knop, *Beware of the English!*, Hamish Hamilton, London, 1939, pp 91–92.
18. S.D. stood for *Sicherheitsdienst*, the security service of the SS.
19. Marlis G Steinert, *Hitler's War and the Germans. Public mood and attitude during the Second World War*, Ohio Univerity Press, Athens, Ohio, 1977, p 63.
20. William Russell, *Berlin Embassy*, Michael Joseph, London, 1942, p 93.
21. Howard K Smith, *Last Train from Berlin*, Cresset Press, London, 1942, pp 132–133.
22. Harry W Flannery, *Assignment to Berlin*, Michael Joseph, London, 1942, p 125.
23. Nazi Party district leader.
24. Willi A Boelcke, (editor), *The secret conferences of Dr Goebbels, October 1939–May 1943*, Weidenfeld & Nicolson, London, 1970, p 65.
25. Sleeve notes to *Swing under the Nazis : the clandestine recordings of the Frankfurt Hot Club*, Harlequin, HQ 2051, 1986.
26. Grunberger, op cit, p 419.
27. RRG ; the German Broadcasting Company.
28. Derrick Sington and Arthur Wiedenfeld, *The Goebbels experiment : a study of the Nazi propaganda machine*, John Murray, London, 1942, pp 169–170.
29. Louis P Lochner, (Translator and editor), *The Goebbels Diaries*, Hamish Hamilton, London, 1948, p 31.
30. Literally, *People's Observer*, the official Nazi Party newspaper.
31. Sington and Weidenfeld, op cit, p 170.
32. Ibid, p 179.
33. Sleeve notes to *Swing under the Nazis : the clandestine recordings of the Frankfurt Hot Club*, Harlequin, HQ 2051, 1986.
34. Detlev J K Peukert, *Edelweisspiraten*, Bund Verlag, Cologne, 1980, pp 156–157.
35. Detlev J K Peukert, *Inside Nazi Germany. Conformity, opposition and racism in everyday life*, Batsford, London, 1987, p 166. Extracts reproduced by kind permission of the publisher.
36. Ibid, pp 166–167.
37. Hans Peter Bleul, *Strength through Joy : sex and society in Nazi Germany*, Secker and Warburg, London, 1973, p 243.
38. Peukert, op cit, p 168.
39. Ibid, p 167.
40. Bleul, op cit, pp 243–244.
41. Peukert, op cit, p 201.
42. Literally, *Illustrated Observer*, the official Nazi Party weekly illustrated magazine.
43. Peukert, op cit, p 201.
44. Marianne Mackinnon, *The Naked Years : growing up in Nazi Germany*, Chatto and Windus, London, 1987, pp 78–79.
45. Zwerin, op cit, p 59.
46. Erwin Leiser, *Nazi Cinema*, Secker and Warburg, London, 1974, pp 35–38.
47. Literally, 'League of German Maidens', the BDM.
48. Reichsarbeitsdienst.
49. Bleul, op cit, p 244.

Select Discography

1. 'Die Goldene 7. Tanzmusik der 30er Jahre' EMI. Electrola. C.148–30 609/10 M
2. 'Swing under the Nazis: the clandestine recordings of the Frankfurt Hot Club' Harlequin HQ 2051
3. 'Kurt Hohenberger und sein orchester. Swing tanzen verboten' Telefunken-Decca 6.22388.AK
4. 'Cafehaus und Salonorchester der 30er und 40er Jahre-Berlin' EMI Electrola IC 134–260 1263
5. 'Cafehaus und Salonorchester der 30er and 40er Jahre-Munchen' EMI Electrola IC 134–46 645/46
6. 'Cafehaus und Salonorchester der 30er und 40er Jahre-Frankfurt' EMI Electrola IC 134–46 446/47
7. 'Tanzorchester von damals' EMI Electrola IC 148–31308/09M
8. 'Benny de Weille und sein orchester' EMI Electrola IC 178–31512/13M
9. 'Lieblinge einer generation. Bernhard Ette Kurt Widman'. Top Classic BB 45.016
10. 'German propaganda swing 1940–1941 Charlie and his Orchestra' Harlequin HQ 2058

'You Smug-Faced Crowds': Poetry and the Home Front in the First World War

Martin Taylor

Martin Taylor is a research assistant in the Department of Printed Books.

You smug-faced crowds with
        kindling eye
Who cheer when soldier-lads go by,
Sneak home and pray you never know
The hell where youth and laughter go.
('Suicide in the Trenches')[1]

The image of the home front in the First World War is most vividly expressed in the poetry of Siegfried Sassoon. Sassoon's early war poems had echoed the sentiments of Rupert Brooke's '1914' sonnets, but as the fighting wore on and the true nature of the struggle became apparent, the tone of his poems changes from one of chivalrous romance to one of bitter satire. The particular object of his satire was the home front, for it was the atmosphere in England, as much as the horrific conditions on the Western Front, that fuelled his anger. The England Sassoon loved in his youth, a world full of 'meadows pied with sun and chasing clouds',[2] had been overwhelmed by a Babel of shrilling harlots, yellow pressmen and scarlet majors, and *The Old Huntsman* and *Counter-Attack*, published in May 1917 and June 1918 respectively, gave voice to his growing resentment. He felt that the representation of the war as purveyed in Britain was unrecognisable to those who had actually fought. Indeed, to anyone who had seen action, the picture of the war as presented by such magazines as *The War Illustrated*, must have seemed a very poor joke indeed.[3]

Soldiers returning to Britain on leave were astounded at the beliefs about the war held by civilians. Robert Graves wrote in *Goodbye To All That*; 'England looked strange to us returned soldiers. We could not understand the war-madness that ran wild everywhere, looking for a pseudo-military outlet. The civilians talked a foreign language; and it was a newspaper language.'[4] The civilian population, however, had to rely on press reports for information, which were at best highly selective, and at worst positively misleading. The general drift of war reporting seems to have depended upon a few well-worn maxims: that the Allies had no responsibility for starting the war, which was a product of German militarism and lust for conquest; that the Germans were no different from the Huns of old, rapists and pillagers; that the British army was full of loyal, cheerful and uncomplaining soldiers, led by efficient and intelligent generals; and that all were united in the belief that it was necessary to fight the war to victory, regardless of cost, so that German militarism could be crushed forever.[5]

The curtain of evasions and misconceptions that developed as a result of this campaign grew so thick that few

Robert Graves, on leave after seeing action in France in 1916, recalled meeting H G Wells at the Reform Club; he was

'full of military optimism [and] talked without listening. He had been given a "Cook's Tour" to France, and staff conductors had shown him the usual sights that royalty, prominent men of letters, and influential neutrals were allowed to see. He described his experiences at length, and seemed unaware that I and Siegfried [Sassoon], who was with me, had also seen the sights.'[7]

It was against this kind of ignorance and complacency that Sassoon aimed his fantasies of revenge;

I'd like to see a Tank come down the stalls,
Lurching to rag time tunes, or 'Home, Sweet Home', –
And there'd be no more jokes in Music-halls
To mock the riddled corpses round Bapaume.
('Blighters')[8]

And against which Owen levelled his more profound invocation;

But cursed are dullards whom no cannon stuns,
That they should be as stones.
Wretched are they, and mean
With paucity that never was simplicity.
('Insensibility')[9]

The reactions of Sassoon, Owen and Graves were not isolated, but represented a widespread response among the troops at the front. According to Vivian de Sola Pinto, himself a war poet and a fellow officer of Sassoon's, by 1916 there had grown up a new division in British society, not between class, but between the Nation at Home and the Nation Overseas;

The Nation at Home still believed in the patriotic myth of a beautiful, heroic war against diabolic enemies. The Nation Overseas was in touch with the realities of life and death, and was completely disillusioned with regard to the heroic nature of the struggle. Indeed, as the war went on, they became more and more solidly united in sentiment not against the Germans, but against (as it appeared to them) the callous, stupid Nation at Home, the government and, above all, the 'brass-hats' of the staff.[10]

serving soldiers could pierce it even with accounts of their own experiences. As James Norman Hall observed in the poem 'Hate':

Another time I was a-tellin' 'em
'Ow we shout back and forth across the trenches
When the lines is close together,
An' we get fed up with pluggin' at each other.
An' I told 'em about the place
This side of Messines, where we was only twenty yards apart,
An' 'ow they chucked us over some o' their black bread,
Arter we'd throwed 'em 'arf a dozen tins o' bully.
Some of 'em didn't believe me, an' some did.
But sour? S'y! 'Ere! They was ready to kill me
For tryin' to make out that Fritzie's a 'uman being'![6]

Although de Sola Pinto may be overstating his case, it is true that as the war continued, in poetry as well as in conversation (and at a humorous level in the drawings of Bruce Bairnsfather), there were increasing protests against the inefficiency of the General Staff, and more serious attacks on the ignorance of civilians. Even intensely patriotic soldier poets like Gilbert Frankau came to chastise those soldier poets who continued to mislead the public by describing the war as 'a kind of Military Tournament';

> Lord, if I'd half your brains, I'd write a book:
> None of your sentimental platitudes,
> But something real, vital; that should strip
> The glamour from this outrage we call war,
> Shewing it naked, hideous, stupid, vile –
> One vast abomination.
> ('The Other Side')[11]

However, Frankau was also responsible for the following lines, written as late as October 1918;

> Socialists – paid by princes;
> Democrats – Kaiser-wrought;
> 'Ware them, Peoples in Judgement
> Lest they bring your justice to nought.
> Now, lest your children's children
> Shriek to the lash of the Hun –
> Women, our murdered women –
> Answer the Word with the Gun!
> ('Justice')[12]

Frankau exemplifies a sentiment common to many soldiers, that although they thought the war was hell, they also believed that Germany had broken the code of European nations and deserved to be punished. What distinguishes the later war poets like Frankau from the early ones like Brooke, was not that they dismissed the conventional notions of heroism and sacrifice, but that they were determined to report the reality of life in the trenches to the Nation at Home. Ian Hay in *The First Hundred Thousand*, published in 1915 and one of the most widely read books of the war, wrote that all the troops asked of the civilian population,

> Is this. Within your hearts be writ
> This single-line memorial:–
> He did his duty – and his bit![13]

But by 1916 the situation had changed: as Osbert Sitwell was to say in 'Rhapsode';

> You hope that we will tell you that they found

This blinkin' moon will be the death of us"

And to think that it's the same dear old moon that's looking down on him!"

Bystander copyright. "THE SAME OLD MOON"
HER: "And to think that it's the same dear old moon that's looking down on him!" HIM: "This blinkin' moon will be the death of us."

The cartoons of Captain Bruce Bairnsfather were as popular in the trenches as on the home front, presumably because they succeeded in neither condescending to soldiers nor offending civilians. The above cartoon is a demonstration of this balancing act, while providing a humorous slant to the 'two Nations' theme.
Department of Art, POS 230

> their happiness in fighting,
> Or that they died with a song on their lips,
> Or that we shall use the old familiar phrases
> With which your paid servants please you in the Press:
> But we are poets,
> And shall tell the truth.[14]

It must be remembered, however, that the work of Sassoon, Graves and Sitwell was not characteristic of most of the poetry available to the public during the war years, and that much of the great poetry we associate with the First World War, the work of Wilfred Owen, Isaac Rosenberg, Edmund Blunden, Herbert Read and David Jones, was not published, nor often written, until after the Armistice. In an age before Modernism had set the poet apart from the public, and writers were depended upon as commentators on issues of national importance, the poets were, by and large, firmly behind the Government.

The anthologies of poetry published during the war illustrate the general poetic climate on the home front. *Pro Patria: A Book of Patriotic Verse*, published in 1915, which reprinted existing patriotic verse as well as new poems by the 'grand old men', and *The Muse in Arms*, published in 1917, composed entirely of (uncontroversial) work by soldiers, show some development in realism, but only enough to increase respect for the 'fighting men'. Not until July 1918 did an anthology appear suggesting that not all writers shared the commitment to war. Bertram Lloyd's *Poems Written During the Great War* contained pieces by Sassoon, Sitwell, Margaret Sackville and Wilfred Gibson, as well as translations of German poems. Even more remarkable was his 1919 anthology *The Paths of Glory*. In the introduction to the later anthology Lloyd identifies the principal confusion of First World War poetry, which was 'to curse the horror and banefulness of war, and yet to be constantly idealising it (implicitly at least), and lauding its ennobling influence, and the courage and heroism it invokes.'[15]

Of the newspapers and periodicals, only Harold Massingham's *The Nation* regularly published provocative work of a high standard. Between its covers appeared Wilfred Gibson's *Battle* poems in 1914–15, protest poems by Margaret Sackville in 1916, some Sassoon, Graves and Sitwell in 1917, and three poems by Owen in 1918.[16] Most editors and publishers, however, chose verse that would bolster the nation's morale. W H Davies, the one-legged 'super-tramp', who depended upon periodicals for an income, wrote to Edward Marsh in 1914, 'I don't expect to have anything in the magazines, with the exception of a war-poem accepted by the Westminster – until all the trouble's over.'[17] Edward Thomas summarised the prevailing literary trend in 1914;

> The demand is for the crude, for what everybody is saying or thinking, or is ready to be saying or thinking. . . . It is the hour of the writer who picks up popular views or phrases, or coins them, and has the power to turn them into downright stanzas. . . . Most [poems] seem to me bombastic, hysterical, or senseless.[18]

A year later, in November 1915, Thomas wrote to Robert Frost, 'it is a pity Rupert Brooke is the only poet killed. I mean a pity for us readers.'[19] For slim volumes by subalterns were now flooding the market, and works by 'fallen heroes' were especially prized. Rupert Brooke's *1914 and Other Poems* was the most popular, running to twenty-five impressions by the end of the war, and memorial volumes also appeared for Julian Grenfell, W G Streets, R E Vernede, Francis Ledgwidge, W N Hodgson, Leslie Coulson, Charles Sorley and E V Tennant, to name but a few. Their popularity lay in that they symbolised the much advertised virtues of bravery, patriotism and sacrifice; virtues that the poets had not lived long enough to question. And the message they carried was an orthodox one: Julian Grenfell assured the civilian population that 'he is dead who will not fight; and who dies fighting has increase',[20] and W G Streets declared;

> Dauntless, we fling our lives into the van,
> Laughing at Death because within Youth's breast
> Flame lambent fires of Freedom.
> ('Youth's Consecration')[21]

Even a poet like R E Vernede, who lived long enough to see the true nature of the war, excluded this realisation from his poetry in case it weakened civilian morale or caused pointless distress. He wrote to his wife in February 1916, that 'anyone who hereafter shows a tendency towards exalting war ought to be drowned straight away by his country';[22] but his poetry continued to do just that. With such self-censorship on the part of the poets themselves, it is not surprising that the public accepted and supported the official attitude to the war.

In *The Generation of 1914*, Robert Wohl rejects as a myth the theory that the soldiers of the First World War were a generation of innocent youth led to the slaughter by an older and more cynical generation;

> . . . the representations of the war that flourished on the home front could not have survived the generation of returning combatants if they had not corresponded in some way to the experiences and feelings of many soldiers – or, to be more accurate, of many officers and war correspondents who interpreted the war to the English public.[23]

But Wohl fails to give full consideration to the confusion of sentiments evident in the responses of the returning soldiers. Further, he seriously underestimates the effectiveness of the official voice, which sought to capitalise on this confusion by orchestrating a unified approach on all matters pertaining to the war.

On 2 September 1914, a meeting took place at Wellington House in London, at the instigation of C F G Masterman, the newly appointed Head of the Government's War Propaganda Department. Around the table sat William Archer, Sir J M Barrie, Arnold Bennett, A C Benson, R H Benson, Robert Bridges, Hall Caine, G K Chesterton, Sir Arthur Conan Doyle, John Galsworthy, Thomas Hardy, Anthony Hope Hopkins, Maurice Hewlett, W J Locke, E V Lucas, J W Mackail, John Masefield, A E W Mason, Gilbert

Murray, Sir Henry Newbolt, Sir Gilbert Parker, Sir Owen Seaman, George Trevelyan, H G Wells, Israel Zangwill and assorted government officials. Rudyard Kipling and Sir Arthur Quiller Couch were unable to come but sent messages offering their services. It was an unprecedented, and since unrepeated, gathering of writers for an official purpose: being the assurance of a commitment to furthering the Allied cause, which they gave with the same zeal that the younger generation had displayed in entering the armed forces.[24] The example of these writers largely determined the tone of the literary work produced during the war years.

Many of the writers, including Arnold Bennett and H G Wells, actually joined the staff at Wellington House, and later recruits included John Buchan, Ian Hay and Hugh Walpole. The others wrote propaganda pieces at the request of the government, the first of which was Thomas Hardy's *Men Who March Away*;

> In our heart of hearts believing
> Victory crowns the just,
> And that braggarts must
> Surely bite the dust,
> Press we to the field ungrieving,
> In our heart of hearts believing
> Victory crowns the just.[25]

That this should come from the author of *The Dynasts* (1903–8), which had explored the pity of war well before 1914, indicates how the patriotic fervour of the time gripped even the most cautious of writers. With the exception of George Bernard Shaw, Bertrand Russell, D H Lawrence and a few lesser known authors, British writers of all persuasions wrote uncritically in support of the Allied cause.

The acquaintance of most writers with the material of their subject was slight, and this ignorance can in some way excuse their excesses. Conan Doyle, Rudyard Kipling and Arnold Bennett, however, had visited the front. Although under close supervision, they had seen enough to appreciate the reality of the situation, but nevertheless, considered it their duty to exclude this appreciation from the published accounts of their experiences.[26] The same can be said for those writers in uniform, employed to write accounts of the fighting: John Masefield whitewashed the failure at Gallipoli, and John Buchan turned the disaster of the Battle of the Somme into a glorious victory.[27]

A tradition of poets writing propaganda for the state can be traced back to Milton's service under Cromwell, Wordsworth's *Sonnets on Liberty* during the Napoleonic War, Tennyson's defence of the blunders of the Crimean War in 'The Charge of the Light Brigade', and Kipling's advertisements for the Imperial mission in India and during the Boer

War. No one, however, could have foreseen the willingness of poets to write on the behalf of the government in the First World War. Although propaganda work was for some writers the only work available, without doubt patriotic fervour was a major motivation, as well as being one way to assuage any guilt at being too old to fight. As William Watson wrote in 'Duty' in August 1914;

> Give gladly, you rich – 'tis no more than you owe
> For the weal of your Country, your wealth's overflow!
> Even I that am poor am performing my part;
> I am giving my brain, I am giving my heart.[28]

First published in the *Daily Chronicle* of 31 August 1914 and reprinted the next day due to public demand, 'Fall In!' quickly became one of the most popular war poems. Begbie relinquished copyright, as did Hardy with 'Men Who March Away', so anyone could use his lines; it was turned into a song by Sir Roderick Cowen and recorded five times, and distributed as the broadsheet, illustrated below, by the War Office. Department of Printed Books 59(=41). 2/3–8 74622

YOUR COUNTRY NEEDS YOU

FALL IN!
Reproduced from the London "Daily Chronicle."

What will you lack, sonny, what will you lack
  When the girls line up the street,
Shouting their love to the lads come back
  From the foe they rushed to beat?
Will you send a strangled cheer to the sky
  And grin till your cheeks are red?
But what will you lack when your mate goes by
  With a girl who cuts you dead?

Where will you look, sonny, where will you look
  When your children yet to be
Clamour to learn of the part you took
  In the War that kept men free?
Will you say it was naught to you if France
  Stood up to her foe or bunked?
But where will you look when they give the glance
  That tells you they know you funked?

How will you fare, sonny, how will you fare
  In the far-off winter night,
When you sit by the fire in an old man's chair
  And your neighbours talk of the fight?
Will you slink away, as it were from a blow,
  Your old head shamed and bent?
Or say—I was not with the first to go,
  But I went, thank God, I went?

Why do they call, sonny, why do they call
  For men who are brave and strong?
Is it naught to you if your country fall,
  And Right is smashed by Wrong?
Is it football still and the picture show,
  The pub and the betting odds,
When your brothers stand to the tyrant's blow
  And Britain's call is God's?
                          HAROLD BEGBIE.

ENLIST NOW

"FALL IN" has been set to music by Sir Frederic Cowen, and is sold at 1/- by Enoch & Sons, 14, Great Marlborough St., W. The profits of the sale are handed over to the Prince of Wales's Distress Fund.

Printed by United Newspapers, Ltd. 12, Salisbury Square, E.C.

It needs to be said, however, that poems like 'Duty' were not always taken as seriously as their authors intended. 'The Egoist' published its own comment in December 1914, referring no doubt, to such poets as William Watson, Alfred Austin and Henry Newbolt: 'Song in Wartime' by 'Herbert Blenheim';

> At the sound of the drum,
> Out of their dens they come, they come,
> The little poets we hoped were dumb,
> The little poets we thought were dead,
> The poets who certainly haven't been read,
> Since heaven knows when, they come, they come,
> At the sound of the drum, of the drum, of the drum.[29]

Although largely applauded on the home front, the poetry of most civilians invited cynicism and resentment from those who knew what the Western Front was really like. Some civilian poets, however, were extremely popular among the troops. John Oxenham's little khaki-covered books, designed to fit into a tunic pocket, sold in thousands. With an accent on suffering rather than heroism, he managed to avoid most of the pitfalls that beset civilian verse. As the war dragged on, soldiers became uneasy about the whole notion of heroism, and contemptuous of civilians who bandied such concepts about. Even the most patriotic of soldiers were not likely to appreciate effusions on the theme of sacrifice by high-minded poets writing comfortably at home. 'The Short Road to Heaven' by Katherine Tynan is characteristic of the genre;

> The long road is dusty and never a streamlet sings,
> The dust lies on the hedgerows and on the birdies' wings;
> The longer that you travel the wearier you are
> And the farther off is Heaven and the stars are far.
>
> But the wise lads, the dear lads, the pathway's dewy green,
> For the little Knights of Paradise of eighteen and nineteen;
> They run the road to Heaven, they are singing as they go,
> And the blood of their sacrifice has washed them white as snow.[30]

The idealisation of slaughter and disablement perhaps was inevitable, for in no other way could it be made bearable: martyrdom presupposes a worthy cause. Maurice Baring wrote to the mother of Julian Grenfell, after hearing that the son of a mutual friend had been killed; 'I am sorry for us, but not for him. For him it is a privilege and a prize beyond anything he can have dreamed before the war. To say it is a waste is to me like saying the frankincense, gold and myrrh of the Three Kings was a waste.'[31] Baring's sentiments sound rather less fine, however, from the pen of the 'Little Mother', published in *The Morning Post* in 1916;

> Our ears are not deaf to the cry that is ever ascending from the battlefield from men of flesh and blood whose indomitable courage is borne to us, so to speak, on every blast of the wind. We women pass on the human ammunition of 'only sons' to fill up the gaps, so that when the 'common soldier' looks back before going 'over the top' he may see the women of the British race at his heels, reliable, dependent, uncomplaining.[32]

Graves found it enough to quote the 'Little Mother's' letter as proof of civilian madness in the First World War, and for many soldiers, this sort of patriotic excess seemed to be most frequently enacted by women on the home front. Sassoon was moved to complain: 'Poor heroes! If only they would speak out . . . and ask their women why it thrills them to know that they, the dauntless warriors, have spilt the blood of Germans. Do not the women gloat secretly over the wounds of their lovers?'[33]; and he wrote in 'Glory of Women';

> You love us when we're heroes, home on leave,
> Or wounded in a mentionable place.[34]

Inevitably, women became identified in the minds of the soldiers with the prevailing civilian ethos. Although many women served with distinction, and were killed in action, the enduring images of women from the First World War are of the 'Little Mother', the recruiting chorus girls and the ladies handing out white feathers to men not in uniform. These were the women who became the particular focus of the soldier poets' attack on the home front.

Women were, without doubt, cynically exploited by the propagandists. In urging men to go and fight, they could only have earned the soldiers' scorn for their ignorance of what they were actually sending the soldiers to. And those soldiers who had enlisted to the strains of 'I'll make a man of you', very soon realised that the only thing they were likely to be made was a corpse. Some women, however, did embrace the cause with an appalling enthusiasm. What soldiers must have thought of the following can be imagined;

> They shot Flynn's eyes out. That was good.

Eyes that saw God are better blind.
(Katherine Tynan 'The Vision')[35]

No wonder Sassoon was prompted to write;

Does it matter? – losing your eyes? . . .
There's such splendid work for the blind;
And people will always be kind,
As you sit on the terraces remembering
And turning your face to the light.
('Does it matter?')[36]

The most famous of the women poets on the home front was Jessie Pope. Two drafts of Owen's poem 'Dulce et Decorum Est' were dedicated 'To Jessie Pope' and 'To a certain Poetess', and an extract from 'The Beau Ideal' should demonstrate why she deserved such a tribute;

The lad who troth with Rose would plight,
    Nor apprehend rejection
Must be in shabby khaki dight
    To compass her affection.
Who buys her an engagement ring
    And finds her kind and kissing,
Must have one member in a sling
    Or, preferably, missing.[37]

But women did not lack critics of their own sex. Both Margaret Sackville and Helen Hamilton condemned civilian warmongering, blaming women in particular;

Reap we with pride the harvest! it was sown
By our own toil. Rejoice! it is our own.
This is the flesh we might have saved – our hands,
Our hands prepared these blood-drenched,
dreadful lands.
What shall we plead? That we were deaf and
blind?
We mothers and we murderers of mankind.
(Margaret Sackville 'Nostra Culpa')[38]

When the last man has gone.
And if and when that dark day dawns,
You'll join up first, of course,
Without waiting to be fetched.
But in the meantime,
Do hold your tongue!
You shame us women.
Can't you see it isn't decent,
To flout and goad men into doing,
What is not asked of you?

(Helen Hamilton 'The Jingo-women')[39]

Other women, like Maud Anna Bell and Sybil Bristowe,[40] conscious of their isolation in Britain, sought to bridge the gap between themselves and the soldiers in France by imaginative, if wholly inadequate, attempts to portray trench life. Those women, like Vera Brittain, who served in theatres of war and saw the immediate results of fighting as VAD nurses, grew to feel something of the soldiers' alienation from the home front themselves, and their poetry can be seen as honourable additions to the accounts of trench life by the soldier poets. But the most successful of the poems by women were those that drew upon the parallel, if not comparable, agony of millions of women who had to survive the deaths of lovers, brothers, husbands and fathers. Their pain led them to question the purpose of the whole endeavour, and although there were comforts in religion, patriotism and optimism, not all were convinced. Margaret Postgate wrote in 'Recruited – Poplar, March 1917';

They made a man of you this year, the sort
That England's rich and proud to own . . .
And so they went and killed you. That's their
way.[41]

Perhaps most effective of all in its finely controlled despair, is 'Easter Monday' by Eleanor Farjeon, about the death of Edward Thomas. The very admission of an ignorance of conditions in France imparts to the poem a power most elegaic poetry of this type lacks;

Then you spoke
Of the coming battle and said, 'This is the eve.
Good-bye. And may I have a letter soon.'
That Easter Monday was a day for praise,
It was such a lovely morning. In our garden
We sowed our earliest seeds, and in the orchard
The apple-bud was ripe. It was the eve.
There are three letters that you will not get.[42]

Margaret Sackville's poetry of protest was an extension of her political activities as a member of the Union of Democratic Control, formed as soon as the war began to bring an end to hostilities by non-violent means. Although this and other pacifist groups exerted little influence on the public consciousness, they did at least act as a focus for pacifist feelings during the war and as a reminder that not all writers fell under the influence of Wellington House. When not interned in camps for conscientious objectors, and thus effectively muzzled, pacifist poets were published in a few periodicals, and in book form through at least two pacifist publishers,

Stanley Unwin and C W Daniel.

Unshackled by a dependence on press reports and impervious to the call of patriotism, many pacifist poets displayed a historical and psychological perspective of the war that quite escaped other commentators. W N Ewer, in default of any comment from Hardy, in '1814–1914: On Reading the Dynasts', written in November 1914, recalls at the outbreak of war how Englishmen who fought against Napoleon for the liberties of Europe, later found their own liberties disregarded at Peterloo;

> Once again the statesmen bid the silent Englishmen
> Die for freedom's sake.
> Stern, stupid Englishmen, nowise disbelieving them,
> March cheerfully away,
> Heedless of the story of their fathers' 'War for Freedom'
> Under Pitt and Castlereagh.[43]

Even some patriotic poets came to express concern over the monster they had helped to create. J C Squire, who wrote in support of the Allied cause, was also aware of the ironies of patriotism;

> God heard the embattled nations sing and shout
> 'Gott strafe England!' and 'God save the King!'
> God this, God that, and God the other thing –
> 'Good God!' said God, 'I've got my work cut out.'
> ('The Dilemma')[44]

What is most obviously lacking in the poetry of civilians, whether patriotic or pacifist, is a sense of the reality of the trenches as experienced by the troops. The trench experience was the central experience of the First World War, and most of the great poetry of the period comes from the tension between the soldiers' expectations and the reality of that experience. Of the civilian poets who attempted to visualise conditions in France, the most successful was Wilfred Gibson, who was admired by such soldier poets as Ivor Gurney and Siegfried Sassoon;

> We ate our breakfast lying on our backs,
> Because the shells were screeching overhead.
> I bet a rasher to a loaf of bread
> That Hull United would beat Halifax
> When Jimmy Stainthorp played full-back instead
> Of Billy Bradford. Ginger raised his head
> And cursed, and took the bet; and dropt back dead.

> We ate our breakfasts lying on our backs,
> Because the shells were screeching overhead.
> ('Breakfast')[45]

Although he enlisted in 1917, Gibson never went to France, and 'Breakfast', published in October 1914, is a remarkable attempt at imaginative realism. As a Georgian his interest in realism is not surprising, and most of the successful soldier poets, like Gurney, Graves, Owen and Sassoon, at some stage considered themselves to be Georgians. Rupert Brooke was the first of the Georgian brotherhood to enlist and the first to die. At the outbreak of war, Georgian poetry had very quickly gone out of fashion, and it was not until the death of Brooke that the fortunes of the school revived. Brooke's vision of an England worth dying for restored to popularity poems about the countryside, and the longer the war lasted the more necessary were images of pastoral tranquillity as reminders of exactly what was being fought for. From being propagandists for the English countryside the Georgians became, by extension, propagandists for the Allied cause.

Lascelles Abercrombie, Walter de la Mare and John Drinkwater, none of whom served at the front, throughout the war wrote poetry that expressed their love for the English countryside;

> I love my land. No heart can know
> The patriot's mystery, until
> It aches as mine for woods ablow
> In Gloucestershire with daffodil,
> Or Bicester brakes that violets fill.
> (John Drinkwater 'The Patriot')[46]

The effect of the war on many of the Georgian poets was to encourage them to provide dreamy, escapist verse depicting an unchanging peaceful rural Arcadia, which eventually led them away from any interest in realism. According to Robert Graves, they finally succumbed to a surfeit of nightingales.[47] As a positive force in poetry, they barely survived the war.

Edward Thomas's poetry, which was all written after the outbreak of the war and before his departure for France in January 1917, presents a rather different picture of the English countryside. For Thomas even the landscape carries an awareness of the events on the other side of the English Channel. In 'Fifty Faggots' everything seems fragile and impermanent, including his own chances of survival;

> This Spring it is too late; the swift has come.
> 'Twas a hot day for carrying them up:
> Better they will never warm me, though they must

Light several Winters' fires. Before they are done
The war will have ended, many other things
Have ended, maybe, that I can no more
Foresee or more control than robin or wren.[48]

Thomas's response to the landscape is altogether less sentimental and more persuasive than those of his Georgian contemporaries. The intensity of his expression suggests a level of integration with the English countryside that communicates a wholly honourable and humane patriotism. Something of this relationship emerges in the poem 'Lob', where Thomas describes the sort of countryman with whom he identified: 'as English as this gate, these flowers, this mire', with a face 'by life and weather cut and coloured'. Throughout the centuries he has offered his life in defence of his land;

    Although he was seen dying at Waterloo,
    Hastings, Agincourt and Sedgemoor, too –
    Lives yet. He never will admit he is dead.[49]

Thomas felt he could do no less. Eleanor Farjeon recalled an incident that probably best explains Thomas's patriotism. When she asked him, 'Do you know what you're fighting for?', he bent down, picked up a handful of earth and, crumbling it between his fingers, replied, 'literally, for this.'[50]

When Thomas was commissioned in 1915 to compile a patriotic anthology of poetry and prose to be called *This England*, his choice fell to literature of 'indirect praise' rather than 'professed patriotic writing', the latter being usually bad.[51] The writers represented included Hardy, Chaucer, Cobbett, Shakespeare and Thomas himself. What may have seemed an assumption at the time, has proved to have been one of the wisest decisions of all. Of the poets under discussion, Thomas was one of the few to write about the war without sacrificing the traditional and all-important detachment and integrity of the writer. His most propagandist poem, 'This is no Case of Petty Right or Wrong', is a refutation of the facile patriotism of the time, and a testimony of commitment to his own artistic integrity;

    This is no case of petty right or wrong
    That politicians or philosophers
    Can judge. I hate not Germans, nor grow hot
    With love of Englishmen, to please newspapers.[52]

Bertrand Russell claimed in *Justice in War-Time*, published in 1916, that 'Allegiance to country has swept away allegiance to truth', and few authors and poets responded to his plea not to be used, either directly or indirectly, by the state for propaganda purposes.[53] Those that raised their voices in protest went largely unheard, or if too significant to be ignored, like Bertrand Russell and George Bernard Shaw, were harried and baited by the employees of Wellington House. All were drowned by the fierce wave of patriotism that swept Britain.

The combined efforts of the British writers who advocated the Allied cause were to create a propaganda myth which prevailed until the end of the war. Censorship ensured that little bad news would pass, but the writers exceeded mere complicity in the illusions created by the press and the Government, by manufacturing dubious moral benefits from the waste, squalor and bloodshed of the trenches. Enshrined in a language full of sonorous platitudes and romantic cliches, they spoke of gallant soldiers laying down their lives on the field of honour, of sacrifices not made in vain, of resolute and resourceful generals, and of the need for total victory over the barbarous and blood-thirsty Hun. The language distorted the sordid reality of the war, and prevented any real understanding of the issues at stake. When the war was over, the younger writers found that the old men of literature had so bankrupted the language that they had lost the trust of the public, and the authority of authorship had been seriously undermined. Never again were writers to be so influential in forming and changing public opinion, and the old rhetoric based on a widely held set of common values and aspirations had gone for good.

The Armistice and ensuing peace celebrations saw the revival of the spirit of 1914, with victory poems by the 'grand old men' in *The Times* and other newspapers. The soldier poets were simply glad it was over, as were the civilian poets of protest. One final poem, however, is worth quoting. Published in *The Nation* in October 1918, and the only known verse of the unknown Philip Johnstone, the poem confidently predicted the time when the scenes of so much death and destruction should become tourist sights for patriotic civilians, ensuring that the romantic distortions of the war were carried into the years of peace;

    As I was saying, all is as it was,
    This is an unknown officer,
    The tunic having lately rotted off.
    Please follow me – this way ... the path, sir,
    please,
    The ground which was secured at great expense
    The company keeps absolutely untouched,
    And in that dug-out (genuine) we provide
    Refreshments at a reasonable rate.
    You are requested not to leave about
    Paper, or ginger-beer bottles, or orange-peel,
    There are plenty waste-paper-baskets at the gate.
    ('High Wood')[54]

Notes

1. Siegfried Sassoon, *Counter-attack and other poems*, Heinemann, London, 1918, p 31.
2. Siegfried Sassoon, 'The Old Huntsman', *The Old Huntsman and other poems*, Heinemann, London, 1917, p 10.
3. An interesting comparison of civilian and trench journalism can be found in J M Winter, *The Great War and the British people*, Macmillan, London, 1985, pp 285–289.
4. Robert Graves, *Good-bye to All That*, Penguin, London, 1979, p 188.
5. See Cate Haste, *Keep the Home Fires Burning: Propaganda in the First World War*, Allen Lane, London, 1977, for an account of propaganda on the home front.
6. *Poems written during the Great War 1914-1918: an anthology*, edited by Bertram Lloyd, Allen & Unwin, London, 1918, pp 51–52.
7. Graves, *Goodbye*, op cit, p 205.
8. Sassoon, *Old Huntsman*, op cit, p 31.
9. Wilfred Owen, *War poems and others*, edited with an introduction and notes by Dominic Hibberd, Chatto & Windus, London, 1974, p 90.
10. Vivien de Sola Pinto, *Crisis in English poetry 1880–1940*, Arrow, London, 1963, p 161.
11. Gilbert Frankau, *The poetical works, Volume two: 1916-1920*, Chatto & Windus, London, 1923, p 35.
12. Ibid, p 191.
13. Ian Hay, *The First Hundred Thousand, being the unofficial chronicle of a unit of 'K(1)'*, Blackwood, Edinburgh, 1915, p vii.
14. *Poems*, Lloyd, p 71.
15. *The Paths of Glory: a collection of poetry written during the War 1914–1919*, edited by Bertram Lloyd, Allen & Unwin, London, 1919, p 6.
16. Graves recalled receiving a letter from Sassoon in April 1917 in which 'He had seen the last issue of *The Nation*, and commented what fun it was for us two to appear as a military duet in a pacifist organ.' *Good-bye*, p 210.
17. Quoted in Caroline Dakers, *The Countryside at War*, Constable, London, 1987, p 50.
18. Edward Thomas, 'War poets', *Poetry and Drama*, Vol II, no 8, 1914, pp 341–345.
19. Quoted in Dakers, op cit, p 14.
20. Julian Grenfell, 'Into Battle', *Up the line to death: the war poets 1914–1918*, an anthology selected and arranged by Brian Gardner, Methuen, London, 1964, p 34.
21. W G Streets, *The Undying Splendour*, Erskine Macdonald, London, 1917, p 9.
22. R E Vernede, *Letters to his wife*, Collins London, 1917, p 59.
23. Robert Wohl, *The Generation of 1914*, Weidenfeld and Nicolson, London, 1980, p 93.
24. For a fuller account of the activities of Wellington House see M L Sanders and Philip M Taylor, *British propaganda in the First World War, 1914-18*, Macmillan, London, 1982, and Peter Buitenhuis, *The Great War of words: British, American, and Canadian propaganda and fiction, 1914–1933*, University of British Columbia Press, Vancouver, 1987.
25. Gardner, op cit, p 7.
26. The published accounts were: Arnold Bennett, *Over there: war scenes on the Western Front*, Methuen, London, 1915; Rudyard Kipling, *France at War*, Macmillan, London, 1915; and Arthur Conan Doyle, *A Visit to Three Fronts*, Hodder & Stoughton, 1916.
27. The published accounts were: John Buchan, *The Battle of the Somme: first phase*, Nelson, London, 1916; and John Masefield, *Gallipoli*, Heinemann, London, 1916.
28. William Watson, *The Man who Saw: and other poems arising out of the war*, John Murray, London, 1917, p 80.
29. Quoted in Dakers, op cit, p 50.
30. Katherine Tynan, *Herb O'Grace: poems in war-time*, Sidgwick & Jackson, London, 1915, pp 18–19.
31. Quoted in Nicholas Morley, *Julian Grenfell*, Weidenfield and Nicolson, London, 1976, p 116.
32. Graves, op cit, p 189.
33. Siegfried Sassoon, *Diaries 1915–1918*, edited and introduced by Rupert Hart-Davis, Faber, London, 1983, p 175.
34. Sassoon, *Counter-attack*, op cit, p 33.
35. *Poems of the Great War: an anthology*, edited by Dominic Hibberd and John Onions, Macmillan, London, 1986, p 20.
36. Sassoon, *Counter-attack*, op cit, p 29.
37. Jessie Pope, *More war poems*, Grant Richards, London, 1915, p 43.
38. Lady Margaret Sackville, *The Pageant of War*, Simpkin, Marshall, Kent & Co, London, 1916, p 39.
39. Helen Hamilton, *Napoo! a book of Bêtes-Noires*, Blackwell, Oxford, 1918, p 92.
40. See *Scars upon my Heart* edited by Catherine Reilly, for a selection of the more sensitive women's poetry from the First World War.
41. Margaret Postgate, *Poems*, The Herald, London, 1918, p 35.
42. Eleanor Farjeon, *First and Second Love: Sonnets*, Michael Joseph, London, 1947, p 56.
43. Lloyd, *Poems*, p 33.
44. Hibberd, *Great War*, op cit, p 115.
45. Wilfred Wilson Gibson, *Battle*, Elkin Matthews, London, 1915, p 10.
46. John Drinkwater, *Loyalties*, Sidgwick & Jackson, London, 1919, p 52.
47. See Robert Graves, *A Survey of Modernist poetry*, Heinemann, London, 1927, for a fuller discussion of the decline of Georgian verse.
48. Edward Thomas, *Collected poems*, Faber, London, 1936, p 52.
49. Ibid, pp 60–65.
50. Eleanor Farjeon, *Edward Thomas: the last four years*, Oxford University Press, London, 1958, p 154.
51. Edward Thomas, *This England: an anthology from her writers*, Oxford University Press, London, 1915, p 7.
52. Thomas, *Poems*, op cit, p 154.
53. Bertrand Russell, *Justice in war-time*, Allen and Unwin, London, 1916, p 1.
54. Gardner, op cit, p 157.

Further Reading

Buitenhuis, Peter, *The Great War of Words: British, American and Canadian propaganda and fiction, 1914–1933*, University of British Columbia Press, Vancouver, 1987.
Dakers, Caroline, *The Countryside at War*, Constable, London, 1987.
Motion, Andrew, *The poetry of Edward Thomas*, Routledge & Kegan Paul, London, 1980.
Wohl, Robert, *The Generation of 1914*, Weidenfeld and Nicolson, London, 1980.
Poems of the Great War: an anthology, edited by Dominic Hibberd and John Onions, Macmillan, London, 1986.
Scars upon my heart: women's poetry and verse of the First World War, edited and introduced by Catherine Reilly, with a preface by Judith Kazantis, Virago, London, 1981.

'I Know What it is to Kill a Pig; I Won't Kill a Man': The Museum's Oral History Programme on Conscientious Objectors of the First World War

Margaret Brooks

Margaret Brooks joined the Museum as a research assistant in the Department of Sound Records in 1973, and has been Keeper of the Department since 1983.

'The essence of freedom, as we know it and value it, is that the individuals of a nation shall be able to think what they believe to be true and to do what they believe to be right'
The Times 21 November 1914.

'Recruiting for the Regular Army is lacking in enthusiasm in London and the provinces'
Daily Telegraph 25 November 1914.

Before the First World War there had never been a statutory universal military service in Britain. General public opinion was by no means pacifist, but it was widely felt across all sections of society that quality rather than quantity was what counted and that there was no positive benefit in compulsory service. The National Service League, founded after the Boer War in 1902 had acted as focus for conscription demands on the grounds of discipline, fitness and efficiency. The part-time Territorial Force was formed in 1908 both for home defence and to give the regular Army greater capacity at short notice. During the later Edwardian period, debate about and pressure for conscription grew in the press and later in Parliament where five unsuccessful conscription bills were defeated before 1914. Herbert Asquith, Prime Minister since 1908, rejected conscription as did his Liberal party. The Conservatives were divided on the matter, but within their ranks there was increasing support for conscription and military expenditure in response to increasing German war production and commercial competition. The new Parliamentary Labour Party was also split with some believing – as did many Continental socialists – that universal military service was more democratic and that there was merit and advantage in a broadly-based citizens' army. Others held conscription to be a tool of imperialism. The Independent Labour Party had consistently taken a stand against conscription, considering it to be militaristic and anti-libertarian.

Asquith's government formed a coalition with the Conservatives in May 1915. This change in political complexion increased the prospects of conscription, particularly as the public was now more aware of the likely lengthy duration of the war. The thin edge of the wedge for conscription was the National Registration Act of summer 1915 under which everyone in Britain between the ages of 18 and 65 was required to register and which showed the government that nearly two million men of an age and fitness to qualify for military service had not enlisted. The Cabinet committee on war expenditure had recommended a major increase in the number of divisions in the field but the recruitment boom of August–September 1914 was short-lived and over the previous twelve months enlistments had fallen from 300,000 to 80,000 new servicemen per month with casualties running at some 30% of those in the armed forces.[1] With more men in the armed forces the government also came to see conscription as a means of regulating labour supply in key categories.

Another measure which helped to pave the way for conscription was the Defence of the Realm Act, actually a series of legislative measures the first of which was passed without debate by the House of Commons three days after the declaration of war. DORA gave the police and military broad powers to prevent 'assistance to the enemy' including acting 'in a manner prejudicial to public safety' such as possession of suspicious publications, and allowed civilians to be tried and sentenced by courts martial. This infringement or suspension of civil liberties was considered acceptable if not essential in wartime.

Lord Derby's recruiting scheme, an attempt in the autumn of 1915 to stave off conscription by means of classification of all eligible men into categories of availability, failed to produce sufficient volunteers and Asquith presented the first Military Service Bill, which became law in January 1916. From the following March military service was imposed on all single men in England, Scotland and Wales aged 18 to 41 except those who were in jobs essential to the war, the sole support of dependents, medically unfit or 'those who could show a conscientious objection'. This later clause, though not unique, was a significant British response and a very important one as it defused opposition to conscription. Further acts included married men, tightened occupational exemptions and raised the age limit to 50. Whether or not men attended their recruiting offices they were 'deemed to have enlisted'.

Ultimately there were approximately 16,000 British men on record as conscientious objectors to armed service in the First World War. Naturally this figure does not include men who may have had anti-war sentiments, but who were unfit, were in reserved occupations or who joined the forces anyway. Of a total wartime enlistment of nearly six million men, this is clearly not a large number. But the impact of these men on public opinion and on future governments was to be profound.

The Imperial War Museum's Department of Sound Records has been keen from its establishment in 1972 to include in its oral history programme examples not only of experiences at various levels of active participation in all theatres of our wars but also the broader effects of these conflicts on our society. In 1973 the Department began to record reminiscences of people involved in the anti-war movement of 1914–1918. An initial approach was made to the Society of Friends and the Fellowship of Reconciliation – both active during the period in question – and the Peace Pledge Union and War Resisters' International, neither of which was established during the First World War, but which succeeded other similar organisations and included First World War 'veterans' among their members.

There was no point in trying to produce a statistical sample of the anti-war movement some sixty years after the event, had we even wished to do so. But care was taken to include people representing the very different religious, political, moral and philosophical objections raised to armed service during the First World War. The interviews ranged in length from one to seven hours, and were normally recorded in more than one session. The approach adopted for each interview was flexible, but we were particularly interested in the following topics: the influences, beliefs, role and activities of various groups, recollections about personalities who were prominent in the movement, the formalities of registration and tribunals, the experience in prison or alternative service, the treatment of COs by their relatives and the public, and the aftermath of the war. The Department's emphasis was always on individual personal experience rather than an historical overview.

The people interviewed ranged in age, in 1916, from 17 to 42 and at that time held various positions including: insurance clerk, civil servant, newspaper editor, piano tuner, Church of Scotland clergyman, land agent, farmer, postal clerk, tailor, accountant, YMCA staff, shop assistant, bank clerk, composer, publisher, secretary, ambulance driver, trade union organiser, university student, teacher and student teacher.

Though a wide range of society is represented it appears from the above that conscientious objectors were likely to have more formal education than average. Undoubtedly an educated and articulate person would have found it easier to gain conscientious objector status. Such a person may also have been more likely to come forward to participate in a national oral history programme and people in the semi-skilled/unskilled socio-economic groups would have been likely to have died younger and not to be available for recording some sixty years on. Our contributors have reminisced about other conscientious objectors who were a miner and a building labourer, for example. Oral history can give a voice to the (for whatever reason) voiceless and most of the Department's informants had not published or recorded their experiences. They agreed to put their personal stories on record for the benefit of future students of the period, and because in some cases they still felt set apart and affected by their experiences.

Britain's public response to the outbreak of the First World War was so unanimous that society tended to view men who would not fight – and the men and women who supported them – as a distinct and separate species, virtually as enemy aliens. One of our informants said, referring to the outbreak of war: 'I had no hope of surviving the war. I remember going back to Glasgow with this in mind: that all those who wouldn't fight would be shot.'[2] And another, at the time aged eighteen, was told by Geoffrey Fisher, the headmaster of his school and later Archbishop of Canterbury: 'I don't suppose there are two hundred people in the whole country who think as you do. You're one of the loneliest people I've ever known.'[3]

None of the conscientious objectors we recorded was given a white feather for cowardice – a phenomenon that seems to have been less widespread in practice than in the popular imagination. But to become a conscientious objector in 1916 was a difficult decision, apparently involving a rejection of the whole of conventional society and everything it stood for. Wartime propaganda made it all too plain that a person was either *with* the national effort or against it and if against it, by implication either not concerned with the sacrifices of others or actually undermining their willingness to serve. The conscientious objector was trapped psychologically: he felt guilty if he shared the soldiers' ordeal, and guilty if he did not.

Broadly speaking there were four reasons why men objected to armed service in the First World War. The most common grounds were religious or political ones and this is reflected in the people whom we recorded. Pacifism was a time-honoured tenet of the Society of Friends (Quakers) though some eligible Quaker men did enlist. Some Christian fundamentalists and others simply took the Bible at its word: Thou shall not kill. Other members of both the non-conformist and established churches rejected the Christ in khaki concept rather than following specific dogma.

The next largest group of COs were political activists of the left who saw an imperialist war and an example of the age-old theory – that the ruling classes make wars which the workers must fight. The left was split over the war with the Parliamentary Labour Party generally supporting the war and the government. The radical left who opposed the war were not necessarily pacifists; they reserved the right to go to the barricades for a cause in which they believed. Some First World War conscientious objectors later fought in or supported the Spanish Civil War, for instance. Many of the middle class religious pacifist COs were greatly influenced by the radical socialists they met at anti-war meetings or in prison and many were later to join the Independent Labour Party.

Thirdly, there were what might be termed humanists who felt it wrong to kill, although not on religious grounds. For instance, one former naval rating, who had gone to work as a butcher, became a conscientious objector because, he said, 'I know what it is to kill a pig; I won't kill a man'.[4] Another man explained his ethics:

The very things which you try to accomplish by the use of force you bring onto yourself because you must have something even worse or more powerful in order to combat the evil which you are trying to overcome. The result is that at the end of the period you've got not only the very thing which you are trying to oppose but you've got something worse. You cannot overcome evil with evil.[5]

The fourth group were those who objected to the government ordering their lives, particularly as the war had nothing to do with them personally; some might have fought if the United Kingdom had been directly threatened. Some were anarchists, some were artists or craftsmen. Amongst this group were men who simply disappeared rather than serve in the armed forces. The police stopped likely-looking men in the streets seeking both deserting soldiers and men who had not registered at all. The three eligible men in a London anarchist commune, for example, lost themselves in the Scottish mountains rather than be conscripted. One then went abroad, but the others were discovered by the police and arrested. Their sentence was 21 months imprisonment.[6] Most First World War COs, however, preferred to make a positive statement of their views than to slip away.

The prescribed procedure for a conscientious objector was to apply to his local tribunal for exemption from military service. The tribunals of local worthies had already been set up to decide on exemptions under the unsuccessful Derby Scheme, so they were available, when actual conscription came in, to assess candidates' conviction and sincerity. The tribunals were poorly briefed for their difficult task and in many cases merely used the hearings to state their own views. One of our informants was asked his age. On hearing that he was eighteen the tribunal chairman said, 'Oh in that case you're not old enough to have a conscience. Case dismissed.' The CO was sent to prison. Another witnessed a tribunal which used a similar line of questioning to that which Lytton Strachey made famous:

[The chairman] said the Germans were doing such bad things that they ought to be stopped by any means. He said, 'What do you think you would do if it was a case of a German officer molesting your wife and taking her away?' And the CO said, 'He couldn't do it, Sir'. 'Of course he could.' And the CO said, 'He could not do this.' And they went on like this for two or three times until the CO got the chairman to say, 'Well why couldn't he do it?' 'An English officer has already done it.'[7]

At the tribunal's discretion the exemption might be absolute or from combatant service only or conditional on undertaking work of national importance. COs were frequently rejected by the local tribunal or offered an unacceptable position. They could then go before an appeals tribunal and if they were refused again could appeal to the Central Tribunal in London, at this tribunal's discretion. In practice, having been rejected on appeal, a conscientious objector was a soldier absent without leave and, as such, subject to arrest. He was taken to the camp or barracks of the regiment of which he was deemed to be a member and put in the guardroom. A problem for the CO was where to draw the line in his stance and whether there was a difference in principle between combatant and non-combatant service:

> We went down [to the regiment at Newhaven], my friend and I, taking the absolutist point of view. We said 'No' and that's that. Well now when we got down there there was a man I remember who did his best, one of the NCC [Non Combatant Corps] people – he'd been presumably through the tribunal and so on – to persuade us to carry on. He said 'Oh but this is all right, you're not killing, you're non-combatant'. And we said 'No' and we went off for the first sentence. When we came back he himself was in the guardroom for refusing because he was a Seventh Day Adventist and they'd asked him to do some work on a Saturday and he'd refused, so that was that. But then another chap there was quite prepared to carry on and was trying to persuade him to carry on and this was ludicrous. And the next time we got out this other chap was in the guardroom because he'd refused to load munitions. I mean it was easy for us. We'd said 'No' to this because we on principle are not prepared to accept anything. These people had to think it out every time.[8]

A conscientious objector might be with 'his' regiment for a few days or a few weeks. It depended upon how unwilling he was to obey any orders and how much his commanding officer wanted to be rid of him. Sooner or later he would disobey an order and be tried by court martial, following which he would be sentenced to a prison term. However, thirty-four conscientious objectors were actually taken with their regiments to France where one could be shot for refusal to obey a military order.

> In its most extreme form [of punishment for disobedience] a man can be tied up to a gun-carriage, which isn't at all a pleasant thing, but normally he's sent to what is known as a field punishment barracks, and there the prisoners are tied up for three nights out of four. They're tied up maybe to a fence, or to ropes, with their arms extended, and their feet tied together, or they may be tied back to back. It varies in form; and that's done for two hours. But finally we had the second court martial, and the whole business was: each of the four of us, it was all gone through, all read and taken down in longhand. Each took about a day, these court martials, and it must have been very annoying to the base commandant who had to come down from his office in each case to give evidence. I think the poor, wretched man must have been thoroughly fed up with this business. Anyway, after a few more days, we were taken out to the parade ground. There was a big concourse of men, mostly of the Non-Combatant corps and the labour battalions, lined up in an immense square. We were taken to one side of it, and then under escort taken out one by one to the middle of the square. I was the first of them. An officer in charge of the proceedings read out the various crimes and misdemeanours; refusing to obey a lawful command, disobedience at Boulogne and so on and so forth, and then: 'The sentence of the court is to suffer death by being shot.' Then there was a suitable pause. And one thought, 'Well, that's that.' Now the second thing: 'Confirmed by the Commander in Chief'. That's double-sealed it now. Then another long pause, 'But subsequently commuted to penal servitude for ten years.' And that was that. And the thing that interested me and the others particularly was that penal servitude meant your return to England, and would get us into the hands of the civil authorities at a civil prison. You see as long as we were in the hands of the military authorities we were subject to military punishments. We could only go on offending.[9]

They were returned to British prisons and work camps. Of the 16,000 COs over one-third went to prison at least once and 1500 absolutists were imprisoned virtually for the duration. The initial standard sentence for COs was 112 days third division hard labour, the most severe level of prison sentence at that time under English law. This began with one month in solitary confinement on bread and water and meant arduous, boring manual jobs like stone-breaking, mailbag sewing by hand and picking oakum. This length of sentence

Left, a Conscientious Objectors' stonebreaking crew at Dyce near Aberdeen in the summer of 1916, Q 103669 and right, a CO's prison cell, probably at Wormwood Scrubs. SR398

actually came to about three months with good conduct remission. When he was freed after serving this sentence the conscientious objector was immediately again arrested as a deserter, court-martialled once more and returned to prison – the 'Cat and Mouse' treatment previously used on the Suffragettes. As the war went on the sentences handed down to Conscientious Objectors were increased – up to two years' hard labour. A sentence of penal servitude could be imposed for any number of years, but it was accepted by the courts that a greater duration of hard labour than two years carried a serious risk to health or sanity.

At first, Conscientious Objectors were sentenced to military prisons because they were, after all, considered to be soldiers. Of course if the CO didn't feel able to obey military orders at the barracks he wouldn't be likely to feel able to obey military orders in prison and he would bring even greater and longer punishment upon himself. It was a minor triumph for the anti-conscription movement when a mid-1916 Army order ruled that Conscientious Objectors who had been court martialled were henceforth to be sent to civil prisons – where there was plenty of room because the prisons were without a lot of their usual clientele who were in the armed forces. When Harold Bing was in Winchester Prison, there was one wing for ordinary convicts, one for women and two for conscientious objectors:

> I was in a cell by myself the whole time. The cell was about six feet by thirteen feet with one small window above one's head so that you couldn't see out of it except by standing on your stool – for which of course you might be punished if you

were found doing it. In the door there was a little spy-hole with a cover on the outside so that the warder could come along and open the spy-hole and spy on you at any time to see what you were up to. So that you had the sense of being watched the whole time which gave you a very uncomfortable feeling at first until in time you grew indifferent to it.[10]

These conditions were the same as those for ordinary criminal prisoners of the time. The daily menu was: breakfast – skilly (watery porridge) and bread; mid-day dinner – meat or savoury, vegetable and bread, on a seven-day rotation; tea – skilly and bread; evening – cocoa. Conscientious objectors succeeded in getting the prisons to offer a vegetarian diet. Vegetarianism was common and has an obvious affinity particularly with humanitarian pacifism. The conscientious objector prisoners were allowed a very limited number of censored letters (though one of our informants said 'filling the notepaper was quite an art': there was nothing to say after months or years in prison). They had no calendars, no newspapers, few visits – and those through a grille. They were limited to a few books, not likely to be of high literary quality, from the prison library at infrequent intervals. After a while the COs were able to have books sent in, with the provision that they donate them to the prison library when they'd finished with them. So later CO prisoners were impressed to find prison libraries stocked with titles by William Morris, Sidney and Beatrice Webb and the like. Life was circumscribed to levels which would have been amusing if they were not so degrading. Harold Bing recalled the following exchange:

'I'd like a toothbrush'.

'Oh you'll have to put yourself down sick.'

'But I'm not sick.'

'Yes but unless you're put down sick you can't see a doctor and if you don't see the doctor you can't get a toothbrush.'

So I put myself down sick which meant I lost my exercise. Then when they came to open the cell to go to see the doctor: 'take your pint pot'. I said, 'What for?'

'That's for your medicine.'

'I don't want any medicine, I'm going to ask for a toothbrush.'

'You've got to take your pint pot if you see the doctor.'[11]

Universally severe physical brutality to Conscientious Objectors seems to be a First World War myth. Certainly several of our informants experienced or witnessed very harsh treatment and in all seventy-three COs died as a result of physical abuse.[12] But the most likely physical damage were weakened eyesight and lungs and the development of rheumatism. For many COs the pressures and hardships strengthened their resolve. The primary punishment, in most cases the most severe, was psychological rather than physical. The fortunate COs were those who could devise ways to cope with loneliness, doubt, depression and loss of the ability to concentrate, for instance with mental exercise. One of our informants, a musician, played an imaginary piano on his knees and even did some composition of which he gave us a sample.[13] Some of our informants practised Esperanto; many recited poetry from memory; several went on long, imaginary, remembered walks. One man held races on the floor between bits of cobbler's wax. And one man gained comfort from talking to the spiders on his wall and the bolts on his door, as they too were forced to be there.

Some conscientious objectors coped best by taking a more active role and challenging the situation in which they found themselves. This could be clandestine activity:

One had no writing facility – the only writing facility in a cell was a slate and the slate pencil and therefore if you filled your slate you had to rub it all out again. There was no writing material except periodically when you were allowed temporarily to have the notepaper in your cell and a pen and ink to write your monthly or fortnightly letter. But here again a little ingenuity was used and some prisoners managed to make

little inkwells by taking a block of cobbler's wax – which was used for waxing the thread for making mail bags – making a hole in it, sinking a thimble into the wax and then covering it up with another piece of wax. So that what appeared to be a block of wax was in fact a block of wax with a lid. And that thimble you filled with ink when you had your fortnightly or monthly ink for writing your letter. With ink pots of that kind there was produced in Winchester prison a periodical called the *Winchester Whisperer*.

I used as a pen a needle writing with the hollow end – dipping the hollow end into the ink. This meant of course one had to be always dipping the needle into the ink for almost every word. But it did produce thin writing so that you could get a good deal on one small sheet of toilet paper. It was written on the small brown sheets of toilet paper with which we were supplied – different people writing little essays or poems or humorous remarks, sometimes little cartoons or sketches. And all these bits of paper were passed surreptitiously from hand to hand and reached the editor who bound them together with a bit of mail bag canvas used for repairing – bit of old canvas – for a cover and this issue of the *Winchester Whisperer* was then again passed round secretly hidden under people's waistcoats or up their sleeves. And as it happened, despite many searches, no copy of that *Winchester Whisperer* was ever captured by the warders, though I think some of them suspected its existence. Most prisons where there were COs managed to do something similar. Canterbury Prison ran a little surreptitious magazine called the *Canterbury Clinker* and others with, again, similar names in other prisons.[14]

Or the challenge could be open resistance as described by Fenner Brockway:

We found the prison system was absolutely inhuman and denying human rights. As I've said, we were not even allowed to speak to each other. Of course we did but we always had the sense of doing something which was prohibited and which if we were found doing it would lead to punishment – bread and water, solitary confinement. And the point arose when many of us thought that it was wrong to accept this absolutely inhuman system. For example, we had a heating

During the war COs' supporters produced a number of postcards; some sentimental, some humorous . . .'. Q102926 and Q102928

pipe going right through our cells – going up to the next floor. We had a complete telephone system. We learned the Morse code in reverse and by tapping on the pipe we had a prisoner at the end acted as a kind of switchboard; he could actually put our message through on the pipe to the floor above. I played chess this way with a boy in the next cell. We only had a slate and a slate pencil but we could rub out the moves and a whole game would take a week.

But a point came when many of us felt that it was undignified and humiliating to accept the system itself and we decided openly to resist it. For ten glorious days sixty of us ran our own hall in prison. Speaking openly on the exercise ground instead of marching five steps behind each other and not saying a word – round and round. We took arms, we played games, we organised concerts every night. We were shut in our cells but we had lots of Welsh boys who could sing beautifully – they would sing at the window and every-

one down the side would hear. But the effect became disastrous in Walton Prison, Liverpool, because not only did our own boys hear but the ordinary prisoners heard as well. And so the five leaders were isolated and then we were transferred to other prisons. I was transferred to Lincoln Prison. I had eight months solitary confinement at Lincoln Prison. Three months bread and water treatment until the doctor wouldn't allow more. And yet one had an extraordinary sense of personal freedom which I can't describe.[15]

Work strikes and hunger strikes were also held by COs including Clifford Allen (Lord Allen of Hurtwood) chairman of the No-Conscription Fellowship and Sir Francis Meynell. People like those quoted above managed; some didn't. One informant felt permanently defiled by his prison experience: 'Every day I had to apologise to my own body and say I'm so sorry to have brought you to this'.[16] Some men couldn't take it:

There was a CO in prison. He was a man who had kept to himself and I should think he had a rather obsessive mind. I begged of the warders that that chap needed looking after; you must pity him. Still, it had the best of him. And he had gone mad and started shouting in his cell. The warders tried to get in but he had put his table against the door and the warders banged and shouted at him and couldn't get in. Ultimately when they got in their anger was so violent . . .

I couldn't meet his wife and tell her that things would be all right because I didn't believe that things would be all right. I never cheered them with false hopes because I had no hope at all, ever, at that place. I didn't see the war ending at all. I thought it had come as a way of life; it seemed like it the way people were accepting war.[17]

Whilst they were in prison the conscientious objectors were offered so-called 'work of national importance' in a scheme put forward by the Home Office. This work took place in prisons empty of their usual inhabitants during wartime and in special camps. It was generally agriculture, forestry or unskilled manual labour. Walter Griffin, imprisoned at Dartmoor Prison calculated that it cost three times more to produce food by Home Office COs at Dartmoor than to buy it on the open market.[18] But 'useful work' was a useful lie to induce many conscientious objectors to co-operate. Whether they were in prison or not, conscientious objectors – and their families – did have a common experience in many respects in the pressures they felt from society.

There was a bit of a riot when we arrived there and a number of the fellows were smothered with mud and that sort of thing. I was in the middle of it but I didn't get anything at all; they must've thought I was the boss. Of course they'd heard about COs and knew we were COs and they were going to take it out on us. You see, when we went down as individuals the majority of them didn't know who we were. It was just when we arrived as a crowd on that one train. (Brockenhurst, Hants)[19]

I remember two or three of the COs at Princetown going up to the church for communion service and being stoned away, with the parson standing on a flat tombstone – I won't say actually cheering them on but at any rate encouraging. (Dartmoor, Devon)[20]

I wouldn't like to say it was the attitude of the church but the attitude of the minister was that he did his best to separate my fiancée and me. We were both of us workers in the church. The minister used to make a practice of going to the door and shaking hands with people as they went out and when he saw me he refused to shake hands. (Watford, Herts)[21]

My father was a very quiet and humble and scholarly sort of man and I'm sure he was a pacifist at heart but he never was outspoken. I think I brought upon him without knowing it a good deal of unpopularity because I was away but it was known that I was a conchie and that was something that was very unpopular, the last word in disgrace. (Blackford, Perthshire)[22]

It had a very bad effect on my mother. She came from a very united family and as soon as they realised that my brother wasn't going to fight for his country they just cut us dead completely even after the war was over. They wouldn't have anything to do with us at all, a clean cut but it never healed. And they didn't even come to her funeral. (Croydon, Surrey)[23]

Women were not conscripted during the First World War, but many did have roles in the anti-war movement. They were elected to 'shadow' positions in the No-Conscription Fellowship branches and other organisations so that when the president or secretary were arrested a woman was ready to carry on the work of each officer. Women also attended COs' tribunals taking notes on the proceedings, and kept track of the comings and goings of COs in guardrooms and magistrates' courts. They worked on the No-Conscription Fellowship newspaper *The Tribunal* and monitored press coverage of the COs in national and local newspapers. Some women smuggled messages to or from imprisoned COs. Some raised money for COs' dependents, who, of course, had no official support.

In spite of the fellowship of supporters and new-found friends in prisons and work camps, each conscientious objector was ultimately alone. The COs were not released and demobilised until about six months after the end of the war, in order to give most soldiers a head-start when looking for a job. They were also disenfranchised until 1926. With the passage of time most did find a way to fit back into society – some very successfully indeed. None of our informants suggested any bitterness, but they seem to remain, through their First World War experience, permanently set apart.

Notes

1. For statistics on enlistment, etc see Beckett, Ian and Simpson, Keith, *A Nation in Arms: a Social Study of the British Army in the First World War*, Manchester University Press, Manchester, 1985, and Hirst, Francis, *Consequences of the war to Great Britain*, OUP, London, 1984.

2. Department of Sound Records, Lewis Maclachlan interview, 1975, 565/6 Reel 1.

3. Department of Sound Records, Joseph Hoare interview, 1974, 556/5 Reel 1.

4. Department of Sound Records, Stephen Winsten interview, 1976, 784/18 Reel 10.

5. Department of Sound Records, Walter Griffin interview, 1977, 9790/8 Reel 2.

6. Department of Sound Records, Lilian Wolfe interview, 1974, 668/1 Reel 1.

7. Department of Sound Records, Walter Griffin interview, 1977, op cit, Reel 2.

8. Department of Sound Records, Philip Radley interview, 1974, 642/8 Reel 2.

9. Department of Sound Records, Howard Marten interview, 1974, 383/8 Reel 4.

10. Department of Sound Records, Harold Bing interview, 1974, 358/11 Reels 4–5.

11. Department of Sound Records, Harold Bing interview, 1974, op cit, Reel 9.

12. One of our informants was able to clarify a minor mystery: some historians – and COs – have wondered about the location of a wooden plaque carved in memory of the 73 who died. It was taken from London by Martha Steinitz, a German pacifist who was later persecuted by the Nazis, fled with it to Denmark and subsequently fled to Sweden whence it was returned to Britain by a former conscientious objector.

13. Department of Sound Records, Frank Merrick interview, 1974, 318/4 Reel 2.

14. Department of Sound Records, Harold Bing interview, 1974, op cit, Reel 6.

15. Department of Sound Records, Fenner Brockway interview, 1974, 476/4 Reel 2.

16. Department of Sound Records, Stephen Winsten interview, 1976, op cit, Reel 4.

17. Department of Sound Records, Stephen Winsten interview, 1976, op cit, Reel 11.

18. Department of Sound Records, Walter Griffin interview, 1977, op cit, Reel 2.

19. Department of Sound Records, Percy Leonard interview, 1974, 382/6 Reel 4.

20. Department of Sound Records, Joseph Hoare interview, 1974, 556/5 Reel 5.

21. Department of Sound Records, Percy Leonard interview, 1974, op cit, Reel 1.

22. Department of Sound Records, Lewis Maclachlan interview, 1975, op cit Reel 1.

23. Department of Sound Records, Dorothy Bing interview, 1974, 555/9 Reel 1.

Further Reading

General

Beckett, Ian and Simpson, Keith, *A Nation in Arms: a Social Study of the British Army in the First World War*, Manchester University Press, Manchester, 1985.

Boulton, David, *Objection overruled*, Macgibbon and Kee, London, 1976.

Ceadel, Martin, *Pacifism in Britain 1914–45*, Oxford University Press, Oxford, 1980.

Graham, John Winston, *Conscription and Conscience*, Allen & Unwin, London, 1922.

Hayes, Denis, *Conscription Conflict*, Sheppard Press, London, 1949.

Hirst, Francis W, *Consequences of the War to Great Britain*, OUP, London, 1934.

Marwick, Arthur, *The Deluge: British society and the First World War*, Bodley Head, London, 1965.

Rae, John, *Conscience and Politics*, Oxford University Press, Oxford, 1970.

Weller, Ken, *Don't be a soldier: the radical anti-war movement in North London*, Journeyman, London, 1985.

Simkins, Peter, *Kitchener's Army: the raising of Britain's New Armies 1914–1916*, Manchester University Press, 1988.

Personal experience accounts

Some individual conscientious objectors have published their memoirs and the Museum's Department of Documents has a growing collection of letters, diaries and other papers donated by First World War conscientious objectors and the men and women who supported them. These include, for example, an exchange of letters between P Wall and other members of the Aberdare branch of the No-Conscription Fellowship while he was in Wormwood Scrubs and Liverpool prisons, a diary kept by non-combatant W Knott in which he records his experiences and treatment and a large collection of papers and pamphlets relating to the pacifist movement collected by Reverend S J Haggis, himself a conscientious objector. In addition the archive contains a number of references in the writings of servicemen to their attitudes towards conscientious objectors which provide an interesting counterpoint to the views expressed by the COs themselves.

A printed catalogue summarising the Department of Sound Records' recordings of conscientious objectors is available from the Department for £3.60.

Change: The Indian Army before the Demise of our Indian Empire in 1947

Brian Montgomery

Colonel Brian Montgomery MBE was commissioned in the Royal Warwickshire Regiment before transferring to the Kings' African Rifles and the Indian Army. He served under Field Marshal Slim during the British Army's retreat from Burma. Later as commander of the 6th Battalion the Rajput Regiment he took the surrender of the 33rd Japanese Army in 1945. After the partition of India he joined the Diplomatic Service.

Colonel Montgomery is author of *A Field Marshal in the Family*, a personal view of his famous elder brother, Field Marshal Montgomery's, life, *Monty: a Life in Photographs*, *Shenton of Singapore*, the life of Sir Shenton Thomas, and a biography of his grandfather entitled *Monty's Grandfather*.

I was asked to choose whatever subject I liked for my Reflections, and I have therefore written what in part is autobiographical, and otherwise is based on my own research, including invaluable information in the Imperial War Museum.

I believe the majority of British regular officers who volunteered to join the Indian Army before 1939, generally did so for either family or financial reasons, or both. Certainly in my case it was both. My grandfather spent nearly forty years in the East India Company and Indian Civil Service, followed by another twenty years at the India Office; my father was born in India and so were his brothers, my uncles. I certainly joined for both reasons, for I badly needed the far higher rate of pay in the Indian Service. I believe I was finally convinced by an uncle, in the Royal Indian Marine, and another in the ICS who rose to become a Commissioner; both these painted a glowing picture of the strong financial advantages.

But it was not all 'family history or money-grabbing'. There were stronger reasons, deeper than those, which appeared from the moment you disembarked from the troop ship at 'The Gateway to India', at Bombay. There were some memory-pictures, as it were, which struck and remained. In my case it was the vast crowds of people in the bazaars and elsewhere. People needing work, or wanting to be servants, and who wanted to be *your* servant because they knew your father and mother – astonishing to a newcomer. I had already served in East Africa so I recognised the climate, but not the relative paucity of the white man.

My grandfather, who had risen to become Lt-Governor of the Punjab (1859–1865), responsible for an area as large as the whole of the existing Punjab, with the present North West Frontier Province and all Baluchistan, had ruled this vast region with far less than 50 British administrators. These comparatively few white men had in a very short time seized control of this whole huge area and replaced the already crumbling power of, first, the Maratha Empire, followed by the even greater (Muslim) power of the Mughals. It is well worth taking a brief look at the immense achievements of our British ancestors, both economic and military, before and after the significant events of the Mutiny Years 1856–1859.

It is often assumed that our highly profitable ownership of the State Capital and Port of Bombay were originated by the efforts of the East India Company. But this is not so. It was the Portuguese to whom we owed this possession, not the Company. In 1662 King Charles II married Katharine of Braganza, daughter of the then King of Portugal. Fortunately Katharine brought with her, as her marriage dowry, all of Bombay, which had been in Portuguese possession since late in the fifteenth century but had not been developed. Charles II then gave Bombay to the East India Company on charter in 1668. Look at what then happened, and went on throughout the land.

Production of crops in all India and Pakistan is still very largely dependent on British irrigation, or that originated by Britain. This included construction of many thousands of miles of canals, which supply water to regions lacking rainfall and are served by the great railway systems. These, again British built, provide for the famine periods which occur periodically when the monsoons fail.

Production of coal, steel, petroleum, manganese, cotton, jute, and other textiles, are all British made industries; but I should mention by name some of the great soldiers and Governors-General who kept the peace and made the essential administrative regime proceed without hindrance, either internally or from outside.

Robert Clive's great triumph at Arcot against *inter alia* the French, turned this victory in our favour, and from that time British military and civil influence increased. Warren Hastings (1772–1785), and Lord Cornwallis overhauled the East India Company; Marquis Wellesley made our friendships with the Princes. Lord William Bentinck and Lord Dalhousie introduced railways, telegraphs, and cheap postal services. Then followed the Mutiny period, but all those I have named are pre-Mutiny yet seldom get the recognition they deserve.

Against that mixed background I do not apologise for provoking myself into a eulogy for our British ancestors in India, for any period including the two world wars. But I think it true to record that we kept the peace in India in spite of many distractions, some of which must be mentioned here.

All our history books, from the Victorian era onwards, have emphasised that the potential and hostile danger to British India was, and always would be, the operational threat of Russian invasion; over the mountain passes of the Afghan North-West frontier, out into the great plains of the Ganges and its sister rivers. It was the same traditional way taken by the historic invaders of India from the days of Alexander the Great until the Muslim invasion of the eleventh century AD, followed by our own wars with Afghanistan in the nineteenth and twentieth centuries. There is no difference today.

Indeed the threat to both new nations now winds its way along the whole stretch of the great Himalaya Mountain Range, from its Iranian and Chinese passes to its Eastern ending at the Burmese frontier. But my reflections concern the old historic frontier passes, known always as the North

West Frontier Province (NWFP) covering in particular the North West frontiers of Pakistan and of new India. But there is one big change and a vital one. No land frontier can ever again be described as impassable – no mountain is any longer an impassable obstacle.

This particular (frontier) threat always preoccupied the whole garrison of British India, and every commander had an obligation to keep all ranks under his jurisdiction familiar with Frontier Warfare, and well trained therein. It mattered not where you were stationed, Madras or Peshawar, you had to be ready to move to NWFP, either wholly as a regiment, or individually – and both happened not infrequently.

Furthermore you had to simulate Mountain Frontier Training topographically; if you were stationed, say, in a flat desert training area (eg Sind desert country) you had to simulate high mountain territory at a supposed height of, say, 9000 feet, and act (behave) accordingly. You generally had your mountain artillery battery with you for mountain training – even if you had no mountains! Ironically enough this particular threat came temporarily from Germany during the Second World War; whilst, saddest of all surely, as I write Pakistan and New India are each a threat to each other – in real terms.

My immediately preceding reflection leads me to emphasise that training for war in the Indian Army was long, continuous and hard. It is also true that our training for the NWFP generally had the first priority; the reasons for this was that those (NWFP) operations meant actual training with live ammunition; against well armed and skilled tribesmen intent on shooting you and your men. Death or serious wounds incurred on Frontier operations were certainly not infrequent; furthermore your reputation at all levels of command and action, could depend on your NWFP service.

Be all that as it may, I doubt whether few, if any, of us 'volunteers' for Indian service regretted our decision to go to India for our professional career. Of course there were drawbacks as with all professions, but the Government of India, by and large, gave us generous help in certain matters; particularly with the important problem of meeting the cost of passages home, by sea and air, to and from the Indo-subcontinent, for yourself and all your children. This most important concession, I really believe, ensured that you kept your sense of humour – at all levels, times and places!

Equally important, for everyone, there was ever present a broad and welcoming social life. This covered every aspect of day to day business, duty and sports of every sort; it has been described for and by every writer on India – in history books, novels, biographies, and stories.

At this particular stage in my reflections it would be most inappropriate not to include some record of British shortcomings, indeed vital mistakes. In particular we failed to extend the scope of our own social activities to include the Indian born nationals generally. Looking back, this error was staggering in its scope and its significance. It has been already highlighted, and rightly so, and I need not extent its coverage. But I often marvel at the wonderfully generous scale of hospitality shown now to British officers who revisit India.

Divide and rule. This is the description of British military and civil policy generally, which we certainly applied for generations after the Mutiny, and which may still be held against us. Briefly it meant placing certain restrictions on manning, to ensure that the balance of regimental strength (that is to say in battalions and garrisons, etc) between class, race and religion could be kept under control. To put it another way we tried, with exceptions, to ensure that on average no regiment was recruited all Hindu, or all Muslim, or all Sikh, for internal security reasons. Equally when a large fortress or city was concerned, it was the general rule to keep one battalion, or equivalent unit at short notice, for security duty if necessary; and to rotate that duty between units accordingly.

Who would have thought that, after little more than three hundred years, our Indian Empire would have broken up into four constituent parts each its own Republican State with no question of a paramount power or overruler. And as for our old Indian Army, with which so many British and Commonwealth families have served, or had very close links, that too has gone.

I think that comparatively few of us in India, in 1946–1947, believed that the Empire was ending; or at first refused to accept it. I certainly did not. We knew that for centuries the British had ensured that all the races, classes and creeds – Hindus, Muslims, Sikhs, Christians (be they Punjabis, Jats, Mahrattas, Dogras, Pathans etc) would obey the *sahib's* first, absolute law. This was to subordinate, if required, all racial, religious, caste, social and other class prejudices to their loyalty to their King Emperor, whom they had never seen. This was the *sahib's* greatest achievement, and no previous ruler (Mughal, Maratha, Rajput or otherwise) had ever done it.

It was not until His Majesty's Government announced that Lord Mountbatten would come, and end British rule in three months, that the 'scales dropped from our eyes' and the full horror of the initial implications, and the likely results, burst upon us all. For the few thousand British, particularly their families, the dangers and problems for all were obvious. But we should all recognise the many more immediate changes, to life and property, flowing from the creation of new national countries and frontiers, for the millions of the indigenous populations.

Come to think of it, it was His Majesty's Government who gave the order to end British rule and partition the Empire, and it was the timing they chose that caused one million or so casualties with appalling loss and damage to property! History has yet to have its say on all this, and historians will no doubt reflect on that timing decision. Wavell said he would do it in eighteen months.

Be all that as it may, by 15 August 1947 no British professionals of the Indian Service, military and civil, were left in any doubt that their Indian career services were finally ended. With a suitable career compensation, their lives in the Indian Sub-Continent were finished, except for those who opted to remain under contract.

An Army Surrenders

I am ending these reflections with the following story of how one famous regiment of the old Indian Army spent its last days of active service under the Raj.

VJ Day, 14 August 1945, when Japan surrendered unconditionally, brought no immediate change for troops of the 14th Army fighting in Burma. Communications between Tokyo and South East Asia were very poor, and six weeks or more passed before all local Japanese commanders finally accepted the news that their Emperor had ordered them to stop fighting, and surrender to their enemy on the battle field.

Then, on the last day of September, I received the following, to me very surprising, orders by field telephone line from Brigade Headquarters:

'You are to move your battalion, with all its transport, as fast as possible across the Sittang River. Having landed on the East Bank you will proceed with all speed to Thaton, about 50 miles to the South-East, where you will contact the Japanese 33 Army under General Honda. It will then be your duty to disarm the Japanese 33 Army and take their surrender.'

I was the commanding officer of the 6th Battalion in a very famous and historic regiment of Indian Infantry of the old Indian Army – the Rajput Regiment – with a reputation for loyalty, courage and fighting in battle second to none. Half the 600 young sepoys were high caste Hindu Rajputs from the Ganges Valley in what is now Uttar Pradesh; the remaining half were Muslims from the Eastern Punjab, yeoman farmers, all with a long tradition of military service. All ranks were Indian nationals except for myself and four other British officers.

At that time we were in South Burma, mopping up pockets of Japanese who were still trying to break out from the hills and dense jungles of the Pegu Yomas, to find sanctu-

A pay parade of troops of the 7th Indian Division in the Egyptian theatre during the First World War. Q12499

Casually dressed British soldiers lounging on the roof of the Alumbagh in January 1858, probably waiting for the final advance to the relief of Lucknow in March 1858. Q112129

Sikh recruits training at Nowshera military school near the North West Frontier. Photographed by Cecil Beaton during his tour of Burma and India as an official photographer in January 1944. IB1042

ary east of the Sittang River with the rest of the Japanese forces. Significantly we had now begun to take wounded prisoners; previously the Japanese custom was to kill their own wounded rather than let them suffer the ignominy of capture alive, and become a risk to Japanese security!

My orders emphasised that speed to contact the Japanese was imperative; and there was no opportunity to consult about *how* or *where* to 'take the surrender', about which I felt woefully ignorant! All I knew was that the strength of a Japanese army generally exceeded 10,000 men. We must move at once, and that we could do, for the battalion was fully motorised, albeit with jeeps, 30-cwt Dodge trucks and 3-ton lorries (those old work horses of load-carrying vehicles in the army). We moved the next morning by rail (a special train laid on for us) to the site of the old steel railway bridge over the Sittang River, which we had destroyed three years earlier during our disastrous retreat back to India. Boats had been laid on to ferry us across the river; some high authority had given us priority and by that evening we had begun our 'fast as possible move to Thaton'. We camped that night in the jungle but everything seemed quiet and peaceful and we saw no one. To the best of my knowledge we still had no troops east of the Sittang River.

My orders had also stressed the great importance of showing and maintaining the highest possible standards of foot drill and turn-out by all ranks, particularly when in contact with the Japanese; a smart appearance at all times must be kept. So I mounted a double-sentry battalion quarter-guard at my headquarters, day and night, from that date – even in dense jungle.

When we reached Thaton the local population appeared very glad to see us and were most co-operative; better still, they 'knew all about the Japanese and said they were in camp' some miles further on, due east on the road towards the Salween River.

'Never camp in town or village' was an absolute rule in Burma so my battalion camp was sited beyond Thaton on the axis of that road to the Salween. I decided I must contact the Japanese at once, and therefore sent out a strong motorised patrol, commanded by a British officer, with orders 'to find the Japanese and report back to me'! To my surprise and pleasure the patrol soon returned bringing with them an English-speaking Japanese non-commissioned officer. He was very polite and said 33 Army knew about their surrender and now awaited our orders. That was a great relief!

Thereupon I wrote out my own *Instrument of Surrender* (no doubt very amateur and unprofessional!) in which 'I charged the Officer Commanding Japanese 33 Army that from this date, 2nd October, he was entirely responsible to me for compliance with my orders, wheresoever and whatsoever.' He was to send an English-speaking liaison officer to my headquarters which would be linked by field telephone to Japanese HQ. Meanwhile no Japanese of any rank would move beyond the limits of their current concentration area, without my personal permission. He was to send me forthwith a strength return of 33 Army, by units in detail, with a map showing each unit location. In due course he would be notified of the time and place when all his weapons, arms, ammunition, equipment and war-like stores of all nature will be surrendered into the keeping of my force.

Space does not allow me to include further details of the surrender document. But I added that Japanese officers might continue to wear their swords, *within their concentration area* when on duty, until the time of their surrender of arms referred to in the immediately preceding paragraph. Finally I made it clear there would be frequent inspection by my medical staff (one captain in the Indian Medical Service!) of all Japanese accommodation, rations and water supply with special emphasis on hygiene and sanitary control.

My next act was to have word sent to General Honda, commanding 33 Army, that I wished to interview him and his Chief of Staff, Major-General Sawamoto, at their headquarters and would arrive . . . . giving him time and date. Forty years have passed and memories have grown dim, but the events of that day are still clearly etched, as it were, in my vision. During the drive to Japanese HQ I wondered how this General would react at our interview. I too had experienced defeat, for I had marched back in the long retreat from Rangoon to India in 1942, but that would be minor compared with this General's fate. It was an integral part of Japanese philosophy that nothing was more disgraceful than to surrender, either as an individual or as a group, or as a country, so how would this army commander react now? Of course he could cling to the fact that his own Emperor had ordered him to surrender.

When we reached the headquarters, where everything was neat, clean and garnished to perfection, I was shown in to his personal office and, except for an interpreter, we were left alone; I did not take any officer with me. He was very well turned out in his uniform, not wearing his sword, of slim appearance, and looking what presumably he was, an experienced, proficient, professional officer. I waited for him to salute (I was not going to salute my prisoner-of-war!) which, after a pause, he did and I returned his salute.

I began by saying that I was glad to meet him, for I knew he had received my orders. I would always treat his army fairly within the rules, including rights and privileges, for the treatment of international prisoners-of-war. We were both professional soldiers and I would deal with him on that basis; I felt sure he knew that. He replied saying he fully understood, and would I please deal with his Chief-of-Staff (in all relevant matters) who would always comply with

my orders. I then left him, and somehow I think we were both glad the interview was over. I took away with me the picture, and very strong impression, of a Japanese General who had decided it was his duty to submit entirely to any orders issued on behalf of the British Supreme Allied Commander in South-East Asia. (I had signed my orders to him 'for' Lord Mountbatten.) Yet, with all his complete submission, General Honda never once lost his composure and, more importantly, there was no apparent loss of dignity or self-confidence.

I only saw him once again, I cannot remember for what reason.

The day soon came when we held the parade at which all ranks in 33 Army surrendered to 6th Battalion the Rajput Regiment every Japanese weapon in their possession, including all stock of ammunition and military stores of every kind. During this parade (it occupied one whole day) tact, courtesy and common sense demanded that every Japanese officer should personally surrender his sword to myself as the senior British commanding officer present; and this was done in complete silence and with perfect discipline.

For the rest it required a very large building, kept under constant armed guard with orders to shoot on sight any unrecognised intruder, to house such a multitude of military equipment. There must have been many thousands of rifles, bayonets, revolvers, mortars, light machine guns, as well as artillery guns, and all their associated stocks of ammunition supply and replacement.

We were fortunate in having a large empty Burmese rice mill as storage space for this vast collection of military equipment, and it was from that time that I began, increasingly, to learn and appreciate Japanese efficiency. For them submission meant not only complete military surrender, but also complete obedience and compliance with orders. It was they (Japanese soldiers), who included expert carpenters and craftsmen, who cleaned up that rice mill and fitted within it all the necessary racks, shelving, cupboards and the like, appropriate for military storage purposes. I was astonished by their competence; indeed, looking at today's world scene, I now see no need for that surprise.

We wanted a very strong ramp built, of sufficient size and strength to allow for end-loading of 3-ton vehicles, as well as an inspection pit for transport vehicle maintenance. All these were provided and it became true to say that for all short and long term routine (military) maintenance and repair, other than British uniform and armament, I found no need to place demands on my higher authority. We needed a strong and comfortable hut built for an officers' mess; it was provided. The Japanese 33 Army had a number of horses, clearly well schooled, and what I would call Japanese country-breds. I demanded six and they were provided, each saddled with what resembled an English-type hunting saddle, and bridled with a big ring snaffle. From that day my officers and I were able to enjoy our morning and evening hack. Life became pleasant indeed.

More than four months passed, a period of constant inspection and attention to turn-out, which I had been ordered to maintain. There must be no question of British loss of face, and that meant that sepoys of the Rajput Regiment must be seen, frequently and always well dressed in uniform, by their prisoners-of-war.

Then one day I received the following letter which I have judged it right to quote in full. It came as a complete surprise, but I am glad I kept it; it was written in Japanese script with the accompanying English translation. Of course, I could not follow up his offer to give me a present!

Skeletal human remains in front of the devastated Secondra Bagh, Lucknow, 1858. Q69824

33rd Army H.Q.
Zemathwe, 18 Jan. '46

Dear Colonel Montgomery,

At this time, our 33rd Army has been ordered to evacuate our present site, and move in the direction of Moulmein, thus leaving your command.

During the encampment of our Army under your command we were able to enjoy a far more wholesome and profitable existence than the one we expect, far exceeding our maximum wishes. I wish to thank you on behalf of the entire Army for your unbiased and sympathetic treatment, which made this possible.

Now at this very time when they are about to step off on their first leg Eastward, the hearts of all the men are throbbing with excitement at the expectancy of being able to see Home. At the same time the officers of the 33rd Army Staff, who have come into contact with you, have all expressed a most unexplainable feeling of not wanting to part from you, which surprises me very much.

In continuing, I would like to express the thankfulness of our Army by some token. However, being that under the present limited conditions, such a thing cannot be done, let me at this time state that if there is anything in the way of handicraft work, you would like to have our men make, please do inform our Staff Officer, Major Fuchi.

Before letting my brush be, I would like to wish you continued good health, and to pray for your future successes. In closing, I remain

Yours most sincerely,
Major General Rekichiro Sawamoto,
Chief of Staff, 33 Army,

Troops of a Kashmiri regiment on the Shagai plateau near the eastern end of the Khyber Pass. Photographed by Cecil Beaton during his tour of Burma and India as an official photographer in January 1944. IB1341

Tochi Scouts, part of the frontier militia, clambering up a mountain on the border between India and Pakistan. Photographed by Cecil Beaton in January 1944. IB1010